WHEN JESUS RETURNS

Also by David Pawson

The Challenge of Islam to Christians
Jesus Baptises in One Holy Spirit
The Normal Christian Birth
Once Saved, Always Saved?
The Road to Hell
When Jesus Returns
Word and Spirit Together

When Jesus Returns

J. David Pawson

Hodder & Stoughton
LONDON SYDNEY AUCKLAND

First published in Great Britain in 1995 by Hodder & Stoughton
This edition first published in 2003

10 9 8 7 6 5 4 3 2 1

British Library Cataloguing in Publication Data

ISBN 0 340 61211 8

Typeset by Hewer Text Ltd, Edinburgh
Printed and Bound In Great Britain by
Bookmarque Ltd, Croydon, Surrey

Hodder & Stoughton Ltd
A Division of Hodder Headline
338 Euston Road
London NW1 3BH
www.madaboutbooks.com

Contents

B. THE REVELATION RIDDLE

Foreword

While working on this book I preached at two funeral services, a rare experience for me since I began a travelling ministry. One was for my mother-in-law, who died at the age of ninety-eight; the other was for my daughter, who died some months later at thirty-six. Both lived and died with a personal trust in Jesus as Saviour and Lord.

On each occasion I spoke of their present situation. They are fully conscious, able to communicate with others (though not with us) and, above all, enjoying the presence of Jesus.

But I went on to speak about their future prospects. One day they will have new bodies, subject to neither the frailty of brittle bones nor the ravages of septicemic leukemia. But they will not get them until they come back to live here on earth. This is not the 'reincarnation' of their souls, since they come back as themselves, but the 'resurrection' of their bodies.

It will happen when 'the Lord himself will come down from heaven' again (1 Thess 4:16), for 'God will bring with him those who have fallen asleep in him' (1 Thess 4:14). This event lies at the heart of Christian hopes for the future and shifts the focus of expectation in time and space.

The New Testament says very little about our existence immediately after death. While it is true that Christian believers 'go to heaven to be with Jesus' (language which even unbelievers dare to use when explaining death to children), this is not the main thrust of apostolic comfort. For heaven is only a waiting-room! The supreme moment will be the gathering of *all* believers, already dead or still alive, to 'be with the Lord for ever' (1 Thess 4:17).

But this will not be in heaven. It will be on earth – or, at first, just above it, in the air, in the clouds (1 Thess 4:17). If our immediate destiny after death is heaven, our ultimate destiny is earth, though we and it will have been completely recycled, restored to our original condition.

Christianity is a very 'down-to-earth' religion. It began when the Son of Man came down to earth. It continued because the Holy Spirit was sent down to earth. It will be consummated when the Father himself changes his address ('our Father who art in heaven') and makes his 'dwelling-place', his residence, 'with men' (Rev 21:3). At the very end, which is also the real beginning, we do not go to heaven to live with him; he comes to earth to live with us.

Before this can happen, the Son must pay a second visit. There are more things he needs to do here on earth before history can be wound up. This is the basic theme of *When Jesus Returns*, of which there are four parts.

The first is a reprint of a booklet with which some readers may already be acquainted: *Explaining the Second Coming* (Sovereign World, 1993). I am grateful to both publishers for agreeing to share this material. It represents what I preach about this subject. For reasons of space and objective I had to omit the controversies associated with this topic and simply present my conclusions, which is what I believe we should do in the pulpit. Faith is not aroused by tentative opinion but by confident declaration. But many have enquired how I arrived at my convictions. This volume attempts to answer that by sharing the thinking that went on in my study. There is therefore a radical contrast in style, content and vocabulary in the rest of the book. If the first part is condensed milk, the remainder is minced meat!

The second is an introduction to the book of Revelation, the only book in the New Testament to major on the second coming. The aim has not been to write a commentary, though many puzzles and problems are faced, hopefully clarifying them.

The hope is that a fairly detailed overview will familiarise the reader with a book that has intimidated too many. I hope the reaction will be: 'Oh, now I can see what it's all about'.

The third tackles a major difference about what has come to be called 'the rapture'. Most Christians who have at some time been taught about the return of Christ are usually told to expect him at any time and that he is coming to take believers out of the world before the 'Great Tribulation' erupts. I have had to give the reasons why I believe this to be a false and dangerous assumption.

The fourth plunges into a theological minefield! The 'millennium' has caused so many discussions and even divisions that many Christians don't even want to hear about it. The tragedy is that more know what they don't believe about it than what they do. I believe the main reason is that the options set before them have not included the view universally held in the church of the first few centuries, which we have called: 'classic premillennialism'. I am convinced that this is 'an idea whose time has come' and make no apology for my impassioned advocacy.

I am no stranger to controversy (anyone who writes books about hell, water baptism and male leadership must expect it); but I have not sought it for its own sake. Of all the characters in Bunyan's *Pilgrim's Progress*, I identify most readily with Mr Valiant-for-truth. That does not mean that I think I've got a monopoly on the truth or have always grasped it. But I find that honest debate sharpens my own mind and, I believe, that of those with whom I disagree.

And I do not think divisions from fellow believers are justified by differences in this particular area. The wise words of another writer spring to mind: 'Suppose you are not convinced. Shall we who are relying on the same Redeemer, begotten by the same God, inhabited by the same Spirit, incorporated in the same body, entrusted with the same gospel, assaulted by the same devil, hated by the same world, delivered from the same hell and destined to the same glory – shall we who have so much in common allow ourselves to be divided in heart or service because, just because we are of different minds on this secondary matter? God forbid'. (Norman F. Douty in *Has Christ's Return Two Stages?* Pageant, 1956.)

Mind you, I cannot agree that God's promises for the future are a 'secondary matter', though our interpretation of them may be. 'Eschatology', study of the end-times (from the Greek word *eschaton*, which means 'end' or 'last') is regarded as a branch of theology and a somewhat speculative one at that. Actually, the whole gospel is itself 'eschatological'. It is an announcement that the future has broken into the present. Tomorrow has become today. The coming kingdom is already here.

But not all of it. The kingdom of God cannot be fully 'realised' now, though it has been 'inaugurated'. It can be 'entered' now, but can only be 'inherited' later, when it is 'consummated' by being established worldwide. This tension between the 'already' and the 'not yet' is fundamental to understanding the New Testament. It exactly corresponds to the first and second comings of Jesus to planet earth. To emphasise the present at the expense of the future, or the future at the expense of the present is to distort the good news.

I had hoped to include a whole section on the kingdom of God and another on the people of Israel, both topics extremely relevant to my theme. But space forbids; my manuscript has already exceeded the size specified in the publisher's contract. In any case, each deserves a whole book to itself. God willing, I may yet be able to give them that.

My next book is already on the stocks and deals much more fully with what will be for some the most provocative item in this work. If I say that its tentative title is: 'Once Saved, Always Saved? A Study in Perseverance and Inheritance', the reader will understand the issue which I am facing. Few questions could be more crucial to the Christian life. It is raised in an acute form by the purpose of the book of Revelation presented here.

It remains only to add that much of the content of this volume is available in more 'popular' form on cassette and video from Anchor Recordings, 72 The Street, Kennington, Ashford, Kent,

TN24 9HS. Those who prefer to listen as individuals or to look as groups are encouraged to use this facility.

My heartfelt prayer is that my efforts to complete this book under intense family pressures will ensure that some 'meet the Lord in the air' when he returns who would otherwise not be there.

J. David Pawson
Sherborne St John, 1994.

The Fascinating Future

Our attitude to the future is ambiguous, a mixture of fear and fascination. We want to know what is going to happen to us and the rest of the human race – and we don't want to know! Were it possible, which one of us would wish to learn the date of our death or the end of the world?

We are the first generation to live with the possibility that these two dates might coincide. In one survey half the teenagers believed their death and the death of our planet would be simultaneous. Whether through nuclear holocaust (a diminishing fear) or environmental pollution (a growing fear), the days of life on earth seem to be numbered.

Again, our reaction is inconsistent, even contradictory. On the one hand, many try to forget the future and squeeze as much purpose and pleasure out of the present as possible. 'Let us eat and drink, for tomorrow we die' (this is actually in the Bible! Isa 22:13, quoted in 1 Cor 15:32). 'Existentialism' is the name for this philosophy of life and it is widespread.

On the other hand, there is more interest in the future and efforts to change it than ever before, an enthusiasm that hovers on the border of panic. Attitudes cover a wide spectrum from elated optimism to depressed pessimism, sometimes swinging wildly from one extreme to the other, from faith to fatalism.

Broadly speaking, there are three ways in which we can pierce the veil that hides the future from us.

First, the *superstitious* method. Divination is an ancient practice, but still very much alive. Clairvoyants and mediums, crystal balls and ouija boards, tarot cards and tea-leaves – there are

many forms. Six out of ten men and seven out of ten women read
their horoscopes every day; no popular newspaper or magazine
would dare to neglect the stars.

Yet it has been estimated that none of these channels has ever
been more than 5% accurate, which means that they are at least
95% mistaken. Only those willing or wanting to be deceived
forget the errors and focus on the few fulfilments.

Second, the *scientific* method. Deduction from observation is
the basic tool of modern science. To calculate present trends
and project them is the concern of 'futurology', as the tech-
nique is now named. Professorial chairs in the subject are
being established in universities, particularly those majoring in
technology. Industrial, commercial and political spheres have
their 'think-tanks'. More than one computer programme has
calculated the likely date of the end of the world as 2040
(by taking into account population growth, food and energy
resources, environmental decay, etc.).

Average accuracy of published results has so far been around
25% or, to put it negatively, up to 75% wrong. The short-term
forecasts, as one would expect, are much more reliable than the
long-term ones.

Third, the *scriptural* method. Declaration about future events
is a major feature of the Bible. It claims to contain the words
of God ('Thus says the Lord' occurs 3808 times!), the only
person who is in a position to 'make known the end from
the beginning, from ancient times, what is still to come' (Isa
46:10). Over a quarter of all the verses in the Bible contain a
prediction about the future. Altogether 737 separate forecasts
are made, from some only mentioned once to others hundreds
of times.

Of these, 594 (over 80%) have already come true. Since those
that have not are all concerned with the end of the world, which
obviously has not happened yet, the Bible has actually achieved
100% accuracy. All that could have taken place already has done
so, which should be ample grounds for confidence that the rest
will also be fulfilled. (These statistics, with a detailed analysis of

every prediction, may be found in the *Encyclopedia of Biblical Prophecy* by J. Barton Payne, Hodder and Stoughton, 1973.)

How astonishing then that people would rather consult satanic rigmarole or human reason than divine revelation. Part of the blame must lie at the door of the church, which has neither been clear nor confident enough in sharing her knowledge, the result of allowing scientific scepticism about the supernatural to undermine the authority of scripture.

The Bible reveals its secrets to those who read it with reverence and obedience, in a humble and teachable spirit. It yields more to simple intelligence than sophisticated intellectualism. It is written for ordinary people in ordinary language (New Testament Greek is taken from the streets, not the classics). It is meant to be taken at face value and taken seriously. When it is, a clear picture of the future emerges.

Many things are predicted – personal and political, social and environmental, moral and meteorological. But one event stands out above them all: the return to this world of a person who lived here two thousand years ago, a carpenter from the village of Nazareth. Were he simply a human being, this would seem unbelievable. If he was what he claimed to be, divine as well as human, the one and only God-man, his return becomes credible and congruous. Rejected by an unbelieving world, it is only right that he should be publicly vindicated.

This event is more frequently predicted than any other and dominates the biblical preview. The question: 'What is the world coming to?' is changed into: 'Who is the world coming to?' or, better still: 'Who is coming to the world?'

History will be brought to a conclusion. And by a human being. Not by pressing the button of a nuclear attack on earth but by breaking the seals of a scroll in heaven on which is already written the countdown of world events (Rev 5:1; 6:1). At the climax of the crisis, Jesus himself will reappear on the world stage to take personal control of the grand finale.

Such is the heart of the Christian hope for the future. Jesus is the only hope, the only person with sufficient ability and authority, character and compassion, to right the wrongs of this sick, sad and sinful world. On his first visit to our planet he demonstrated that he *could* do it; on his second he has promised that he *will* do it.

In theory, the Church of Jesus Christ gives his return a central place. The most regularly repeated creeds, the Apostles' and the Nicene, include it as a fundamental part of the faith. Bread and wine are regularly taken as a reminder of his former presence and current absence 'until he comes' (1 Cor 11:26). The liturgical calendar includes Advent in December, the first part of which anticipates his return.

In practice, however, neglect of this vital truth is spreading. Even during Advent, any thought about his second coming is quickly forgotten in the celebration of his first, in the festivities of Christmas. Some have become so confused or impatient with the doctrinal differences over it that they have taken refuge in agnosticism on the subject. More have conformed to the world's obsession with the present by concentrating on the application of Christian insights and efforts to the personal and political needs of the day.

Now abideth faith, hope and love; but the weakest of these is hope!

That is a tragedy in a world of widespread depression and despair. The Bible describes unbelievers as 'without hope and without God in the world' (Eph 2:12). In such darkness, Christians should be shining beacons of hope. After all, they are the only ones who know how it will all end. They know that it will all end well, that good will triumph over evil, that their Lord will defeat the devil, that the kingdom of God will come on earth as it is in heaven.

This hope is 'an anchor for the soul, firm and secure' (Heb 6:19). The raging storm of world events will get worse rather than better, until every part of the globe is affected. May the reading of this book help you to get your anchor down now!

A. THE APPROACHING ADVENT

CHAPTER ONE

Making Sense of his Return

With over three hundred references to the second coming in the New Testament, the problem is almost too much material rather than too little. Fitting it all together feels like assembling a jigsaw puzzle with interchangeable pieces.

Perhaps this explains why there are such differences of understanding, even among Christians with implicit confidence in scripture. They all agree on the central fact of his coming, but disagree strongly about what precedes and what follows that event.

Rather than add yet another chart or time schedule to the many already published, this study will take a topical approach. The data will be collected under five basic questions:

Who – will he come as the pre-existent Son of God or the incarnate Son of Man?
Where – will he come to the whole world at once or just to one place in it?
How – will the second coming be like the first or totally different?
When – will he come soon and suddenly or only after clear signals?
Why – what can he only achieve by coming back here, and how long will it take?

Some of the answers may come as a surprise, even a shock, to those who have only been exposed to one school of thought or have already got fixed ideas on the subject. Readers coming

with an open mind and an open Bible will get the most
benefit.

WHO?

Who has not continued gazing into the distance long after a train
or plane has taken a loved one out of sight, especially if that is
expected to be a final parting? Is it a reluctance to acknowledge
the departure, an attempt to postpone the pain? We are not so
likely to do it if we are sure we shall see that person again, that
they will return from their journey.

This is exactly what happened to the men of Galilee when Jesus
went up into the clouds, less than two months after he came back
to them from the dead. Long after he disappeared, they were still
staring at the point of their final glimpse. It took two angels to
reassure them and bring their attention down to earth again.

They assured the disciples that he *would* return, implying that
they would not see him again until then. What interests us is
the phrase they used: 'This same Jesus ... will come back'
(Acts 1:11).

Two things are worth noting. First they used his human name,
not any of his divine titles. Second, they emphasised that he will
not have changed in the meantime.

One of our common fears is that during a long separation
persons may change so much that a former relationship cannot
be resumed. Disciples of Jesus need not worry. They may change,
indeed should change for the better, but he neither will nor
needs to. He is 'the same yesterday and today and for ever'
(Heb 13:8).

It cannot be too strongly emphasised that the divine Christ and
the human Jesus are one and the same person. Both conscious
attempts and unconscious impressions have driven a wedge
between them. Even in Christian circles it has been assumed
that the Son of God was only made flesh, 'incarnated', for
thirty-three years and has now 'gone back' to his former state.

The truth is that he became human and keeps his resurrected body for the rest of eternity. He has retained his humanity. He is the only mediator between God and man precisely because he is still 'the man' (1 Tim 2:5). That is why he is the perfect high priest, who can both sympathise with us and represent us before God (Heb 4:15). Incredibly, a perfect human being is now in control of the universe (Matt 28:18)!

We must not forget that this person, who has 'ascended' to the highest heaven is the same one who 'descended' to lowest earth (Eph 4:9–10). The place of his baptism is, in fact, the lowest point on the earth's surface!

The exalted was first humbled – as a baby in Bethlehem, a boy in Nazareth. He was a woodworker for eighteen years, then a wonder-worker for three (the same proportion of six to one as his heavenly father: Gen 1). The latter period made him famous among his people, the focus of attention for friends and enemies alike. His ignominious death at an early age was terribly public.

All this meant that he was widely known and well-known. Of course, there were varying degrees of intimacy, different circles of acquaintance. Thousands listened to him; seventy were commissioned to spread his mission; twelve were chosen to follow him; three shared unique experiences with him (Peter, James and John at the transfiguration for example); one was closer than any other (John, the 'beloved', into whose care Jesus entrusted his bereaved mother).

This human knowledge of the human Jesus is enshrined in the four Gospels. From these emerges a clear portrait of a unique personality, loved by sinners, hated by hypocrites, adored by the poor and feared by the powerful. His eyes could fill with tears of compassion for the oppressed and blaze with anger against the oppressor. His hands could lift the fallen and whip the greedy. His tongue could be softer and sharper than any other.

It is this Jesus who will return to the planet earth one day. He will not have changed. He will be no less human than he was when walking the dusty roads, reclining at meal tables, sleeping in a boat, riding a donkey or washing feet.

However, it must be pointed out that there had already been one major change in his humanity even before he left the earth. God gave him a new body when he raised him out of the tomb (for fuller details, see my *Explaining the Resurrection* in the series from Sovereign World.

This 'glorious body' (Phil 3:21) has the same appearance, even to the disfigurements of the crucifixion with scars on the head, back, side, hands and feet. But it was no longer subject to the 'natural' processes of aging, decay and death. When he returns it will be no older, still in its prime, still thirty-three – except that his hair will be snow-white (Rev 1:14; a symbol of his sharing the nature of his Father, the 'Ancient of Days'; Dan 7:13).

This transformation of his body did not make Jesus less human but more human, which is what God had intended all human beings to be and, by his grace, what many will be. In this Jesus is our 'pioneer' (Heb 2:10), blazing a trail for us to follow. But he will not leave us to find our own way; he will come back and take us to be with him, for he himself is 'the way' (John 14:3–6).

Then we too will have 'glorious bodies' just like his. But we will be the same persons we have always been (which is why Christians speak about 'resurrection' rather than 'reincarnation'; popular usage of the latter implies a change of identity).

We need to remember that Jesus was not always a human being. Indeed, he was not always 'Jesus'; that was a name he acquired when he was incarnate, embodied, and when he became human (Matt 1:21). Unlike us he existed before he was conceived, and was the only person who ever chose to be born. He was the eternal Son of God, the Lord of glory, the Word. He was the divine being before he was a human being.

It is therefore very significant that the angels used his human name when promising his return to planet earth. It is the 'Son of man' who will appear in the clouds (Dan 7:13; Mark 14:62). It is the embodied Jesus who will return to planet earth, not some intangible apparition of the Son of God (Dan 3:25).

Some, finding such a 'bodily' return difficult to accept, have 'spiritualised' his coming, identifying it with the 'coming' of his Spirit to the church at Pentecost or his 'coming' to each individual believer at conversion. But neither of these interpretations does justice to the promise that 'this same Jesus . . . will come back' (Acts 1:11).

The Jesus who invited the disciples to touch him, who ate fish in their presence, who walked to Emmaus and broke bread, who told Thomas to examine his wounds, who cooked breakfast on the shores of Galilee – it is this Jesus who will return one day.

But we must face one implication of believing this: an embodied Jesus can only be in one place on earth at once. Even with his glorious resurrection body he could only be in Emmaus or Jerusalem or Galilee. He never appeared in two places at the same time.

Therefore, when he returns to this earth, he can only come to one geographical location. Where will that be?

WHERE?

If the return of Jesus is 'physical', it must also be local. His Spirit can be everywhere, but his body must be somewhere. Before he ascended, Jesus could not be in two places at once.

That is why he told the disciples it was for their good that he was leaving them and sending another 'stand-by' to take his place (John 16:7). He had promised to be with them always, even to the end of the age (Matt 28:20); yet they would be *scattered* to the ends of the earth (Acts 1:8). The only way he could do this was to remove his body and replace his physical presence with his ever-present and omnipresent Spirit, unlimited by time or space.

This situation will not be reversed when he returns. Believers will not lose his Spirit but will enjoy his physical presence as well. They will be doubly blessed!

However, since his body, like ours, must always be at one point on the surface of the earth, his return means that his disciples will have to be *gathered* together from every part of the globe. Only thus could they experience his bodily presence. This is precisely what the New Testament promises will happen.

So where will he appear? Where will his people gather to welcome him?

Cities compete to host such prestigious events as the Olympic games. Which of them will have the honour of greeting the King of kings? Will it be one of the political capitals – Washington, Beijing, Brussels or Delhi? Will it be one of the financial centres – New York, Tokyo, London or Hong Kong? Will it be one with ecclesiastical fame – Rome, Geneva or Canterbury?

It will be none of these. They may be important to men but are not significant for God. He chose for his capital a most unlikely city, hidden in the hills, away from roads and rivers, an obscure mountain refuge that would be unknown had not God chosen to attach his name to it. Even today the nations of the world will not recognise it, by refusing to open embassies there. It has known more conflict and tragedy than any other and may yet prove the spark to ignite a conflagration throughout the Middle East.

The most important happenings in human history took place there; they divided time into two parts – BC and AD. It was there that the only Son of God was unjustly executed for crimes he had never committed, actually bearing the sins of the whole world. It was there that he defeated the last enemy, death, becoming the first person to have an immortal body.

It is from this city that he departed to return to his home in heaven and it is to this city that he will return from heaven. He called it 'the city of the Great King' (Matt 5:35). It is the city he wept over, telling its citizens they would not see him again until they said 'Blessed is he who comes in the name of the Lord' (Matt 23:37–39, quoting one of the 'Hallel' psalms sung by Jerusalem pilgrims to welcome their 'Messiah').

The history of this city is by no means over. Future events are unveiled in the book of Revelation, where it is described as 'the great city' (11:8) and 'the city he loves' (20:9). It is to this city that the nations will one day turn for the arbitration of international disputes, enabling multilateral disarmament (Isa 2:1–4; Mic 4:1–5). For this is Jerusalem, or 'Zion', where the Lord will reign.

The city is strategically placed for an international function. It is quite literally at the very centre of the world's land mass and at the meeting-point of three continents – Europe, Africa and Asia. It would seem an ideal rendezvous for the gathering of Jesus' followers.

But how many will there be, bearing in mind that the crowd will include Christians who have already died and are then raised again? Even today, that could be in the region of fifteen hundred million! No stadium on earth could hold such a number. Even the whole city of Jerusalem would be far too small.

The Bible gives a twofold answer.

First, it will take place *outside* the city. Jesus ascended to heaven from the Mount of Olives, a peak to the east with a panorama of the whole city on one side and the wilderness down to the Dead Sea on the other. It was on the slopes of this mountain that thousands of pilgrims to the three annual Jewish feasts used to camp, and it was here that they welcomed Jesus with palm branches when he rode into Jerusalem on a donkey (Mark 11:8–10). The same prophet who predicted that event (Zech 9:9) also foretold: 'On that day his feet will stand on the Mount of Olives' (Zech 14:4). Jesus is returning to the very same spot he left. Yet the mountain can hardly hold the millions on this occasion.

Second, it will all take place *above* the mountain! We 'will be caught up ... in the clouds to meet the Lord in the air' (1 Thess 4:17). There is certainly plenty of room in the sky, but how will the law of gravity be overcome? By then we shall have received our new 'immortal' bodies (1 Cor 15:51–53), just like his 'glorious' body (Phil 3:21), which was equally at home on earth or in heaven, able to eat fish and cook breakfast yet pass through locked doors and step into space without a space-suit!

Imagine this vast multitude floating among the clouds. Few

elements in God's creation give us a clearer picture of his glory.
Those who have flown above cumulus clouds bathed in radiant
sunshine will understand. The sight is 'glorious'.

It means that the wind will be westerly on that day, bringing
moisture from the Mediterranean. East winds from the Arabian
desert bring only dry scorching heat. This was how God blessed
or punished his people Israel (1 Kgs 17:1; 18:44). The return of
their Messiah will be the greatest blessing they ever received.

HOW?

This aspect of his return is best approached by comparing it
with his ascension and contrasting it with his advent. His second
coming will be like his first going, but unlike his first coming.

It was the angels who first drew the parallel between his
ascension and his return: 'This same Jesus . . . will come back in
the same way you have seen him go into heaven' (Acts: 1:11).

In other words, had one of the disciples had a camcorder and
made a video of his departure and disappearance, this could have
been used to portray his return, just by showing it backwards!
The one event is simply the reverse of the other. They belong
together, though one is past and the other future.

Some contemporary scholars dismiss the ascension as a myth,
as fiction rather than fact, as conveying theological truth about
who Jesus was but not historical truth about where he went. They
regard themselves as too sophisticated to accept the idea that
heaven is 'up there'. Not surprisingly, this creates real problems
for thinking about his return. Most of them just don't!

Who do we believe, the angels or the scholars? Will Jesus come
down from a cloudy sky in the same way in which he was taken
up? Or is the whole thing a fairy tale? The choice is yours!

Those who accept the eye-witness testimony of those who
saw him go have no difficulty believing that he will come
back in the same manner. His return will be visible, audible
and tangible.

However, while his part in the picture will be the same, other aspects will be quite different.

There were only two angels attending his ascension but thousands will accompany his return (Matt 25:31; Jude 14). Only eleven men saw him go but millions will see him come back. The whole scene will be crowded.

And there will be more to hear as well as see. One statement about his return has been described as 'the noisiest verse in the Bible' (1 Thess 4:16). God is speaking, the archangel is shouting, the trumpet is sounding – and it is difficult to imagine the millions watching remaining silent when for the first time they see the one whom they have loved for so long.

All this is in sharp contrast to his first coming. For his first nine months on earth he was completely invisible, hidden in the darkness of Mary's womb. Only a few close relatives knew of his presence. His birth was relatively unnoticed, except by a few shepherds, until wise men from the east (probably descendants of the many Jews who stayed in Babylon after the exile) alerted Herod to a potential rival. There were, of course, angels to announce his first advent as they would his second; and there was the star, one pin-point of light in the sky, whose significance was only realised by those looking for it. The 'king of the Jews' was only born in David's royal city, Bethlehem, because a distant emperor introduced a new poll tax. Even then, his cradle was an animal feeding trough.

It is obvious that the world was totally unaware of what was happening or of who had come. It was as if God himself wanted as little publicity as possible for his Son's intervention in history. This was to be a hidden visit to planet earth seen only by the eye of faith.

His second coming could not be more different; no longer as a helpless baby, but as a mature man; not with a single star in the sky, but with lightning from the eastern horizon to the west (Matt 24:27); not in weakness but in power; not in humility, but in glory; not in meekness, but in majesty.

There will be universal awareness and instant recognition.

Everyone will know he has come and everyone will know who he is. It will be the most public and publicised event in history.

New Testament writers searched the Greek language for words to describe this unique occasion. They settled on three, each of which had special associations, both in the Greek translation of the Hebrew scriptures and in the general usage of contemporary society.

Parousia was their favourite. It means 'to be beside' and was used generally when someone 'arrived' to join others who expected them. However, there were two particular applications which made it peculiarly appropriate for the second coming, both connected with royalty. One was when a foreign king 'arrived' with his army at the border of a land he intended to invade, conquer and occupy. The other was when a native king 'arrived' with his court to visit one of his cities; in this case, the leading citizens would go out to meet him well outside the city wall, so that they might honour him by processing through the gates with him. These two images perfectly combine the dual aspect of Jesus' return. Unbelievers will see him as an alien invader; believers will welcome and honour him as their sovereign.

Epiphaneia can best be translated as 'appearing on the scene', with the hint of a sudden rather than a gradual coming into view. Again, it has been used of an invading army or a king visiting his subjects – much as the British royal family 'appears' on the balcony of Buckingham Palace before the assembled crowd below. Its highest use is in the context of worship, when God manifests himself in visual ways – as when the 'Shekinah' glory came down on the Tabernacle or Temple. This last application often carried the nuance of bringing comfort and support. God was appearing on the scene to help his people, especially at a critical time of need. This meaning may be illustrated by 'Western' films, when the cavalry troops come over the horizon in the nick of time to *save* the pioneer settlers from Red Indian attack. That is an 'epiphany', and explains why the word is used of the first as well as the second coming of Jesus.

Apokalypsis takes the notion of 'arriving' and 'appearing' one step further. The root of the word is to hide but the prefix changes the meaning to uncover what has been hidden. Applied to persons, it means to unveil. The English colloquialism: 'to be shown up in one's true colours' is an excellent equivalent. Applied to royalty, it would mean wearing the crown, robes and jewellery befitting a sovereign. It is to be fully revealed as one is for all to see. For obvious reasons, this could not be used of Jesus' first coming, but is entirely appropriate for his second, when he comes 'with power and great glory' (Matt 24:30).

There is a children's story in which an Emperor, disguised as a beggar, mingles with his people the day before an intended visit, to see how they will treat him as a person; the following day is his *apokalypsis*, with full regalia and retinue, causing great shame and embarrassment as the 'beggar' is recognised as supreme ruler. So it will be when Jesus appears as King of kings and Lord of lords. Significantly, the book of Revelation, which says more about his coming than any other, begins with the words 'The apokalypsis of Jesus Christ . . .' (Rev 1:1). It is one of a number of 'apocalyptic' books in the Bible which 'uncover' the hidden future (Daniel and Ezekiel are examples).

These three words together provide a vivid description of this unique event. It is important to note that they are used interchangeably to indicate different aspects of the same occasion and not separate stages of an extended sequence, as some have mistakenly thought.

The common verb that ties them all together is 'come'. Jesus is coming. He is coming as a conquering king. He is coming to save his people.

He is coming as he really is. The world last saw him crucified; now it will see him crowned. At last every knee will bow and 'every tongue confess that Jesus Christ is Lord, to the glory of God the Father' (Phil 2:10–11).

But when will he come? How much longer do we have to wait?

WHEN?

If we knew the answer to this, we would be possessors of the greatest secret in the world. No one knows – except God himself. Even Jesus, when he was on earth, confessed ignorance of this date on his Father's calendar (Matt 24:36). And he told his disciples they would not be able to find it out (Mark 13:33–35; cf. Acts 1:7). It seems important that we should *not* know (paradoxically, as we shall see, we are more likely to be ready if we don't know than if we do).

So is that all there is to be said? Or can we still ask further questions?

Will his coming be sudden, totally unexpected? Or will there be indications of his impending return? To put it another way, will it be a complete interruption of the historical process or the climax of a series of preceding events? If we can't have the exact date, can we work out an approximate one? Quite simply, will we have any warning of his approach?

To this last, the New Testament appears to give two contradictory answers: yes and no!

On the one hand, in addition to the passages emphasising ignorance there are a number picturing his coming as a 'thief in the night', unexpected and unnoticed (Matt 24:43; 1 Thess 5:2; Rev 16:15); there is a well-known Christian film with this very title. Since the essence of successful burglary is surprise, the implication is that there will be no warning of his coming, nor even any indication that he is near. Which means that Jesus could come back at 'any moment' (a phrase now used as a label for this view).

On the other hand, other passages speak of events preceding his return, things that have to happen first which are '*signs*' (or signals) announcing that he is 'at the door' (Matt 24:33), about to step through on to the stage of history again. Consistent with this are frequent exhortations to '*watch*', as well as '*pray*' for his return. This cannot mean living with eyes glued to the clouds in the sky! Apart from the inherent danger, he will only appear above Jerusalem. The context is always one of world events, presaging the end of the age. In fact, the disciples asked Jesus what would be the signs of his coming (Matt 24:3); and he gave them specific details in his reply. The practical implication of this is that he cannot (or will not) return until we 'see all these things' (Matt 24:33). We cannot therefore expect him 'at any moment', or even in the immediate future – though every generation of believers can validly hope it will be within their lifetime.

There is obviously a tension between these two strands of scripture. Bible students have resolved it in different ways. We shall look at three, two of which are questionable.

Some settle the issue by opting for one and ignoring the other. They either take the 'Any Moment' position or the 'Looking for Signs' approach. But building doctrine on only part of what the Bible says on a given subject leads to imbalance and extremism, with unfortunate practical results.

A more popular solution, particularly among North American fundamentalists, is to assume that there are *two* second comings, separated in time. Jesus is coming twice, the first time secretly and unexpectedly for his bride the Church, the second publicly and with preceding signs to establish his kingdom. This theory is relatively recent (it first gained popularity around 1830) and has been widely accepted. This view teaches that believers will be 'raptured' out of the earthly scene before they can 'watch' for the signs of his coming.

There is a much simpler and more scriptural way of under-standing the paradox. There will not be two comings, but there will be two groups of people at the one coming. To one it will be a total shock, to the other no surprise.

Jesus himself compared the day of his return with the days of Noah (Matt 24:37–39). Then, the majority of mankind were feeding and breeding, totally unaware of the impending disaster which came without warning. Yet Noah and seven others were ready, knowing what was coming and knowing it could not happen until the ark was completed. The boat itself was a long-term 'sign', the gathering of animals and storage of food a short-term 'sign'. But those who ignored or disbelieved the signs were completely taken by surprise.

This dual response runs right through the New Testament passages. To *unbelievers* Jesus' arrival will be a total surprise, a dreadful shock. To them he will appear as a 'thief', to rob them of all they have lived for. It will happen as suddenly as painful contractions come on a pregnant woman and will be equally inescapable (1 Thess 5:3). But the very next verse states that *believers* will not be surprised (1 Thess 5:4). They will have kept their eyes open, seen the signs and will be expecting him. They will be like the householder who heard that a burglar was intending to visit his home and stayed awake, 'keeping watch' for every sign of his approach (Matt 24:42–43). However, even believers are exhorted to be self-disciplined, alert sentries, lest they fall into the world's stupor and be caught out themselves (1 Thess 5:6–9).

So what are the signs of his coming? What are we 'watching' for? What events should we particularly notice as we read the newspapers and watch the television?

Here we run into a problem. We have so much data, almost too much, but it is scattered throughout the New Testament – some in the Gospels (particularly the first three), more in the Epistles (particularly the two to the Thessalonians) and a great deal in the book of Revelation.

Where shall we start? How shall we fit it all together? It's like trying to complete a jigsaw puzzle without the guidance of a picture on the lid. What we need is a basic framework into which all the pieces can be fitted. Is there such an outline anywhere in the New Testament?

Many think it is provided by the book of Revelation, which appears to give a sequence of future events (pictured as seals, trumpets and bowls). But the order is very complicated and detailed examination reveals that it is not strictly chronological (past events are recapitulated and future events are anticipated at irregular intervals). Actually the book was never intended to be a blue-print of the future and to treat it as such misses the practical purpose behind every part of it – to encourage believers to be 'overcomers' in the coming crisis (Rev 3:5 and 21:7 are the keys).

That is not to say there is no order in its predictions. In fact, the sequence becomes much clearer towards the end, when the bad news gives way to the good news. But in the middle chapters it is far from simple or clear – which explains why it has led to so many different 'charts' in the commentaries. If we accept that its primary aim is to help believers endure suffering rather than identify signs, we are free to look elsewhere for help with the latter.

Thankfully, the disciples once asked Jesus the very question we are asking: 'What will be the sign of your coming and the end of the age?' Jesus' answer is in each of the 'Synoptic' (similar viewpoint) Gospels (Matt 24, Mark 13 and Luke 21). Unfortunately, they asked another question at the same time – when would Jesus' prediction about the destruction of the Temple come true (presumably they thought it would be at the same time, little dreaming they would be at least nineteen centuries apart!)? Jesus answered both queries together, so that the events of AD 70 are blended with the signs of his coming (which may not be altogether misleading, since the two events have quite a lot in common, the one foreshadowing the other).

Of the three versions Luke concentrates on the earlier event, Matthew on the later. It is in the latter that we find the clearest outline, a fourfold framework of future events signalling his return, into which all the other information can be inserted.

After identifying the four basic 'signs' in the sequence, Jesus adds to each a warning about its attendant peril and counsel about the disciples' proper response to that. So for each sign there is a description, a danger and a duty (readers can easily make their own chart, which will be an aid to the memory). There is special emphasis on the risk that each will bring – namely, the deception of believers, misleading them in both belief and behaviour.

Sign 1: Disasters in the World (Matt 24:4–8)
Three are specifically mentioned: wars, earthquakes and famines.
The list is not exhaustive. Many others are mentioned in
Revelation – for example, polluted rivers and oceans, outsized
hailstones. The 'four horsemen of the apocalypse' cover imperial
expansion and its resultant bloodshed, famine, disease and death.
Clearly, these disasters have both natural and political causes.

An exponential increase in such catastrophes quickly spreads
alarm and insecurity. In such a mood people look for a 'saviour'
to avert tragedy, a situation ripe for unscrupulous claimants who
will delude others and even deceive themselves into thinking that
they are 'Christ'. The danger is a rash of false 'messiahs'.

Disciples must protect themselves from such deception by not
allowing panic to make them vulnerable. They can do this by
understanding these painful calamities in the opposite way to
the world's reaction, not death-pangs of the old but birth-pangs
of the new, not the end of all good things but the beginning of
much better things. The appropriate response is not alarm and
anxiety, but a sense of anticipation.

This sign is clearly visible. There have been over forty international conflicts since World War II, to say nothing of civil
disturbances. Earthquakes are apparently doubling in number
every ten years. Famine is widespread in the 'third' underdevel-
oped world. How long this state of affairs will continue or how
much worse it can get, we cannot guess. But it is the first major
sign of his coming.

Sign 2: Deserters in the Church (Matt 24:9–14)
The changes will be of degree rather than kind, but will be
universal in scale. Again, three features are mentioned, which
relate to each other.

First, *opposition*. Followers of Jesus will be hated by all
nations, which will bring a corresponding increase in martyrdom.
There are approximately two hundred and fifty political 'nations'
in the world today. Christians are under pressure in all but about
thirty, and that number shrinks annually. Churches everywhere

need to prepare their members for suffering and sacrifice. The first three chapters of Revelation provide a curriculum for such schooling; indeed, the whole book is designed as a manual for martyrdom and covers every crisis likely to be encountered by the faithful.

Second, *reduction*. Such pressures quickly reveal the difference between genuine and nominal Christians. Mere churchgoers give up. Their love cools as a result of moral compromise with an increasingly wicked world. They will turn away from the faith, betraying Christ and Christians.

Third, *expansion*. Paradoxically, a church purified under pressure becomes a preaching church. This is confirmed throughout history and is particularly true of China today. This third development will be the completion of the task of world evangelisation. Only then can history be wound up, mission completed.

During this phase the danger shifts from false messiahs to false prophets, who are much more likely to deceive believers since true prophets are a continuing ministry within the church. Discernment will be needed. From the Old Testament we have some guidance about the content of false prophecies. They offer 'Peace, peace – when there is no peace' (Jer 6:14; 8:11). They reassure with false comfort when trouble looms. Their message could be summarised as 'Don't worry, it may never happen'. One current example is the teaching that all Christians will be taken out of the world before the 'Big Trouble' or 'Great Tribulation' begins (see Sign 3 below). This leaves many Christians unprepared for the trials and testings ahead, which some of their brethren are already suffering.

Another characteristic of false prophecy is to make light of the sin in God's people, as if those who are the 'elect', the chosen of God, are eternally secure no matter what their moral or spiritual condition and will not be required to face personal suffering. The cliché 'Once saved always saved', a phrase which never occurs in scripture, encourages this kind of thinking. Jesus makes it quite clear that this is not the case. 'He who stands firm to the end will be saved' (Matt 10:22; 24:13). Apostasy, the public denial of Christ in word or deed forfeits future salvation. 'But whoever disowns me before men, I will disown him before my father in heaven' (Matt 10:33). The book of Revelation takes the same line. The 'overcomers' will inherit the new heaven and earth but the 'cowardly' will be thrown into the lake of fire (Rev 21:7–8).

What proportion will fail to stand firm to the end? It is a sobering challenge to read Jesus' prediction that '*many*' will turn away from the faith and the love of '*most*' will grow cold. The defection will not be negligible.

Yet there is an ever greater crisis to come which could wipe out even the faithful remnant, were it not for the fact that God in his sovereign power will strictly limit its duration.

Sign 3: Dictator in the Middle East (Matt 24:15–28)

The troubles that have always afflicted God's people will reach a climax in a short, sharp crisis known as 'the Great Tribulation' (Rev 7:14) or 'the Big Trouble'.

Jesus said more about this penultimate sign than the other three, but in a less straightforward way. His words need careful examination.

He based his warning on a phrase used three times by the prophet Daniel in the sixth century before Christ: 'the abomination that causes desolation' (Dan 9:27; 11:31; 12:11). A careful study reveals that Daniel was referring to a human conqueror who, in the very city where God had been honoured, would utter blasphemous words and commit obscene deeds provoking great mental and physical distress among God's people.

This prophecy was partially fulfilled by the Seleucid king of Syria, Antiochus IV Epiphanes (= 'Glorious', though behind his back he was called Epimanes = 'Crazy'). In a reign of terror over Jerusalem for three and a half years in the second century before Christ, he ordered the Jews to abandon the laws of God, set up a Greek altar to the god Zeus in the Temple, sacrificed pigs on it and filled the priests' rooms with prostitutes. His tyranny ended in a revolt led by the Maccabees family and he died insane.

Even Daniel realised that there would be another such, even

worse, 'at the time of the end' (Dan 11:35, 40; 12:4, 9, 12, 13). Clearly Jesus, speaking after Antiochus, endorsed this second fulfilment as still future. And there are notable similarities.

It will be for the *same period*. While Jesus simply said the days of this despot would be *'cut short'*, the book of Revelation is more specific: 1260 days, forty-two months or three and a half years ('a time, times and half a time' Rev 12:14).

It will be in the *same place*. Jesus advises all living in Judea at that time to leave as quickly as possible, without even waiting to pack. They must not remain in the vicinity of this man. That this is sound advice was demonstrated by the fact that no Christians died when Jerusalem was destroyed in AD 70 though a million Jews perished; they had fled across the Jordan to Pella the moment the emperor Titus and his troops arrived. Titus was no Antiochus, however. Hopefully believers in and around Jerusalem at the end of time will be as ready to act promptly. They must pray it will not be on the Sabbath when there will be no available transport or in the cold of winter since they will have to sleep out. Pregnant women and nursing mothers will have a particularly hard time keeping up in the flight.

Other passages in the New Testament speak about this last dictator. John alone calls him 'the antichrist' (1 John 2:1; note that in Greek 'anti' means 'instead of', a substitute rather than an antagonist), though this is the title by which most Christians identify him. Paul talks about this 'man of lawlessness', who 'opposes and exalts himself over everything that is called God or is worshipped and even sets himself up in God's temple, proclaiming himself to be God', but he is 'doomed to destruction' (2 Thess 2:3–4). The ultimate blasphemy!

Again, the book of Revelation gives us most information, particularly in chapter 13. Here he is described as a 'beast', as is his religious colleague and co-conspirator, 'the false prophet'. Together they set up a totalitarian regime in which only those who submit to this authority, by being branded with their mark, are allowed to buy and sell food and goods. The mark will be a number (666); the full meaning will be obvious when the time comes, but 6 is the human number, always falling short of the divine perfection of 7.

Since the authority of this tyranny will be universal rather than just local (Rev 13:7), the 'distress' will be unprecedented. Nothing like it will have been experienced before or will be experienced after, said Jesus. It will be the greatest pressure his followers have ever known, terribly fierce but mercifully brief.

However, the greater danger will be the same one of deception. Such conditions will produce a plethora of false prophets *and* false messiahs, as eager to take their pickings as vultures gather around the body of an animal that has been attacked. With supernatural displays of occult power they will try 'to deceive even the elect', mimicking the example of the antichrist and the false prophet (Rev 13:3, 14–15).

There will be many rumours that Christ has returned and believers will be told where they can find him. They must not listen to these rumours. They will see the sign that he has come, wherever they are at the time (see Sign 4 below). Only those in Judea must travel, not to encounter Christ but to escape Antichrist. The rest must stay where they are, keeping their ears shut and their eyes open. They must watch and pray.

This whole extraordinary scenario may be difficult to imagine or believe. But we have Jesus' word for it: 'See, I have told you ahead of time', (Matt 24:25). It is a question of trusting his foreknowledge and truthfulness. How kind and thoughtful of him to prepare us with such detailed information. Those who accept and act upon it will be kept safe when the storm breaks.

Before considering the final sign, there are two very important points to note at the end of the 'Trouble' or 'Great Tribulation'. First, *Christ has not come yet*. There are plenty of rumours that he has, but the truth is that he has not. Second, *Christians have not gone yet*. They are still on the earth, experiencing the wide distress (note 'you' and 'your' throughout these verses). The only ones who escape are those who are martyred, though this will be a 'great multitude' (Rev 6:9–11; 7:9–17; 11:7; 13:15; 20:4). Others will be safely hidden in deserted areas (Rev 12:6,14). The

warning that all who worship the beast and accept his mark will
be 'tormented with burning sulphur . . . for ever and ever' is seen
as a call 'for patient endurance and faithfulness on the part of the
saints' (Rev 14:9–12) lest they share this fate.

But this crisis can be measured in days and will soon be
over. There will be only one more 'sign' before the Lord
returns.

Sign 4: Darkness in the Sky (Matt 24:29–31)
This will follow 'immediately after the distress of those days'.
There will be no more delay. This means that those who live to
see the third sign will have a very good idea about when Jesus
will come back. This knowledge should encourage them to hold
on during those terrible months.

The final sign will be unmistakable. All natural sources of
light will be extinguished, leaving the whole sky black as ink.
Whatever the time of day, it will be the darkest night. Sun,
moon and stars will be shaken out of their orbits, no longer
able to shine upon planet earth. Hebrew prophets foretold it
(Isa 13:10; 34:4; Joel 2:31, quoted in Acts 2:20).

The sky has already reflected key events in the life of Christ.
The brilliant star at his birth and the eclipsed sun at his death
are foreshadowings of the cosmic welcome to his return.

The absence of natural lighting will make the supernatural
'lightning' all the more noticeable. The sky which was pitch-dark
will be filled with brilliant light, the glory of the only begotten
Son of God, glimpsed so briefly by three disciples on Mount
Hermon (Mark 9:3; John 1:14; 2 Pet 1:16–17), now blazed
around the globe and seen by all.

In a theatre, when the house lights are turned off it is a
signal that the drama is about to begin. The excited audi-
ence knows it will not have to wait long before the curtain goes up on a brightly illuminated stage, often a crowd
scene with the main actor centre front. So it will be on 'that
day'.

The nations will see the 'lightning coming from the east and flashing to the west' and they will see Jesus riding on the clouds (just how is not explained; will it be caught by television cameramen?). As full realisation of the significance of what is happening dawns on unbelievers, they will be overcome with grief. How wrong they have been! What opportunities they have wasted! Now they will be the ones to experience unprecedented distress.

Not so the believers who have waited so long for this day to arrive. They too will see the lightning, but they will also hear the sound of a trumpet, loud enough to wake the dead! The ancient ram's horn ('shofar' in Hebrew) was a call to the Lord's people to gather together; this will be the same. Angels will escort believers from all four corners of the earth; for many, their first trip to the Holy Land, for all, their first free flight! They will already have their new bodies, as will the dead believers who precede them to this meeting of all meetings.

It is generally known as 'the Rapture'. In modern English, the word has strong emotional overtones, which are not inappropriate. But the word is actually taken from the Latin *rapto*, *raptere* (which means to be 'snatched up' and is used in the Latin translation of 1 Thess 4:17: 'caught up with them to meet the Lord in the air'). The same double meaning can be found in the synonym 'transported'.

Of course, as believers are transported to Israel, unbelievers will be left behind. As Jesus said, there will be two men working together in the same field, one taken, the other left; the same can happen to two women working together in the same kitchen (Matt 24:40–41). Even families will be forever divided (Luke 12:51–53).

But the faithful followers of Jesus will be forever united, both with each other and with their Lord (1 Thess 4:17). Wherever he is or will be, he has come back so that they can be with him and see his glory (John 14:3; 17:24).

*   *   *   *   *

Such are the 'signs of his coming' which Jesus gave to his disciples and, through them, to us. Their content and sequence are clear, as is the increasing speed and the decreasing duration of their appearance.

Jesus encouraged us to look for these signs of history and to interpret them correctly, just as others interpret the signs of nature. When the sap rises in the fig-tree and the buds burst into leaf, the advent of summer is signalled (Jesus is drawing a simple analogy from the natural world; there is no hint that he is speaking metaphorically of the national restoration of Israel to its own land and political independence, even though the Old Testament occasionally likens the nation to a fig-tree, more usually a vine). The analogy is between the budding leaves and the four 'signs' he has been speaking about. 'Even so, when you see all these things [i.e. up to and including the darkened sky], you know that he [or, it] is near, right at the door' (Matt 24:33).

It is vital to realise that Jesus' purpose in giving this detailed forecast was not to argue dates, but to avoid dangers. His intention was practical application rather than intellectual speculation. Alas, history is full of examples of those who have 'guestimated' the actual date. Martin Luther calculated it would be 1636, John Wesley thought of 1874; both were wise enough to choose a year well ahead of their having to live with their mistakes! Not so William Miller, founder of the Seventh Day Adventists, who chose 1844 or Charles Russell, founder of the Jehovah's Witnesses, who chose 1914; both died shortly after their dates expired. Recently there has been a rash of proposals, many highlighting 1988 (as the fortieth year after the 'fig-tree' State of Israel blossomed).

From all that has been said so far, it is obvious that we do not know the year and cannot know at this stage, when only the more general 'signs' are clearly visible. It is also clear that it cannot be this year, next year or even for the next few years. The hope that it will be in our lifetime depends on the extraordinary acceleration in world events. The end could come more quickly than we think.

However, there is one more thing we can say about the timing of his coming. We may not know what year it will be, but we do know what time of year it will be! God wrote into Jewish ritual foreshadowings of his later redemptive work through Christ, especially into the annual calendar of feasts. The three major festivals, when the people gathered in Jerusalem, were 'signs' of the Messiah. The first was *Passover* (March/April in our diaries), when the lamb was killed at 3 p.m., followed a few days later by presenting the 'first-fruits' of the harvest – clearly fulfilled in the death and resurrection of Jesus. The second was *Pentecost* (May/June), to give thanks for the law given at Sinai fifty days after the first Passover, though it led to the death of 3000 rebels (Exod 32:28) – clearly fulfilled in the giving of the Spirit seven weeks after Calvary, bringing life to 3000 penitents (Acts 2:41; cf. 2 Cor 3:6).

The third, *'Tabernacles'* (September/October), is the 'great' feast when Jews recalled the provision of manna in the wilderness by living in temporary shelters, and celebrated the final ingathering of the harvest. Christians celebrate Passover and Pentecost (as Easter and Whit), though now on differently calculated dates. But consciously or unconsciously, they ignore Tabernacles, because they do not see any connection with Christ. There is much more than they realise.

Jesus was probably born during this feast. He may have been conceived on 25 December, but most know he was not born on that pagan midwinter celebration of the returning sun in the northern hemisphere. A little research into scripture reveals that he was born fifteen months after Zechariah was on duty in the temple in the fourth month (1 Chron 24:10; Luke 1:5,26,36). Tabernacles fell in the seventh month. Is this why John says: 'the Word became flesh and lived for a while [the Greek is "tabernacled"] among us' (John 1:14)?

He certainly visited the feast. His sceptical brothers urged him to use the occasion, knowing that this was the very time of year when the Jews expected their Messiah to appear.

His response is very revealing: 'The time for me has not yet come: for you any time is right' (John 7:6). But he did go, privately. And he did make a public appearance on the last and greatest day, on which water was carried from the pool of Siloam to pour on the altar with prayers that the early and latter rains might come again (there is no rain, only dew, for the six summer months), ensuring the next harvest. In this context, Jesus' shouted message takes on profound meaning: 'If a man is thirsty, let him come to me and drink. Whoever believes in me, as the Scripture has said, streams of living water will flow from within him' (John 7:37–38). This caused a lively debate about his identity. Ironically, the possibility that he was the Messiah was dismissed because he came from Nazareth, not Bethlehem! What self-restraint Jesus showed in remaining silent.

However, the real fulfilment of this feast in Christ is in his second advent, not his first. Just as he died at Passover, sent his Spirit at Pentecost, he will return at Tabernacles. Right on time. God's time.

Every Jew knows this. Their own prophets foretold it. Zechariah predicted that the nations will thereafter 'go up year after year to worship the King, the Lord Almighty, and to celebrate the Feast of Tabernacles' (Zech 14:16). Every year at this time, Jews pray that Gentiles may attend the feast to greet the Messiah. If any further confirmation is needed, the fact that it is immediately preceded by the Feast of Trumpets should settle the matter (Lev 23:23–25; cf. Matt 24:31; 1 Cor 15:52; 1 Thess 4:16; Rev 11:15).

On the eighth day of the feast, Jews hold a wedding ceremony and get 'married' to the Law (a scroll held by a rabbi under the canopy). On that day they begin again their annual reading of the Pentateuch, the five books of Moses. One day it will be the 'wedding of the Lamb' (Rev 19:7). That's just one of the reasons why Jesus is returning – for his bride.

*   *   *   *   *

We began this section by considering what the scripture means by describing the second coming as 'sudden'. We must end by looking at the word 'soon', applied to the same event. 'Yes, I am coming soon' (Rev 22:20). The simple question is: how soon is 'soon'?

At first sight, the word leaves an impression that it could be 'any moment now'. But words need to be seen in the context of the whole teaching of the New Testament on any subject.

Some of its writers clearly held the possibility that Jesus would return in their lifetime. 'We who are still alive and are left will be caught up' (1 Thess 4:17; note 'we', not 'they'). Paul certainly hoped it would be (2 Cor 5:2–3). He did not relish the disembodied state between death and resurrection, though he preferred it to being in his present body.

On the other hand, there are clear indications that they did not expect him back at any moment, that there would be a considerable lapse of time. The disciples had to take their testimony 'to the ends of the earth' (Acts 1:8). Jesus predicted Peter's crucifixion in his old age (John 21:18), though in the same context he gave ground for a rumour that John would live until his return; John himself corrects this misunderstanding (John 21:23).

That generation, and the next, were disappointed. They had believed and preached that Jesus would 'soon' return as king. He had not. It became a topic for ridicule, even before the last page of the New Testament was written. Hecklers mocked the teachers: 'Where is this coming he promised? Ever since our fathers died everything goes on as it has since the beginning of creation' (2 Pet 3:4).

The problem is even more acute for us, after fifty or more generations have come and gone. We may be much *nearer* the event, but such a long delay makes us wonder if we are anywhere *near* it. Does 'soon' make any sense to us today? Dare we use it confidently in our preaching? How do we cope with it?

Some scholars simply dismiss the word as a 'mistake'. They assert that Paul, and even Jesus himself, were wrong to use this word, even if they sincerely believed it. Though this explanation is widely accepted in liberal circles, it is untenable to those who believe the Bible to be the inspired word of God, who would not allow such a misleading error to be left for us to read.

The Bible is a self-interpreting book, one part explaining another. In fact, the same chapter in which the scoffing jibe about his delay is mentioned includes a two-fold answer to it.

First, *time is relative*. To the Greeks, God was outside time. To the Hebrews, time was inside God. Time is real to him (even he cannot change the past); but it is relative to him. It is also relative to us. (When Einstein was challenged to give a simple presentation of this theory of time's relativity, he replied: 'One minute sitting on a hot stove seems longer than one hour talking to a pretty girl'!) It is even more relative to God. 'But do not forget this one thing, dear friends: With the Lord a day is as a thousand years, and a thousand years are like a day' (2 Pet 3:8; quoting Ps 90:4). The day God left his beloved Son alone on the cross must have felt like a millennium, but it must seem only a couple of days since God had him back at his side again.

So we should take 'soon' with God's sense of time rather than ours. The second coming is the very next big event on his calendar, even if it isn't on ours. Just a day or two more, or perhaps even just a few 'hours', from heaven's point of view. Notice the constant use of 'day' and 'hour' in connection with this happening (Matt 24:36; John 5:28; Rev 14:7); this may also explain the 'silence in heaven for about half an hour' (Rev 8:1).

So 'the Lord is not slow in keeping his promise, as some understand slowness' (2 Pet 3:9). He only seems slow to us, who operate on a different time-scale and in an age of 'instant' products seek immediate solutions to tension. We have lost the art of waiting for anything, never mind waiting on the Lord. Yet even saints can get tired of waiting. One such read the verse: 'For in just a very little while, he who is coming will come and will not delay' (Heb 10:37) and cried out: 'But, O Lord, it is a very long little while!'

So why did the Lord leave the word '*soon*' in the scripture, knowing it could be misunderstood (by giving it a human rather than a divine meaning), leading to disappointment and impatience? Actually it does more good than harm. Somehow the word stimulates frequent recall of this future crisis. Life is to be seen in this perspective. In a very real sense, his return is the next big event on our calendar as well as God's. 'Soon' reminds us to start getting ready now. For, as we shall see in the second part of this sections, Jesus is not so concerned about what we are doing when he comes back as with what we have been doing all the time he has been away. We need to keep constantly in mind our accountability to him on that Day. The little word 'soon' does that very effectively.

Second, *delay is beneficial.* Instead of grumbling about it, we should be glad. It means that judgement is also postponed. It is an expression of God's reluctance to close the door of salvation quickly. 'He is patient with you, not wanting any to perish, but everyone to come to repentance' (2 Pet 3:9). This same God waited over a century before sending the flood (Gen 6:3; this was not a reduction in life span, since it was not the average age afterwards); indeed, he waited nearly a millennium, the lifetime of Methuselah, since his first announcement of that judgement to Enoch (Jude 14–15). Today this same God is patiently extending to us the opportunity to change our way of living before it is too late. Note how often Jesus drew a parallel between the days of Noah and the day of his return (Matt 24:37), as did his disciples after him (2 Pet 3:5–6).

In other words, if delay makes Christians disappointed for themselves, they should be delighted for the sake of others! And they might ponder on the thought that had there not been a long delay, they themselves would never have known God's love and all that he 'has prepared for those who love him' (1 Cor 2:5).

But we are human. Having 'tasted the goodness of God and the powers of the age to come' (Heb 6:5), we naturally want the rest as soon as possible. To the promise of Jesus: 'Yes, I am coming soon', our instinctive and understandable reaction is to cry: 'Amen. Come, Lord Jesus' (Rev 22:20).

WHY?

This is by far the most important question to ask about the second coming. Strangely, it is the most neglected!

Many Christians who rejoice in the fact of his return rarely think of its purpose. For them it is apparently enough to look forward to having him with them once again.

But why should this bring pleasurable anticipation when every believer can look forward to being with him in heaven immediately after death, 'away from the body and at home with the Lord' (2 Cor 5:8)? Won't fellowship with him be sweeter outside the context of this sad, sick, sinful world?

Is it that they hope his return will come before their death, thus avoiding death (and burial or cremation) altogether? Certainly, no one relishes being measured up to be put in a wooden box! Or is it that they somehow feel that fellowship with his physical presence is somehow more real and desirable than his 'spiritual' presence in heaven?

Let us suppose that he is not coming back to earth, that he will stay in heaven until all his people join him there, where they will live with him for ever (which is quite a common notion, both inside and outside the church). Ask yourself whether this would really affect your belief or, even more relevant, your behaviour. What is your honest answer?

So far we have been thinking subjectively about the effect on ourselves. Let us look at it more objectively, and the results for the world.

Why does he need to return? Why does the world need him back? What did he not do on his first visit that requires a second? Did he not complete his mission? What will he yet do here on earth that he cannot do from his position of supreme authority in heaven?

To some, such questions are inappropriate, even impudent. They see such delving into the mysteries of divine sovereignty as mere speculation. They are content with the revealed fact of his coming, to 'wait and see' what he does when he comes. However, there are two reasons for going further than this.

First, scripture itself gives a number of clear reasons for his return and hints at others. We are at liberty to follow up all the clues. Second, the more we understand the purpose of his return, the more we can appreciate its central importance to our hope for the future and the more it will affect the way we live in the present (this last aspect will be explored in the next chapter).

To stimulate your thoughts, let me raise two further questions which Christians don't seem to consider very often.

How long will he stay? His first visit lasted a third of a century. Will his second be shorter or longer? Can what he has to do be done quickly or will it take quite a lot of time? Will there be another 'ascension' or will he remain here permanently?

Why do we have to come back? Not only is Christ returning to planet earth; all believers now in heaven are also returning. 'We believe God will bring with Jesus those who have fallen asleep in him' (1 Thess 4:14). Christians expect to live on this earth a second time! When did you last hear that preached at a funeral?

We are now ready to ask why Christ, and Christians, need to come back here. What objectives does the Lord have in mind? There are at least five:

To Complete the Saints
The first thing to grasp is that salvation is a continuing process, not an instantaneous change at conversion. It is not yet complete in any Christian, though it is more developed in some than others.

That is why the New Testament uses the verb 'save' in three tenses – we have been saved, we are being saved and we will be saved. This corresponds to the three phases known as justification, sanctification and glorification, which together constitute salvation.

The process will reach its goal when every part of our being is restored to its original condition, when God created us in his own image. We know what that will be like, for his Son is 'the exact representation of his being' (Heb 1:3).

The transformation will be complete when he returns. 'We know that when he appears, we shall be like him, for we shall see him as he is' (1 John 3:2). As he perfectly reflects his Father, we shall perfectly reflect him.

That is why scripture is able to say: 'He will appear a second time, not to bear sin, but to bring salvation to those who are waiting for him' (Heb 9:28). At last, Christians will be fully 'saved', (and only then able to say with confidence, 'once saved, always saved'!). Their Saviour will have completed his work *in* them, as on his first visit he completed his work *for* them, on the cross ('It is finished', John 19:30). He will see the results of all his suffering and be satisfied (Isa 53:11).

We must be careful not to be too 'spiritual' when we think about 'full salvation'. Western Christians are prone to this distortion in a culture more influenced by Greek thinking than Hebrew, in which physical and spiritual are widely separated, morally as well as mentally. Perfection is defined in terms of a soul in heaven rather than a body on earth. Eastern mysticism has a similar contempt for the material world.

But the creation is basically good, because it came from the hand of the good Creator. He wanted a physical universe and intended human beings to have physical bodies. Though sinful rebellion (angelic and human) has ruined his creation, God intends to redeem it, by restoring its original state.

Salvation, therefore, means transforming every part of us, physical as well as spiritual. It is frustrating to be half saved, trying to live the new spiritual life in our old physical bodies (and brains) programmed over the years with wrong habits. The tension was well expressed by Paul: 'For in my inner being I delight in God's law; but I see another law at work in the members of my body' (Rom 7:22–23).

Of course, death of the body brings some relief. But it is only a partial solution to the problem, for the person God intended is incomplete, 'unclothed', 'away from the body' (2 Cor 5:4,

8). That may be enough for Greek philosophers and Oriental mystics, but it will never satisfy those who know what God is really like and what he really wants for them. 'We ourselves, who have the firstfruits of the Spirit, groan inwardly as we wait eagerly for our adoption as sons, the redemption of our bodies' (Rom 8:23).

What a paradox! Because we have the Spirit, we long for new bodies! Like salvation, our 'adoption' as sons of God is future as well as past (cf. Rom 8:15). The crowning climax of our restoration will be the gift of a brand new body, uncontaminated by our sinful past, unlimited in its expression of the spirit within, unaffected by disease, decay or death. Unlike the old, this new body will develop instantaneously, 'in a flash, in the twinkling of an eye' (1 Cor 15:52). What will the evolutionist make of that?!

It will happen the moment the last trumpet sounds to herald the coming of Christ. His return and our resurrection will be simultaneous. The promise that 'we shall be like him, for we shall see him as he is' (1 John 3:2) covers the whole of us – body, soul and spirit. Our new bodies will be 'like his glorious body' (Phil 3:21). Does that not mean that we shall be neither very young nor very old but, like him, in the very prime of life?

But why do we have to come back to earth to experience this metamorphosis of our flesh? Why could we not receive our new bodies in heaven? For that matter, why do we have to wait until we receive new bodies together, all at once? Why not at the moment each of us dies?

The answer is really quite simple: we don't need bodies in heaven, but we do on earth. Heaven is a place for spirit-beings. 'God is Spirit' (John 4:24). The angels surrounding his throne are 'ministering spirits' (Heb 1:14). The 'heavenly Jerusalem' is crowded with 'the spirits of righteous men' (Heb 12:23).

However, when heavenly beings come to earth they need bodies. The Son of God had to be incarnate – 'a body you prepared for me' (Heb 10:5). Angels have to assume human form (Gen 18:2; 19:1; cf. Heb 13:2). Even the fallen angels we call demons inhabit the bodies of others, human or animal (Mark

5:12–13). To operate in this physical world, a physical body is needed.

The implications are profound. If the 'saints' of all ages receive new bodies down here, that surely indicates that they are being fitted for continued life on earth rather than in heaven. It begins to look as if both Christ and Christians come back to stay, to remain on this planet. That would mean that believers still living on earth when Jesus returns will never go to heaven! Even those who went to heaven when they died were in temporary accommodation!

The Bible clearly depicts 'earth' as the ultimate destiny of all who have been saved. But not this old earth, a new earth. The same almighty power of God redeeming our bodies will also redeem our environment. There will be a new earth for our new bodies to live in (we shall consider this later, as well as the question about how quickly this will come after Jesus returns).

We know that our salvation will be complete when Jesus returns, but God's saving purpose will not be fulfilled until the entire universe has been restored to its original condition.

As well as the individual and universal aspects of God's plans for our world, there is to be one national restoration.

To Convert the Jews

Jesus was and is Jewish. He was born and died as 'King of the Jews' (Matt 2:2; 27:37). He 'was sent only to the house of Israel' (Matt 15:24). Almost his entire ministry was spent in his own land and among his own people. It is true that most of them did not receive him (John 1:11), but from those who did we have received the Bible (all but one of its forty authors were Jewish) and the church (all the twelve apostles and most of the initial members were Jewish).

Many Christians seem to have forgotten that their Saviour is a Jew and 'salvation is from the Jews' (John 4:22). The church seems to have pulled up its Jewish roots (for example, in moving Easter, Whitsuntide and Christmas away from the dates for Passover, Pentecost and Tabernacles). Worse than that,

Christians have set the pace for anti-semitism throughout church history, notoriously in the Crusades. Jews have suffered more in 'Christian' countries than any other, right up to the 'holocaust' in Germany. Behind this attitude lie two gross errors.

First, *that the Jews killed Jesus*. The entire nation, past and present, is held to be guilty of deicide (the murder of God). How can the Jews of today be held responsible, even though they still refuse to recognise Jesus as the Son of God? Even more Gentiles do the same. Are contemporary Christians ready to be found guilty for the Crusades? Even in Jesus' day, the whole nation was not involved in the crucifixion. 'The Jews' in John's Gospel are the inhabitants of Judea, southerners, not Galileans. Jesus made it clear that Gentiles would be his actual executioners (Matt 20:19; Mark 10:33; Luke 18:32). And in a sense we are all responsible for his death, since he was suffering for the sins of the entire human race.

Second, *that the church replaced Israel*. Since the Jews rejected their Messiah, Gentiles who accept him claim to constitute the 'new Israel'. God's covenant purposes have been totally transferred from one people to another. Jews have virtually become Gentiles, just one of the many nations of the world, outsiders to the kingdom of God. God's plans for the future do not include the Jewish people as such. So it is said.

Certainly this seems to be implied by some statements of Jesus (Matt 21:43) and Paul (Acts 13:46; 15:17; 28:28; Rom 9:24-26). Many of the Old Testament descriptions of Israel are given to the church in the New (1 Pet 2:9-10); the same applies to some of the promises made to them (Heb 13:5-6). But that is not the whole story.

God's covenant with Abraham and his descendants was 'everlasting' and therefore unconditional (Gen 17:7). To remove all doubt, God later spelled out what this would mean: 'I will not reject them or abhor them so as to destroy them completely, breaking my covenant with them. I am the Lord their God' (Lev 26:44; cf. Deut 4:31; 9:5-6; 2 Sam 7:15; Pss 89:34; 94:14; 105:8-9; 106:45; 111:5; Amos 9:8; Jer 30:11;

14:21; Ezek 16:60; 20:44; Mal 3:6). Though he would scatter
them among the nations when they broke their part of the
covenant, God would never break his and would bring them
back 'from the four corners of the earth' (Deut 32:26; Isa 11:12).
Such a worldwide dispersion and return did not happen in the
Babylonian exile, but is happening today. It was to a people
restored to their land that he promised a deliverer from Zion,
a new covenant and his outpoured Spirit (Isa 59:20–21; Jer
31:1–40; Joel 2:28–32). Despite all attempts to annihilate them,
these people have survived physically and a 'remnant' of them
have remained spiritually faithful to their God (1 Kgs 19:18).

The New Testament endorses all of this. God is still the 'God
of Abraham, and the God of Isaac, and the God of Jacob' for they
are still alive (Luke 20:37–38). The name 'Israel' is mentioned
over seventy times. It is always applied to Abraham's physical
descendants with one doubtful exception (Gal 6:16, if the Greek
word *kai* is translated 'even', instead of its normal meaning 'and',
as in the New English Bible).

Jesus foresaw both the immediate rejection by his fellow-
countrymen and their ultimate restoration. Even while weeping
over Jerusalem's refusal to accept his protection, he predicted:
'You will not see me again *until* you say: Blessed is he who
comes in the name of the Lord' (Matt 23:39; significantly, this
is one of the 'Hallel' or 'Praise' Psalms 113–118, sung at the
Feast of Tabernacles). He anticipated the fall of Jerusalem in
AD 70, but that it would only be 'trampled on by the Gentiles
until the times of the Gentiles are fulfilled' (Luke 21:24). The
disciples' last question to him before his ascension concerned
the timing of the restoration of the monarchy to Israel. Instead
of rebuking the irrelevance of their thinking (as many Christians
would today), he told them that the date already fixed by his
Father was not of immediate concern to them – they had a
mission to be his witnesses to the ends of the earth, the Gentile
nations (Acts 1:6–8). He had already told them they would one
day govern the courts of the twelve tribes (Matt 19:28; Luke
22:30), but this would have to wait. The one thing certain is

that 'this race will certainly not pass away until all these things have happened' (Matt 24:34 NIV margin; 'these things' are the signs of his coming).

In a passage specifically dealing with the future of the Jewish race (Rom 9–11), Paul clearly teaches that God has not rejected them, even though they have rejected him (11:1). He acknowledges that not all Abraham's physical descendants are his spiritual children sharing his faith (9:6–7; cf. 2:28–29). So many Jews are not 'saved' and need to believe in Jesus (10:1). Paul, with a similar anguish over his people as Moses, would willingly go to hell if it would get them to heaven (Rom 9:3; cf. Exod 32:32).

Nevertheless, Israel cannot 'fall beyond recovery (11:11), because 'God's gifts and his call [to the patriarchs] are irrevocable' (Rom 11:29). There has always been a 'remnant' and there always will be (11:6). Only 'some' of the branches of the 'olive tree' Israel, have been broken off and replaced by grafted 'unnatural' wild olive Gentiles (11:17,24). These hybrid believers (i.e. Christians) need to remember that they, too, are in danger of being 'cut off' if they do not continue to trust in the divine kindness (11:22). And they (i.e. the Jews) can be grafted back in our place, if and when they believe in Jesus, their Messiah, fitting into their own roots much more naturally (11:23–24). Indeed, there has been a Jewish minority in the church of Jesus for two millennia and it is currently expanding.

But there is more. Paul made a startling prediction, which he called a 'mystery' (11:25). The scriptural meaning is: a former secret God has now revealed. The hardening of Jewish hearts against the gospel, which is God's punishment for rejecting his redemptive initiative (as it was for Pharaoh: 9:17–18), is only partial and temporary *until* (that word again!) the full number of the Gentiles has 'come in'. Then it will be removed, the veil lifted from their minds (2 Cor 3:15–16), and 'so *all Israel* will be saved'. This phrase does not include all Jews who have ever lived or even necessarily all Jews still alive at the end. The phrase 'all Israel' is frequently used in the Old Testament of a representative national gathering from all the tribes of Israel, usually in Jerusalem (1

Chron 11:1; cf. Deut 1:1); it is perhaps best translated: 'Israel as a whole'.

Since 'saved' must have the same meaning here as elsewhere (cf. 10:1), this prediction is nothing less than a mass conversion to faith in Jesus of the most resistant people on earth! How could such a thing happen? The answer is obvious: in the same way that it happened on the Damascus road to Saul, the persecutor of the Christians, who became Paul, the preacher of the gospel. The posthumous appearance of Jesus of Nazareth is enough proof for any Jew that he is the Messiah.

This is precisely what will happen when Jesus returns to Jerusalem. The same prophet who predicted his first coming on a donkey, and his second at the Feast of Tabernacles proclaimed this word of the Lord: 'And I will pour out on the house of David and the inhabitants of Jerusalem a spirit of grace and supplication. They will look on me, the one they have *pierced*, and mourn for him as one mourns for an only child, and grieve bitterly for him as one grieves for a firstborn son' (Zech 12:10; cf. Ps 22:16: 'They have *pierced* my hands and my feet'). The same word is taken up in the book of Revelation: 'Look, he is coming with the clouds, and every eye will see him, even those who *pierced* him' (Rev 1:7). One can hardly imagine their anguish over the unnecessary suffering and wasted opportunity of two thousand years – but it will not leave them in hopeless despair. As their fathers looked to a brass serpent on a pole for healing, they will now look to the Son of Man and be saved (Num 21:8; John 3:14–15). What a welcome they will give him as he enters the city again (Matt 23:39).

There are two important implications of this amazing result of Jesus's return:

The first is that the Jews will have been preserved as a people and restored to their land and capital. This has already happened. Many Christians rightly see this as a necessary prelude to the Lord's coming, but wrongly use it as an indicator of an imminent return. As we have seen, this immigration was not specifically included by Jesus in 'the signs of the times'.

Furthermore, it means that Jerusalem will remain in Jewish hands in spite of predicted international assaults (e.g. Zech 12:1–3) and that a representative portion of the people will be supernaturally protected through all their troubles, including the 'Great Tribulation'. This surely is the meaning of the 'sealing' of the 144,000 from all the tribes of Israel (Rev 7:1–8).

The second is that the future destiny of the Jews and the Gentiles who believe in Jesus is identical. Both come into the same salvation through the same Saviour. Jesus, speaking to Jews about Gentiles, said: 'I have other sheep that are not of this sheep-pen. I must bring them also. They too will listen to my voice, and there shall be one flock and one shepherd' (John 10:16).

There is a common misconception that Jews have an earthly destination and Christians a heavenly one. The Bible clearly teaches that they will live together in the new heaven and new earth, in a new Jerusalem that has the names of the twelve tribes of Israel on its gates and the names of the twelve apostles of Jesus on its wall foundations. They will be one people living under one (new) covenant.

To Conquer the Devil

Evil is not an abstract object with an independent existence. That means that the question 'why did God create evil?' is really meaningless. There is no such thing.

Evil is personal, not impersonal, an adjective, not a noun. It describes creatures who rebel against their Creator and do things their way rather than his. God did create beings, both on earth, and in heaven, who were capable of becoming 'evil' by their own free choice. This resulted in evil angels and evil humans, apparently in that order (Gen 3:1). Between them they are responsible for all the 'evils' in nature and history. Such is the biblical diagnosis.

The leader of the heavenly rebellion was the fallen angel we call the devil, known by many names and titles – Satan, Beelzebub, serpent, dragon, lion, murderer, liar, destroyer. He persuaded many fellow angels to join his bid for a rival kingdom to God's (Rev 12:4 indicates a third of the angels). We know them as demons.

Both the devil and his demons are given titles of authority and influence in scripture. He is the ruler, prince and even 'god' of this world. They are principalities and powers. With the superior strength, intelligence and ability of angels they are able to wreak havoc in the affairs of men. They can manipulate us through disease in the body and deception in the mind. Their most potent weapon is death and the fear it brings (Heb 2:15). They can divide us from God and one another – and have done so since the garden of Eden. Their successful bid for power has been even greater on earth than in heaven: 'we know . . . that the whole world is under the control of the evil one' (1 John 5:19).

However, the devil is not God, though he would like to be and may even think he is. He is not omniscient (he doesn't know everything and can make blunders, one of which was to persuade Judas to betray Jesus; John 13:27). He is not omnipresent (he can only be in one place at once, which many Christians seem to forget; Job 1:7; Luke 4:13). He is not omnipotent; his power is strictly limited, in two ways:

First, he is no match for God. From the beginning until now, he can only act by God's permission (Job 1:12). God is still in complete control. Satan is no problem to him, though he is to us. This, of course, means that God allowed him to take over our world. We can see both divine justice and mercy in this, justice because those who refuse to live under the rule of a good king deserve a bad one, mercy because that increases the incentive to desire the original regime.

Second, he was no match for Christ. Jesus began and ended his public mission by confronting the devil on his own territory – and successfully resisting his subtle and seductive temptations. For the first time in history an entire life was lived in freedom from his clutches, breaking his monopoly hold on the human race (John 12:31; 14:30). The cross was a fatal blow to his power, a triumph over the principalities and powers (Col 2:15). Through

Jesus' atoning death and interceding life, it is now possible for men and women to live in freedom from the force of evil and their fear of death (Luke 22:31; Heb 2:14–15).

But the final victory is not yet complete. There are now two kingdoms on earth – of God and Satan, good and evil, light and darkness. They are both growing, quantatitively and qualitatively, side by side (Matt 13:30).

Why the overlap? Why didn't Satan's kingdom end when God's kingdom was re-established? A moment's thought will bring the explanation. If Christ had destroyed Satan and his followers as well as defeating them, the earth would have been uninhabited! God so loved Satan's victims that he wanted to give them every possible opportunity to transfer back to his rule, a liberation made possible through his Son (Col 1:13). Millions have now seized the opportunity. Alas, many more have not realised the door is open or have refused to go through it.

One day it will be shut. The kingdoms will not continue together. The wheat and the tares will be separated at the time of harvest (remember the Feast of Tabernacles?). The poisonous weeds will be burned. A good God cannot allow evil to continue spoiling things for ever. He must call a halt sometime.

So Satan's days are numbered. His doom is decided and dated. When Jesus returns, Satan must leave. The world will finally be rid of him, having suffered his evil tyranny since the very first human beings walked the earth. Human history is proof of his existence and testimony to his character.

Since he knows his fate is sealed, we can expect his frustration to become more apparent as the end approaches (Rev 12:12). He will put all his resources into a final bid to regain his dominion. Fortunately, 'we are not unaware of his schemes' (2 Cor 2:11). With the promise of 'peace and security' (1 Thess 5:3), he will set up one world government with one world religion. In charge of each will be two men who will accept his offer of status and power (once refused by Jesus! Luke 4:6– 8). They will be puppets under the devil's authority.

We have already mentioned this 'unholy trinity' (Satan, anti-christ and the false prophet are a dreadful counterpart of God, Christ and Holy Spirit). They will together rule the world as never before in the last few years before Jesus returns. No wonder it is called the 'Big Trouble' or 'Great Tribulation'.

But this last fling of the devil will still be under God's overruling control and be kept mercifully brief.

Their final joint act of defiance will be to gather an international military force intent on slaughtering the apparently defenceless people of God, now gathered in Jerusalem with their returned Lord, Jesus. This will be the last battle in a history of continuous warfare. Scripture locates it in the plain of Esdraelon, the valley of Jezreel, near the ancient fortress town of Solomon on the small 'hill of Megiddo' (in Hebrew, 'Harmageddon'); Winston Churchill called this site of so many fierce actions: 'the cockpit of the Middle East'. The roads from Europe to Arabia and from Asia to Africa cross here.

It will be the devil's biggest blunder. The most basic tactical error is to under-estimate the strength of one's opponent. Jesus will come fully prepared for the conflict. No longer riding to Jerusalem on a donkey as a symbol of peace, he will come on a horse as a symbol of war (Zech 9:9–10; Rev 19:11).

Jesus will only use, only need to use, one weapon – the sword of his mouth (Rev 19:15–21). It will be the same voice that commanded the wind and the waves to be still (Mark 4:39; the verb 'died down' comes from a root meaning to be smitten, cut off). Now a whole army will be slain – with a word! A field of corpses will be left unburied and provide a feast for vultures (Rev 19:17,21), the final humiliation for this rebel force.

But the two human 'beasts' behind it will not be killed. They will be taken prisoner and immediately 'thrown alive into the fiery lake of burning sulphur' (Rev 19:20). They will be the first two human beings to be sent to hell, even before the day of judgement, too depraved to be allowed to stand trial.

Surprisingly, the devil is not sent with them – not yet. He will be. But God has plans to use him just once more before he is sent to join his henchmen in everlasting torment (Rev 20:10). Meanwhile, he is to be banished from the earth for a thousand years, kept in solitary confinement in the lowest dungeons of the underworld so that he can no longer communicate with and deceive the peoples on earth (Rev 20:3).

So the world will at last be liberated from the devil and his oppressive forces of evil. It is difficult to imagine what that will mean for we have never known such a situation. We shall have to wait and see.

Will there be a world to see? Will it continue for a time or come to an end there and then? If it does go on, who will fill the political vacuum left by the collapse of the world government?

The Bible has yet another surprise for us.

To Command the World
Jesus told his followers to pray every day that God's kingdom, his rule, would 'come . . . on earth as it is in heaven' (Matt 5:10).

How and when will this prayer be answered?

Alas, Christians are deeply divided over this. The many different opinions may be grouped in three categories:

First, the *pessimists*. They believe this world is too far gone to be reclaimed. We can bring individuals into the kingdom (i.e. under God's rule). We can establish colonies of the kingdom (i.e. churches). But this world will remain in the devil's control and they will be destroyed together. Only in the 'new' earth will the kingdom be universally established. So this 'old' earth will 'pass away' immediately after the Lord returns. It will never know the blessings of being under God's government.

Second, the *optimists*. At the opposite end of the spectrum, they believe that the world will be 'Christianised' before Christ returns. This does not mean that everyone will be Christian, but that the church will grow and spread to be large and powerful enough to take over world government. This view also believes that this earth will end when he comes, since the kingdom will already have been established. In passing it may be noted that, on the present state and statistics of our world, the second coming must be a very long way off!

Third, the *realists*. Accepting Jesus' expectation that the kingdoms of God and Satan will 'grow together' (Matt 13:30), they anticipate increasing conflict between the two until the final confrontation between the returning Christ and the reigning antichrist. Of the outcome they have no doubt. Christ's victory over the forces of evil will clear the decks for his rule to be extended over the nations of the world. On this view, the 'old' earth will survive beyond his return, at least long enough for his reign to be demonstrated and appreciated.

Boiling down the debate to its simplest issue, we may propose the motion: that Jesus is coming back to this earth to reign over it. Not just to complete the saints, to convert the Jews and to conquer the devil – but to rule over the world for an extended period of time.

What does the New Testament say about this? The book of Revelation contains more information about the second coming than any other; so it is not surprising that the clearest indications of a reign of Christ after his return and on this earth may be found here. Quite early on, there is a prediction that when the last trumpet sounds, the angels in heaven will sing and shout in celebration of a change of government: 'The kingdom of the world [note the singular] has become the kingdom of our Lord and of his Christ' (Rev 11:15).

However, it is at the end of the book, where the chronological order of events is very much clearer, that we find the fullest and clearest statement about a reign of Christ (20:1–10). We must take this passage in its context (chapters 19 and 21); chapter divisions, like verse numbers, are quite late and man-made, often putting asunder what God has joined together.

In its proper setting, this reign of Christ follows his return but precedes both the day of judgement and the creation of a new heaven and earth. Its location in time is therefore clear, as is its location in space. The action takes place on earth, not in heaven (20:1–9).

The duration of his reign on earth is even clearer. The phrase 'a thousand years' is emphatically repeated six times in this short passage, twice with the definite article: 'the thousand years'. The Greek word is *chilioi* (from which we derive the label: 'chiliast', used of those who believe in this earthly reign of Christ); the Latin word is *millennium* (source of the more familiar label: 'millennialist'). Those I have called 'pessimists', who don't believe Christ will *ever* take over the government of this world, are usually known as 'A-millennialist' (non-millennialist would be more easily understood). The 'optimists' are known as 'Post-millennialist', because they believe Christ will return *after* Christians have established a millennial rule on his behalf. The 'realists' are known as 'Pre-millennialist', because they expect Christ to return *before* his worldwide rule is actualised.

Whether the 'thousand years' are taken literally or symbolically, it is obviously a considerable period. Much can happen during it. What will the world be like when the devil is out of it and Jesus is in full control of political and natural events? Imagination is limited by the absence of any previous experience of such conditions; only Adam could tell us and his knowledge was severely restricted in time and space! Revelation is also limited. Scripture throws out many tantalising hints, but we may conclude that the Lord knows it would be unsettling for us to know more.

For example, the Hebrew prophets looked forward to the time when 'the earth will be filled with the knowledge of the glory of the Lord, as the waters cover the sea' (Isa 11:9; Hab 2:14); when every knee will bow to the Lord and every tongue confess his name (Isa 45:23, a prediction applied to Jesus in Phil 2:10–11), when 'the Lord will be king over the whole earth' (Zech 14:9).

They also foresaw some of the results of this just and benevolent reign; a time of unparalleled peace and prosperity would result from the settlement of international disputes by divine arbitration and multilateral disarmament; it is in this context that we find the memorable couplet: 'They shall beat their swords into ploughshares and their spears into pruning hooks' (Isa 2:4; Mic 4:3) – words engraved in granite outside the United Nations headquarters in New York, but lacking any reference to the word of the Lord going out from Zion!

An abundance of food will be a source of health, in turn contributing to longevity. Death at one hundred years will seem a premature tragedy (Isa 65:20). There is an ancient Jewish notion that an ideal length of life on this planet would be one thousand years, based partly on the ages of their pre-flood fathers (none of whom quite made it, even Methuselah) and partly on the statement that 'a thousand years is like a day' to God (Ps 90:4; 2 Pet 3:8).

Even nature will reflect the change of government, with fertility in the vegetable world and harmony in the animal world: 'The wolf will live with the lamb, the leopard will lie down with the goat, the calf and the lion will feed together; and a little child will lead them. The cow will feed with the bear, their young will lie down together, and the lion will eat straw like the ox' (Isa 11:6–7). Carnivores will become herbivores, as God originally intended (Gen 1:30). Nature 'red in tooth and claw' was not his doing. The animals were never intended to be 'wild'. Children will safely play among them one day (Isa 11:8).

It is easy to dismiss all this as 'myth', as metaphysical fable rather than material fact. That is often a cover for our inability to imagine and therefore to believe in such a transformation. It is to question either the Creator's ability or his intention. If he once made a universe that was 'good' in every way, he *can* surely do it again. And if the purpose of redemption is to restore creation, he *will* surely do it again.

Let us return to the New Testament. Two aspects of the 'millennium' are specifically mentioned – one good news, the other bad news.

The good news is that believers, both Jews and Gentiles, will 'reign on the earth' with Christ (Rev 5:10). Men 'from every tribe and language and people and nation' (Rev 5:9) will administer the government among their countrymen. Singled out for special honour will be those who successfully resisted the pressures of the last and worst totalitarian regime, even to the point of martyrdom (Rev 20:4; note that this group is only one section of the company of those seated on 'thrones'). What a reversal! 'The meek will inherit the earth' (Matt 5:5).

This rule by the saints is frequently referred to in scripture – not just in Revelation (2:26 is another example) but in Daniel (7:18), in the Gospels (Matt 19:28; 20:21–23; Luke 19:15–19) and in the Epistles (1 Cor 6:2; 2 Tim 2:12). The prime qualification for responsibility then will be faithfulness now, trustworthiness as opposed to dishonesty, especially in such practical matters as money and property (Luke 16:10–12). Jesus will need many deputies to whom he can entrust key positions in his administration.

The bad news is that in spite of having the best government the world has ever seen and enjoying such ideal conditions, there will still be many who want to opt out of this kingdom of Christ. It is a lie that a perfect environment will produce perfect people, that prosperity brings contentment, that deep down everyone prefers peace to war. Human nature can only be changed from the inside, not the outside.

This sad fact will be amply proved at the very end of the millennium, in an extraordinary development. The devil will be released from his detention for one final opportunity to deceive the nations. He will find people wanting their 'freedom' from God and his people in every part of the globe. He will delude them into thinking that a military attack on the seat of government in Jerusalem will gain their political autonomy (has he not learned the lesson of Armegeddon or is this a suicidal act of defiance intended to take as many others with him as possible?). He will gather a huge army, perhaps the biggest ever, marching under the banner of 'Gog and Magog' (Rev 20:8). There is a very detailed prophecy about this in Ezekiel 38–39 which places the event *after* the restoration of the Davidic monarchy in Israel (the names will become meaningful in the light of the event).

The attempt will be utterly futile. Fire from heaven will put an end to it and to all involved. Why should it have been allowed to happen at all?

The millennium can be considered from two perspectives as a finale to world history and as a prelude to the day of judgement. It will have conclusively demonstrated the sovereignty of God and the sin of man; his goodness and our badness – the two sides of historical reality that must finally be brought together to be eternally separated.

On the one hand, the world will have seen what life can be like under divine rule, when God acts as man has wanted him to act and constantly criticised him for not doing so, by forcefully removing evil powers from the earth. But what will happen when the human cry for liberation from suffering is heeded?

On the other hand, the world will be exposed as having no desire to be set free from the sin that has caused the suffering. There is still a race of rebels, still a mutinous desire for moral independence, still an ambition to be like gods (Gen 3:5), to be landlords of the earth rather than its tenants.

The human race is without excuse. Given the very best opportunities and incentives, human beings still choose a godless existence which cannot remain neutral towards God or his people but must become hostile to both. The need for a day of judgement has been made abundantly apparent. The verdicts have been justified even before they have been announced. The stage is set.

To Condemn the Ungodly

Those whose beliefs are largely shaped by reciting creeds in church will be very familiar with this reason for his return. Both the 'Apostles' and the 'Nicene' creeds remind us that he will come to judge the quick (i.e. those still living) and the dead (already). Unfortunately they give the impression that this is the main, even the only, point of his second advent. As we have already seen, it is one of a number. Nevertheless, it is fundamental to his winding up of this 'present evil age', as the Jewish people called it.

It is necessary for history to conclude with a day of judgement. A little thought will reveal why.

The injustice of life demands it. It is so unfair that the wicked should prosper and the innocent suffer. Most crimes are undetected and unpunished. There seems to be little correlation between personal character and circumstance, integrity and prosperity, holiness and happiness. The universe appears to be based on blind chance – unless there is more to our existence than is bounded by cradle and grave. Instinct demands a time when good is rewarded and evil punished.

The justice of God demands it. If he never rights the wrongs he has permitted, his goodness is in question. If he is truly 'King of the universe', that position carries the responsibility of Judge as well. If it is true that: 'God cannot be mocked. A man reaps what he sows' (Gal 6:7), there *must* be a day of reckoning, when accounts are settled and bills paid in full.

But why a 'day' of judgement? Since death ends the opportunity and fixes a gulf between the good and the bad (Luke 16:26), why is each person not judged at that moment but kept waiting until the whole human race stands in the dock?

Because God must be publicly vindicated. He must be seen to be just in his decisions about our destiny. He has been so frequently accused of being unfair. These criticisms must be silenced, so that all will say, with Abraham: 'Will not the judge of all the earth do right?' (Gen 18:25).

Because Jesus must be publicly vindicated. His execution was the greatest injustice of all, the darkest day (quite literally) in human history. The last sight the world had of him was of a criminal in disgrace. All must witness the reversal of that verdict.

Because the Lord's people must be publicly vindicated. They made the right choice, took the side of God and right, yet in a wicked world paid the price for taking their stand, often with their lives. These, whom Jesus is not ashamed to call his 'brothers' (Heb 2:11; cf. Matt 25:40), must be honoured in the presence of those who treated them with contempt and hatred.

There is, then, to be a 'day' when justice will be done. Every human being has two future engagements, neither of which can be entered in a diary or marked on a calendar. 'Man is destined to die once, and after that to face judgement' (Heb 9:27). The first date is different for each; the second is the same for all.

Where will this great assize be held? There is a widespread impression that it will be up in heaven, perhaps due to the common but mistaken notion that everybody 'goes to heaven' when they die. Among Christians, there may be some confusion between 'the throne' (in Rev 4–5) and 'a great white throne' (in Rev 20:11; note the indefinite article), which are two different thrones, in two different places, occupied by two different persons. One is the throne of God in heaven and the other is the throne of Christ on earth.

Human beings will be judged on earth. This is where they have lived and where they have sinned. This is where their fate will be decided. How could a holy God allow sinners to enter heaven, even for a day? Actually, even the earth will have 'fled' (Rev. 20:11).

Of course, many will have already died and will need to be brought back to life in order to stand trial. The Bible anticipates the resurrection of the wicked as well as the righteous (Dan 12:2; John 5:29; Acts 24:15). Hades, the abode of departed spirits, will give up its inhabitants to be re-embodied. Everyone, whether buried, cremated or lost at sea will stand before their judge (Rev 20:12–13).

Discerning readers will have already concluded that there will have to be *two* resurrection days, separated by the millennium. This is precisely what the New Testament teaches (Rev 20:4–6). Actually, there are *three*, if the first Easter Sunday is counted (1 Cor 15:23–24; note the twofold 'then', indicating sequence).

Human beings will be judged – by a human being! This comes as a real surprise to those who expect God himself to be the judge. But he has delegated that function to one of us: 'For he has set a day when he will judge the world with justice by the man he has appointed' (Acts 17:31). It is Jesus who will sit on the 'great white throne' (Rev 20:11; note the unidentified 'him'). 'For we must all appear before the judgement seat of Christ' (2 Cor 5:10).

During his life on earth, Jesus frequently claimed to have the authority to decide the eternal destiny of nations and individuals (Matt 7:21–23; 13:41–43; 25:30–33). Such a claim can only be explained in one of three ways – that he was mad, bad or God; lunatic, liar or Lord. Only if he was the God-man, divine as well as human, is he perfectly qualified to be the Judge of all. And he has already done everything possible to save us from trial.

His dual nature enables him to apply perfect justice. His humanity gives him understanding. He has lived in our circumstances, under our pressures, with our temptations, without any advantages – yet without sin. His divinity gives him knowledge. He knows us through and through, our secret sins, our careless words, our hidden motives, our deepest emotions. His judgement will be absolutely just.

On the one hand, he will take into account our knowledge or ignorance of what is right and wrong in God's sight. The Bible makes it clear that we shall be judged according to the light we have received – whether the full light of the gospel, the half light of the ten commandments or the lesser light shining through creation outside and conscience inside (Rom 1:20; 2:12–16).

On the other hand, our entire life will be exposed, every thought, word and deed (Rom 2:6). Everything we have done while 'in the body' (2 Cor 5:10). It has all been recorded in 'books', somewhat like the television programme. *This is Your Life*, except that God's account is exhaustive, not a selection of the commendable bits! These books will be opened on that day (Rev 20:12).

What verdict can there be but: 'Guilty'? Who, confronted with such damning evidence, could argue with that verdict? Who has always done what they knew to be right, even if their only guide was their own conscience? Who has avoided everything they have criticised and condemned in others (Matt 7:1)? Truly, 'there is no-one who [consistently] does good, not even one', (Rom 3:12); 'all have sinned and fall short of the glory of God' (Rom 3:23).

None of us has been what God meant us to be or even what in our best moments we know we could and should have been.

The sentence is a living death in the place called hell, separated from God, the source of everything good, shut out of the new heaven and earth, shut in with the devil, demons and all who share their anger with their Creator, tormented, body and soul, day and night, for ever and ever in a 'lake of fire' (Rev 14:11; 20:10) with the anguish and frustration of knowing that wasted opportunities will never be repeated . . . no wonder Jesus spoke with horror of such a fate, warning his disciples of the danger and willing to sacrifice himself to save them from it. (Since this awesome subject is really beyond the scope of this book, readers are commended to the author's *The Road to Hell*, Hodder and Stoughton, 1992).

So is there no hope for anyone? Will the entire human race be condemned in that court? Look again at the scene. In addition to the millions of biographical volumes, 'another book was opened, which is the book of life' (Rev 20:12). Everyone listed in this book will be acquitted, escaping from the verdict and the sentence. Whose names are there and how did they get there?

It is a book that has existed from the beginning of time. It is mentioned in both the Old and New Testaments (Exod 32:32–33; Phil 4:3), but most frequently in Revelation (3:5; 13:8; 17:8; 20:12,15; 21:27; 22:19). God himself writes the names down. It is a list of the people whom he has given to his Son (John 17:6); it is therefore called: 'the Lamb's book of life' (Rev 21:27).

How did they qualify for inclusion? They trusted in Christ as their Saviour. They lived by faith. They trusted and obeyed God's words. Their deeds were evidence of their faith. Some names even date back before Christ (Heb 11). Abraham is the classic example; his faith, proved by his actions, was 'credited to him as righteousness' (Gen 15:6; Ps 106:31; Rom 4:3; Heb 11:8–12; Jas 2:21–24). Most names come after Christ, as many more trusted and obeyed 'the Word' whom God had sent.

It must be said that true faith is not a single step but a long walk. It is of the essence of believing in a person to go on believing in them whatever happens. 'Faith' and 'faithfulness' are exactly the same word in both the Hebrew and the Greek languages. 'The righteous shall live by faith' (Hab 2:4) means 'those whom God reckons as righteous will survive by faithfulness' (note how this continuity of faith is brought out in Rom 1:17 and Heb 10:38–39). The Old Testament heroes of faith were 'still living by faith when they died' (Heb 11:13).

It is possible to depart from the faith, to make shipwreck of it (1 Tim 1:19–20). It is possible for names in the book of life to be 'blotted out' as God made clear to Moses (Exod 32:33). Only those who remain faithful, who 'overcome' all the pressures to distrust and disobey, will keep their names in until the day the book is finally opened (Rev 3:5).

These will be acquitted or, to use the term from Roman courts, 'justified' – not because they are innocent, but because they have *consistently* trusted in Jesus, who has already paid the penalty for their sins. Only because of the cross can God 'be just and the one who justifies' (Rom 3:26). Both his justice and his mercy were fully expressed at Calvary.

* * * * *

With the day of judgement over, the stage is finally set for the redemption of creation. By returning to planet earth the Lord Jesus Christ will have done all that needs to be done to make this possible. He will have completed the saints, converted the Jews, conquered the devil, commanded the world and condemned the ungodly.

A new humanity has been created out of the old race. 'Homo Sapiens' has been replaced by 'Homo Novus'. They are new creatures, part of the new creation. They have not evolved by themselves into this new species; they have been changed by the power of the gospel of God. 'The old man has gone, the new has come' (2 Cor 5:17).

The same thing will now happen to the entire universe. New creatures need a new environment. The 'first' heaven and earth, still bearing the residual damage of angelic and human sin, will pass away (Rev 21:1). They will be 'destroyed by fire' (2 Pet 3:10). Since the discovery that every atom is packed with energy that can be released in fire, this scenario becomes entirely credible. From the ashes, like the mythical phoenix, will emerge the new heaven and earth, beautiful beyond imagination.

That the carpenter from Nazareth will be involved in this reconstruction is beyond question. He was engaged in the first creation. Before he made tables and chairs, doors and window frames, he made the trees from which he would later get the timber. Before he preached the Sermon on the Mount, he made the mountain for his pulpit. The wind and the waves obeyed him because they were his handiwork. 'Through him all things were made; without him nothing was made that has been made' (John 1:3).

Where he (and his) will be during this transformation of the universe, we are not told. So we can only speculate. Maybe in that new metropolitan city of Jerusalem God has designed and built out in space, known about as long ago as the time of Abraham (Heb 11:10).

One thing is certain. This vast urban construction, though erected in heaven, will be planted on the new earth (Rev 21:2, 10). It will be the permanent home of all God's people, Jewish and Gentile.

It will also be the eternal residence for the people's God! Father, Son and Spirit will live *here* with human beings (Rev 21:3,23). We are used to thinking of the Son and the Spirit with us, but have always prayed to: 'Our father in heaven' (Matt 6:9). We have imagined we would go to heaven and live with him there for ever and ever. But he is coming to earth to live with us! As at the beginning, his footsteps will be heard down here (Gen 3:8). Even his face will be seen (Rev 22:4).

All this may seem a little irrelevant to the second coming. Actually it is very significant. Too many Christians have concentrated their attention on heaven. It is the earth which is at the centre of God's purpose in creation and re-creation.

It is a renewed earth which will be his and our everlasting home.

The earth is the focus of our expectations for the future. That is the basic reason why Jesus is coming back here to wind up history as we know it. His return to earth is the very hinge of our hope, on which everything else turns.

Perhaps more than any other people, Christians are thoroughly 'down to earth' in their thinking – or should be. In the next chapter we shall consider how this belief in the future affects behaviour in the present.

CHAPTER TWO

Making Sure of our Readiness

Why are we told so much about the second coming? We know more about it than any other future event predicted in scripture. There must be a reason.

On the other hand, why are we not told more? Tantalising hints leave us full of unanswered questions. There is so much we'd like to know, but don't.

There must be one explanation to cover both our knowledge and our ignorance, some purpose for which we now know all we need to know, neither too little nor too much.

The purpose is practical. In a word, it is to be *ready* for his return.

Revelation about the future is given to affect the present; not to satisfy mental curiosity, but to stimulate moral consistency; not for information, but for incentive.

We live by hope. That is why it 'springs eternal in the human breast' (to quote Alexander Pope). The future influences the present in all of us. What we believe will happen in the future profoundly affects how we behave now.

This is particularly true of Christians, for whom hope is confident certainty rather than wishful longing (the Greek word *elpis* has this very definite assurance). Sinners are more influenced by their past, with the habits of mind and body. Saints are more influenced by their future, with the hope kindled by the Spirit (Rom 8:23–25). This is a stabilising factor in a changing world, an 'anchor for the soul, firm and secure' (Heb 6:19).

Christians are the people of tomorrow. They are the children of a new age that has already dawned for them and will one day

come for the whole world. They look for, long for and live for
this cosmic rescue. They may be described as those who have
'turned to God from idols, to serve the living and true God, and
to wait for his Son from heaven, whom he raised from the dead
– Jesus, who rescues us' (1 Thess 1:9–10).

God has made many promises to send his Son back to complete
the deliverance. But the promises are always accompanied by
precepts. His people must be ready for the return of their
rescuer.

In the New Testament, the hope of Christ's coming is a major
motive for godly living in this 'present evil age'. Even the book
of Revelation, containing more predictions than any other, has
this practical purpose – not so much that its readers may know
what's coming, but that they may be ready for it when it does.

The only time we have to get ready for the future is the present.
To delay is to run the risk of being too late.

How, then, can we be ready for his return? There are
seven ways.

INDIVIDUAL FAITH

'When the Lord Jesus is revealed from heaven in blazing fire
with his powerful angels . . . he will punish those who do
not know God and do not obey the gospel of our Lord
Jesus' (2 Thess 1:7–8). It is not fanciful to find here two
groups among the guilty – those who have not responded
rightly to God and those who have not responded rightly to
the gospel.

God put men in place on the earth so that they 'would seek
him and perhaps reach out for him and find him, though he
is not far from each one of us' (Acts 17:27). To seek means to
'make search or enquiry for, try or be anxious to find or get,
ask, aim at, pursue an object, endeavour to do, make for or
resort to' (*Oxford English Dictionary*). Jesus himself exhorted
people to 'Go on seeking and you will find . . . for everyone who

goes on seeking does find' (Luke 11:9–10; I have translated the verb tenses quite literally).

As we have already seen, God has put enough evidence for his power and divinity into creation, the work of his hands, to leave atheists and agnostics 'without any excuse' (Rom 1:20). Though this is adequate proof of his existence, there are two more requirements to discover his presence.

One is faith. 'And without faith it is impossible to please God because anyone who comes to him must believe that he exists and that he rewards those who earnestly seek him' (Heb 11:6).

The other is repentance. 'Seek the Lord while he may be found; call on him while he is near. Let the wicked forsake his way and the evil man his thoughts. Let him turn to the Lord, and he will have mercy on him, and to our God, for he will freely pardon' (Isa 55:6–7).

Whether there will be many, or even any, who seriously seek God like this, without any knowledge of the gospel, we have no way of knowing. God himself will be the judge of that.

From observation, the general pattern seems to be that human ambition seeks pleasure, wealth, fame, power – everything but God. Human thirst for knowledge covers cooking to computers, DNA to dinosaurs, psychology to sociology – everything but God.

It is unlikely that this book will fall into the hands of someone who has never heard about Jesus, though if it should, they should start looking for God right away. If they don't find him before he finds them out, it would be better for them if they had never been born.

What about those who have heard the gospel? This is an added privilege and responsibility, since we are judged by the light we have received. But it is not enough to have heard it or even to have believed it to be true. The verse with which we began this section talks about *obeying* the gospel. We have to *do* something about it.

Initially, we need to repent and believe, expressing these in an active way by being baptised in water and receiving the Holy

Spirit (see my *Explaining Water Baptism* in the series from Sovereign World, or my book *The Normal Christian Birth*, Hodder and Stoughton, 1989). But that is not the end, only the beginning. Alas, many have the impression that, having begun the Christian life, they are now ready for Jesus' return. That would only be the case if his coming immediately followed their conversion (which obviously has not been so for anyone yet!).

The earliest name for the Christian religion was 'The Way' (Acts 18:25–26; 19:9,23). The gospel is the way to life and a way of life. It cannot be worked for, but it must be worked out (Eph 2:9–10; Phil 2:12–13). After stepping into this 'narrow' way (Matt 7:14), it is necessary to continue walking in it (Isa 30:21; 35:8–10; Eph 4:1; 5:2,8). It is those who are walking with God who are ready to meet him. Enoch is a classic example (Gen 5:24).

So it is not enough simply to have become a 'believer' in God and in Christ. That is certainly the basic requirement, but Jesus himself made it clear that some believers will be ready for his return and some will not.

What else is necessary?

CONTINUAL SERVICE

After giving the signs of his coming to the disciples (in Matt 24, already expounded), Jesus very significantly went on to the subject of readiness for it (in Matt 25). He told a number of parables, which are all variations on a single theme: 'so you also must be ready' (24:44). This urgent imperative is illustrated from different spheres – a household, a wedding, and commercial trading.

The stories have the same plot as well as the same point. In each someone has gone away but is expected to return, though the exact time is not known. It is clear that in the character of the householder, bridegroom and businessman, Jesus was portraying himself. By the same token, those left behind were his followers.

There is the same division of the latter into two types or groups: the wise, who are ready for the return – and the foolish, who are not. Note that 'wise' means sensible rather than clever, and 'foolish' means silly rather than simple.

There is the same test of their readiness. In each parable there is an indication that the return of the key figure is *later* than expected – the bridegroom was 'a long time coming', the master returned 'after a long time'. This is a key point in understanding and applying these stories. The real test is not what people do if they think the return is soon, but what they do if they think it will not be soon (Matt 24:48). That which is born of persistence is of far more value than that which springs from panic. Real readiness is motivated by the fact of the Lord's return, not its timing.

There is the same virtue in the 'wise' – faithfulness. They behaved the same way in the absence of the key figure as they would in his presence. Even a prolonged absence made no difference; they were fully prepared for that. They proved their trustworthiness. They thus gave joy to the one to whom they were accountable. Their reward was both to share in that pleasure and be promoted to greater responsibility. They 'lived happily ever after'.

There is the same vice in the 'foolish' – negligence. In only one case is a bad thing actually done (the housekeeper bullying the other servants and indulging himself). In the others, it is a case of good things left undone – sins of omission rather than sins of commission, as they have been called, neglected duties. The Bible has a lot to say about the sin of sloth, or laziness, especially in the book of Proverbs (6:6; 10:26; 12:24; 15:19; 19:24; 21:25; 26:15; etc.). It is a serious offence.

Jesus uses very strong language in describing the punishment meted out to such sluggards. 'He will cut him to pieces and assign him a place with the hypocrites, where there will be weeping and gnashing of teeth' (Matt 24:51). 'Throw that worthless servant outside into the darkness, where there will be weeping and gnashing of teeth' (25:30). This is the vocabulary of hell and speaks of the endless regret and remorse in that dreadful place.

Who are these lazy people who have wasted their opportunities? Complacent Christians have too readily identified them as unbelievers. But they are servants in the household, bridesmaids invited to the wedding, employees entrusted with their employer's assets. Such descriptions are far more appropriate to believers. And we need to remember that these parables were not addressed to the general public, but to the twelve disciples – of whom one (Judas) had already shown himself to be untrustworthy, even though he had preached and healed in the name of Jesus.

However, there is more than a hint that behind such unreliability lies a failure in relationship, an inadequate knowledge of the returning person. The wicked servant's claim: 'I knew that you are a hard man . . .' (25:24) was rebuked with: 'So you thought you knew me; had you done so, you would also know what I wanted you to do and would have done myself in your place . . . but you didn't'. To the bridesmaids unprepared for his delay, the bridegroom says: 'I tell you the truth, I don't know you' (25:12; not, this time: 'You don't know me', which they obviously did; nor even: 'I never knew you', as in Matt 7:23; but simply, 'I don't recognise you now as having anything to do with me').

Faithful service, then, is an essential ingredient in readiness for the Lord's return. It has often been said that the Lord will commend those who have been *faithful*, rather than successful. This is a false dichotomy and has been used to rationalise persistence in useless activity. The Lord wants servants who are both faithful and fruitful, giving him some return on his investment – though even at our best we are still 'unprofitable' (Luke 17:10).

The quality of our service is also important, not just the quantity. 'If any man builds on this foundation [Jesus Christ] using gold, silver, costly stones, wood, hay or straw, his work will be shown for what it is, because the day will bring it to light. It will be revealed with fire and the fire will test the quality of each man's work' (1 Cor 3:12–13). It is not always the busiest who produce the best results.

One further misunderstanding must be dealt with. Faithful service to the Lord is not limited to 'spiritual' activities in our spare time and for the church or gospel. Our daily work can and should be done for the Lord. Adam was a gardener. The Bible evaluates manual labour much more highly than the world does. Shepherding, fishing, tentmaking and carpentry figure prominently. Man was made to work with his hands (Ps 90:17; 1 Thess 4:11).

The Lord is more interested in *how* we do the job we have than with *what* job we have. He would rather have a conscientious taxi-driver than a careless missionary. He is more concerned about character than career. He must be frustrated to be asked for guidance only when a change of employment is considered.

All work ranks the same with God, as Martin Luther said. Every Christian is in full-time service for the Lord. Every form of employment, provided it is neither illegal nor immoral, is a sacred vocation. In the way we do our daily work, we are writing our future reference, our C V ('curriculum vitae', Latin for 'a brief account of one's previous career'). On it will depend our role and responsibility in the kingdom set up by Christ at his coming.

He will look for dependability, not just ability. He will employ those to whom he can say: 'Well done, good and faithful servant! You have been faithful with a few things; I will put you in charge of many things. Come and share your master's happiness' (Matt 25:21,23).

PERSONAL HOLINESS

The gospel is good news about holiness, as well as forgiveness. It is not just an offer of forgiveness and a demand for holiness – a widespread impression, often fostered by preachers. Both are on offer. It is now possible to have sins conquered as well as cancelled. We can have the ability as well as the appetite to live right, to be righteous.

Gifts must be received. Both forgiveness and holiness are

available, but both need to be appropriated. Too many claim one without the other. They want to be justified now and sanctified later!

Of course, they will be. 'We know that when he appears, we shall be like him, for we shall see him as he is' (1 John 3:2). When we meet him in our new glorious bodies, we shall be perfect, complete, totally transformed in every part of our being. At last we shall live up to the title he gave us when we began to follow him: 'saints' (Rom 1:7; 2 Cor 1:1; Eph 1:1; etc.). The word means 'holy ones'.

But John draws a very practical implication from this future expectancy. 'Everyone who has this hope in him purifies himself, even as he is pure' (1 John 3:3). In other words, if we are really convinced that our future destiny is to be holy, this belief will be evidenced in our present behaviour.

It would be quite unnatural for someone expecting to inherit a large fortune not to want as much of it as possible as quickly as possible. If part of it could be obtained in advance, they would surely apply for it, especially if they were in real need of it.

In other words, it is a question of genuine desire. If we really welcome the hope of being utterly Christlike one day, we will pursue that goal right now. We will have no desire 'to enjoy the pleasures of sin for a short time' (Heb 11:25).

We will want to be holy here and now, if that is possible. And it is possible, though its achievement will be neither easy nor quick. It will involve 'effort', that combination of energy, enthusiasm and endurance.

Frequent thoughts about 'the day' when we look into his face and his eyes look into ours, provides the incentive. Those who have made little effort to be holy, revealing no real desire to be, will be deeply embarrassed, unable to meet his penetrating gaze. How terrible to have him say: 'I could have done so much with you, but you didn't want me to'.

Again, we must emphasise that it is those who persevere who will be approved. 'And now, dear children, continue in him, so that when he appears we may be confident and unashamed before him at his coming' (1 John 2:28).

The New Testament grounds its appeal for many qualities of sainthood on the fact of Jesus' return. Sobriety, fidelity, moderation, patience, sincerity, obedience, diligence, purity, godliness, brotherly love – all these and more are stimulated by the thought of seeing Jesus again. This appeal becomes particularly effective when believers are collectively represented as a bride for whom the bridegroom is coming.

Jesus was not married during his first visit to earth, but will be at his second! In a very real sense, believers are only 'betrothed', engaged to Christ in the present. When he returns, the relationship will be consummated and celebrated in 'the wedding supper of the Lamb' (Rev 19:9; cf. Matt 22:2).

This metaphor runs right through the Bible. It is applied as much to Israel in the Old Testament as to the church in the New. God's covenant with his people is seen in terms of a marriage vow. The metaphor of bride and groom is applied in two different ways.

Negatively, unfaithfulness is seen as adultery, even prostitution. If committed during betrothal, that was grounds for divorce, which nearly happened to the mother of Jesus. (Matt 1:19). To prepare for a wedding is to preserve one's virginity. A bride to be will keep herself only for her future bridegroom. 'I promised you to one husband, to Christ, so that I might present you as a pure virgin to him' (2 Cor 11:2).

Positively, a bride will also be concerned about her appearance at the wedding as well as her abstinence before it. The church will want to be what Christ wants for her on that day: 'to present her to himself as a radiant church, without stain or wrinkle or any other blemish, but holy and blameless' (Eph 5:27).

This will include her clothes as well as her complexion. Clothing figures in a number of statements about the second coming. 'Behold, I come like a thief! Blessed is he who stays awake and keeps his clothes with him, so that he may not go naked and be shamefully exposed' (Rev 16:15). Even the desire to be married in white, the symbol of purity, has its moral counterpart: 'For the wedding of the Lamb has come, and his bride has made herself ready. Fine linen, bright and clean, was given her to wear. [Fine linen stands for the righteous acts of the saints]' (Rev 19:7–8). Note the balance between 'given her' and 'made herself ready'. Clothes may be a gift, but they must be put on and worn at the wedding. Jesus told a parable to warn those invited to participate but who don't bother to change that hell awaits such presumption (Matt 22:11–13).

It is therefore essential to 'make every effort to live in peace with all men and to be holy; without holiness no one will see the Lord' (Heb 12:14). Only by so doing will 'your whole spirit, soul and body be kept blameless at the coming of our Lord Jesus Christ' (1 Thess 5:23).

COMMUNAL FELLOWSHIP

Holiness, or wholeness, has a corporate as well as an individual application. The 'bride' is one person as well as many. 'Christ loved the church and gave himself up for her to make her holy' (Eph 5:25–26).

Believers are called to be 'a chosen people, a royal priesthood, a holy nation, a people belonging to God' (1 Pet 2:9). They are to demonstrate a corporate identity in a decadent world, a convincing unity in a divided world. Jesus wants to find such a people on his return. What are the implications?

At the very least, it means that Christians must not isolate themselves from other believers. 'Let us not give up meeting together, as we are in the habit of doing, but let us encourage one another – and all the more as you see the Day approaching' (Heb 10:25). There is safety in numbers and, as pressures on God's people increase toward the end, it will be vital to stay together.

There is a responsibility for mutual service, as well as moral support. Servants have duties to each other, as well as to their master. Jesus spoke of a servant given the task of feeding his fellow servants during his master's absence. He not only neglected this task, but was guilty of drunken assaults on them. At the master's return, he was thrown into hell for abusing his position in this way (Matt 24:45–51).

On the same occasion, Jesus told the 'parable' of the sheep and the goats (actually, it is not a parable at all but a predictive prophecy containing an analogy). 'When the Son of man comes in his glory, and all the angels with him, he will sit on his throne in heavenly glory. All the nations will be gathered before him, and he will separate the people one from another *as* a shepherd separates the sheep from the goats' (Matt 25:31–32).

The principle of judgement is whether 'the least of these my brethren' were cared for in a practical way, whether their needs were met and their trials shared. Of course, the application depends on the interpretation of 'my brethren'. Who are they? To say they are Jesus' fellow-countrymen, the Jews, is too narrow. To say they are his fellow-humans, the whole race, is too broad. The title is consistently applied to his disciples, out of all nations (Matt 12:49; 28:10; cf. Heb 2:11). It is the neglect of his disciples that qualifies the rejected 'goats' on his left hand.

That this group could include some of the disciples themselves is indicated by their calling Jesus 'Lord' (Matt 25:44; cf. 7:21) and by the fact that this 'parable' was not spoken to the general public, but to his inner circle of the twelve. The theme of negligence among his own followers runs through all the parables in this chapter, as does the awful penalty to be paid for it.

Positively, the 'sheep' are those who have ministered to his brethren, even 'the least' significant of them, in their hour of need. They have been motivated by love of the brethren, without even thinking that it was as good as doing it for Jesus himself (Matt 25:37–38). Their deeds were acts of compassionate spontaneity, not calculated self-interest.

The need to be ready covers the church as a whole, as well as its individual members. Those who truly hope for his return will want as much holiness as is attainable now for all his people, as well as for themselves.

They will have a concern for the *unity* of the church. When all are gathered to meet their Lord in the air, all differences will fade into insignificance. Denominational labels, liturgical styles, ecclesiastical structures, theological arguments – all will disappear from sight when we see his face. There will be an atmosphere of total harmony on that day, which will be reflected in united worship.

Whoever has this hope will both want and work for an anticipation of it here and now. They will take seriously the prayer Jesus prayed on the last evening before his death, which was precisely for just such a demonstration of what was to come (John 17:20–24).

Of course, unity must be defined his way. It is neither union nor uniformity but the unanimity of heart, mind and will, such as he had with his Father. It is based on truth rather than tolerance. Those who seek it will not be indifferent to things that are wrong.

They will have a concern for the *purity* of the church. In matters of belief and behaviour, they will seek to cleanse defiled churches and keep them consistent with the gospel they preach. This will involve confrontation and conflict (1 Cor 11:19).

How significant it is that the book of Revelation, whose whole message centres on the second coming, should open with commands to local churches to deal with heresy and immorality in their midst. The threat of punishment is matched by the promise of rewards at his return (Rev 2:7,10,17,26; 3:5,12,21). However, while whole churches may be 'removed' for not putting things right, the rewards are offered to individual members who seek to do something about it. Anyone can open the church door to let Jesus back in (Rev 3:20, a verse that has nothing to do with personal regeneration and everything to do with communal restoration).

This joint concern for the unity and purity of God's people as a whole is an essential ingredient in readiness for his return.

The bride, which is his church, needs to 'make herself ready' (Rev 19:7).

GLOBAL EVANGELISM

It has been rightly said that the church is the only society on earth that exists primarily for the sake of its non-members! It has a task to be completed before Jesus returns; indeed, before he *can* come back. 'This gospel of the kingdom will be preached in the whole world as a testimony to all nations, and then the end will come' (Matt 24:14). There is even a possibility that tackling this task with urgency and enthusiasm could 'speed its coming' (2 Pet 3:12; though the verb can be translated 'wait eagerly' as well as 'hasten', and the context is not mission).

All four Gospels conclude with this 'Great Commission' to the apostles (Matt 28:18–20; Mark 16:15–18; Luke 24:47–48; John 20:21–23) – and through them to the church throughout time and space, since the twelve could not possibly complete the job themselves. The gospel is to be preached to every creature and disciples made of every 'nation' (this means ethnic groups, not political states).

It is God's desire and intention to have within his family, the new humanity living on the new earth, men and women 'from every tribe and language and people and nation' (Rev 5:9; 7:9). He made them all 'from one man' (Acts 17:26) and will merge their variety into unity again by bringing them 'together under one head, even Christ' (Eph 1:10). We are not encouraged to believe that whole nations will be saved; the objective is to 'save' some from every nation.

So the mission is worldwide, 'to the ends of the earth' (Acts 1:8; cf. Isa 45:22; 49:6; 52:10). Not until every corner of our planet has heard the good news in its own language will the work be finished.

The approach of the twenty-first century, the third millennium since Jesus was here, has stimulated a renewed interest in evangelism by reminding us how long it is taking us to complete the task he gave us and how little time may be left to do so.

However the passing of time should not be our main motive. It should be enough that we have been commanded by our Lord to do this. The simple obligation of obedience is always relevant. But gratitude to the Lord for our own salvation will do more than stimulate a willingness to do what he tells us to do. It will also give us a burning desire to share what we have found with those who are 'lost', whether they know it or not. 'For Christ's love compels us' (2 Cor 5:14). This was said by a man who felt himself under a curse if he kept such good news to himself: 'Woe to me if I do not preach the gospel' (1 Cor 9:16).

Quite simply, those who are really looking forward to meeting Christ personally when he returns will not be content to come alone. They will want to bring as many others with them as possible.

Those who are most ready will do most to get others ready! They will be inspired by the thought of making it possible for more to share in the sheer joy of living with God in a brand new earth. They will also be influenced by the horror of their destiny if they do not hear and respond. This urgency will not lead them into offensive methods which are counter-productive in communicating the message; but it will alert them to every opportunity for doing so with a love that is wise and sensitive.

The joy of introducing others to faith in Christ now is just a foretaste of what we shall feel when we see them meeting him face to face. And if the angels celebrate now when just one sinner repents (Luke 15:7,10), what will they be like 'when the saints go marching in'?

SOCIAL ACTION

It is now generally accepted that evangelism and social action belong together in the mission of the church, though many would rightly give priority to the former.

There is a clear biblical basis for service to an unbelieving world. Jesus endorsed the second 'great' commandment to love our neighbours as ourselves (Mark 12:31); and he interpreted 'neighbour' to cover anyone in need whom we can help (Luke 10:29–37). Paul exhorts us: 'Therefore, as we have opportunity, let us do good to all people' (Gal 6:10); he adds: 'especially to those who belong to the family of believers'. Though it is the most common scripture quoted in this connection, we have already noted that the so-called 'parable' of the sheep and goats is not strictly relevant, since 'brethren' and 'neighbour' are not equivalent terms; but the case should not rest on that passage.

Let it be clearly stated that we are not saved *by* doing good deeds (a widespread but mistaken notion) but we are saved *for* doing good deeds (Eph 2:9–10). We are saved to serve – and to serve indiscriminately whoever needs us, whatever their relationship or response to us. Such unconditional love has a special word in Greek: *agape* (pronounced 'agapay'). Infrequently used in the ancient world, it came into its own when describing God's love for the world expressed in Christ and the consequent love exercised by Christians, both of which included even enemies.

Love of neighbours can be applied at three levels of social activity:

First, in *work*. Provided it is meeting a real need in society, our daily work can and should be seen as a practical expression of neighbourly love. So often it is regarded as a means to our own ends – to get money, status or satisfaction for ourselves. Actually, it is far more likely to be fulfilling, as God intended it to be, if we see it primarily as a way of helping others. Obviously, this is easier with some jobs (nursing, for example) than others (repetitive factory operations) but they can all be done to meet a need, to benefit people.

Second, in *welfare*. Christians have a good record in voluntary service to the distressed. They have pioneered care of the sick, the elderly, the handicapped and those who have been abandoned to their fate by a selfish society. James, Jesus' brother, has stimulated much of it with his definition: 'Religion that God our father accepts as pure and faultless is this: *to look after orphans and widows in their distress and to keep oneself from being polluted by the world*' (1:27; note that active philanthropy is no substitute for moral integrity).

Third, in *reform*. It is at this point that Christians have real differences. There is unanimity over relieving suffering, but not over reforming systems. For this involves political activity, at local or national level. This is so often a matter of compromise, especially under democracy, constantly finding a mean between moral absolutes and material necessities, between what is ideally applicable and what is socially acceptable (reducing the period of pregnancy in which abortion can take place is a typical example).

While acknowledging that legislation cannot impose good, it can restrain evil – and therefore reduce suffering. To relieve the exploited or oppressed victims of an evil system is one thing. To seek to change the system itself is another. It is a less direct and more impersonal way of dealing with the problem. But if it achieves the same end, relief of suffering, and perhaps on a greater scale, can this not also express love of our neighbour?

Paul exhorts us to do good to *all* people, 'as we have opportunity' (Gal 6:10). Christians who are in a position of responsibility for others, in commerce and industry, in civil service and politics, have such an 'opportunity' to change the system for the better.

They will be aware of the danger of imposing distinctively 'godly' behaviour with legal sanctions (for example, to observe Sunday as a holy day or holiday). But they will seek just laws that counter inhumanity. It was for such things that the Hebrew prophets denounced the nations outside Israel, not for breaking the laws given to the redeemed people of God (for example, Amos 1:3–2:3).

Those who believe in a millennial reign of Christ on earth after his return are highly motivated for social reform. As with the hope for perfected individuals and a perfected church, the expectation of a perfected society stimulates the desire to claim as much of this as possible in the here and now. The certainty that one day there will be a perfect world order, spurs them to greater efforts to work for peace and justice now.

Not that they hope to achieve this, either on a universal or even national scale, before the King returns to set up his kingdom. But they can at least demonstrate the nature of that kingdom by applying its principles to contemporary situations. This in itself commends 'the gospel of the kingdom' (Matt 24:14).

It is even more personal and practical than that. If the world is to be governed by Christians 'reigning with Christ' and public offices are to be in their hands (for example, the law courts, 1 Cor 6:2), then the more experience they can gain in these positions of responsibility the better.

Let us close this section with an example of one such believer in the nineteenth century.

In the west end of London, Piccadilly Circus to be precise, stands an aluminium statue. Its resemblance to Cupid, the agent of love, has given it the popular nickname 'Eros' (the Greek word for sex appeal, from which we derive 'erotic'). This is grossly misleading. It should be called 'Agape'. It represents the angel of mercy and is a memorial to Anthony Ashley Cooper, better known as Lord Shaftesbury.

He did more perhaps than anyone else in his day to relieve the suffering caused by the 'Industrial Revolution', which transferred a huge population from rural to urban areas, putting them to work in factories and mines under unhealthy, even inhumane, circumstances. They were simply 'hands' to be exploited by unscrupulous employers. His tactics were to arouse sufficient guilt in public opinion to enable legislation to be passed which limited the potential abuse.

Few are aware that behind these public endeavours lay a constant and conscious expectation of Christ's return to rule for which he sought to be ready. At the top of every letter he wrote were the words: 'Even so, come, Lord Jesus', a prayer to be found on the last page of the Bible (Rev 22:20).

LOYAL ENDURANCE

Is the world likely to get better or worse? At the beginning of the twentieth century, the general opinion was optimistic; the key word was 'progress'. Now at the end of it, the outlook is pessimistic; the key word is 'survival'.

Christian and Communist share an 'apocalyptic' view of history. They both got it from Jewish sources, where it originated – one through Jesus Christ and the other through Karl Marx.

Simply put, two future phases of history are anticipated. First, things will get much worse before they get better. Second, things will get much better after they get worse. This is the basic structure of the book of Revelation (in chapters 4–17 the situation gets worse; in chapters 18–22 it gets better).

As things get bad in the world, it gets even worse for God's people in the world. Indirectly, they suffer the general troubles, but in the 'Great Tribulation' at the end they will suffer specific attacks directed at them, primarily because of their refusal to submit to a totalitarian regime with divine pretensions.

Many will pay the price with their own blood. The number of martyrs will rapidly increase as the climax approaches. Indeed, at times the book of Revelation seems to assume that nearly all believers will die for their faith, so that 'overcomers' and 'martyrs' are almost synonymous. It is significant that the Greek word *martus* or *martur* originally meant 'witness', but now means someone who maintains a faithful testimony at the cost of life itself.

But there has been a 'noble army of martyrs' for nearly two thousand years, ever since the stoning of Stephen (Acts 7:54–60). Not a decade has passed without people dying for their faith in Jesus. The coming 'Big Trouble' or 'Great Tribulation' may be on a wider scale than ever before, but it has already been experienced at local and even national levels.

In the godless world, suffering is one of the sure signs of a genuine disciple. 'Everyone who wants to live a godly life in Christ Jesus will be persecuted' (2 Tim 3:12). The early church taught its converts to expect trouble (Acts 14:22). They even counted it an honour (Acts 5:31). After all, Jesus had promised it: 'In this world you will have trouble' (John 16:33).

What enables believers to survive such pressures, even to overcome them and be 'more than conquerors' (Rom 8:37)? It is their sure hope of his return, when they will receive their reward and share his reign. Not least will be their public vindication in the eyes of the world that expelled them.

The New Testament is full of such encouragement. One of the favourite sayings of the early church was: 'If we died with him, we will also live with him; if we endure, we will also reign with him' (2 Tim 2:11). Martyrs will sit on thrones (Rev 20:4). They will wear crowns given to those who are 'faithful, even to the point of death' (Rev 2:10). Paul, awaiting execution, knew he would be entitled to one: 'I have fought the good fight, I have finished the race, I have kept the faith. Now there is in store for me the crown of righteousness, which the Lord, the righteous judge, will award to me on that day' (2 Tim 4:8).

Overcomers will be heaped with rewards – the right to eat from the tree of life, the hidden manna, the white stone, a new name, authority over the nations, the morning star, white robes, a permanent position in God's temple and many more (Rev 2:7, 17,26; 3:5,12).

All this will be theirs at his coming. In that perspective, suffering is reduced to size and loses its power to intimidate. 'For our light and momentary troubles are achieving for us an eternal glory that far outweighs them all' (2 Cor 4:17).

As well as these positive incentives, there is also a negative deterrent associated with his coming. The 'faithful saying' already quoted continues: 'If we disown him, he will also disown us' (2 Tim 2:12). This warning is based on Jesus' own words: 'But whoever disowns me before men, I will disown him before my Father in heaven' (Matt 10:33).

This is precisely the danger addressed in the letter to the Hebrews. Believing Jews were tempted to leave the church and return to the synagogue in order to avoid the growing persecution of the Christians. To be accepted back they would be required to renounce belief that Jesus was their Messiah. They are warned that it is impossible to repent of such apostasy (Heb 6:4–6; cf. 2:1; 3:12–14; 10:26). When he returns, Jesus will 'not be pleased' with those who shrink back (literally, 'lower their sails') – and are destroyed (Heb 10:37–38).

The book of Revelation is full of such warnings. The 'cowardly' will have their names blotted out of the Lamb's book of life and be thrown into the lake of fire (Rev 3:5; 21:8). The everlasting torment awaiting those who give in to the pressures of hostile authorities calls for patient endurance on the part of the saints who obey God's commandments and remain faithful to Jesus (Rev 14:12). The whole book is addressed to believers about to face such a test of their faith and is intended to enable them to come through it with flying colours. Perhaps this is why readers not facing such a crisis find the book difficult to understand!

When persecution breaks out, few things enable believers to endure as much as the conviction that Jesus will come to vanquish the oppressor and vindicate the oppressed. They know that 'he who stands firm to the end will be saved' (Matt 24:13).

*   *   *   *   *

These, then, are the ways to be ready for his return – individual faith, continual service, personal holiness, communal fellowship, global evangelism, social action and loyal endurance.

Facing such an agenda, many may feel daunted, even discouraged. Let us remember that the issue is not whether we have reached these goals by the time he comes, but whether we are still pressing on towards them (Phil 3:14).

Can we ever reach the stage when we know we are ready? There is one very simple measure of this, namely: how soon we want him to come!

True believers not only 'wait for his Son from heaven' (1 Thess 1:10). They long for his appearing (2 Tim 4:8; literally, 'having loved his appearing'). They not only have thoughts about it. They have feelings about it. They yearn, even pine, for that day. They wish it could be tomorrow at the latest, today if possible.

As a bride, preparing for her marriage, longs for the day of the wedding, wishing it could be brought forward, so the church should look forward to the bridegroom's return. 'The Spirit and the bride say, come!' (Rev 22:17). How many romantic novels have ended with the words: 'so they got married and lived happily ever after'. The Bible is no exception!

The shortest prayer in the early church was composed of two words in the Aramaic language: '*marana tha*'. It means simply: 'Lord, come!' Perhaps the best indication of our readiness to meet him is the frequency with which the phrase, in whatever language, comes spontaneously into our minds and out of our mouths.

It seems appropriate to conclude this chapter with some wise words of Augustine, many centuries ago: 'He who loves the coming of the Lord is not he who affirms it is far off, nor is it he who says it is near; but rather he who, whether it be far off or near, awaits it with sincere faith, steadfast hope and fervent love'.

B. THE REVELATION RIDDLE

CHAPTER THREE

Differences of Opinion

Opinions about the book of Revelation cover a huge spectrum. When put together, it seems impossible that they all refer to the same piece of literature.

HUMAN

opinion varies enormously. The reaction of unbelievers is understandable, since it is not intended for them. It is probably the worst book to use as an introduction to Christian scriptures. The world assumes it is the result of 'indigestion at best or insanity at worst', to quote a typical comment.

Yet even among Christians there are diverse attitudes, ranging from the fearful who can't get into the book to the fanatical who can't get out of it! Bible scholars have made many negative comments: 'as many riddles as there are words'; 'haphazard accumulation of weird symbols'; 'either finds a man mad or leaves him mad'.

Surprisingly, most of the Protestant Reformers (the 'magisterial' ones, so-called because they used the civic authorities to achieve their objectives) had an extremely low view:

Luther: 'neither apostolic nor prophetic . . . everyone thinks of the book whatever his spirit suggests . . . there are many nobler books to be retained . . . my spirit cannot acquiesce in this book.'

Calvin: omitted it from his New Testament Commentary!

Zwingli: said its testimony can be rejected because 'it is not a
          book of the Bible'.

This down-grading has influenced many denominations which
sprang from the Reformation.

There had, as we know, been some debate in the early
church about its inclusion in the 'canon' (rule or standard)
of scripture; but by the fifth century it was confidently and
universally included.

Some commentators are very positive in their assessment: 'the
only masterpiece of pure art in the NT'; 'beautiful beyond
description'. Even William Barclay, who collected these varied
comments but was himself inclined to a 'liberal' view of scripture,
told his readers that it was 'infinitely worthwhile to wrestle with
it until it gives its blessings and opens its riches'.

SATANIC

opinion is consistently negative. The devil hates the first few
pages of the Bible (which reveal how he gained control of
our planet) and the last few pages (which reveal how he will
lose control of it). If he can convince humans that Genesis is
composed of impossible myths and Revelation of impenetrable
mysteries, he is content.

This author has remarkable proof of Satan's particular hatred
of Revelation 20. Many cassette recordings of an exposition of
this chapter have been damaged between despatch and receipt.
In some cases the section dealing with the devil's doom has been
wiped clean before reaching its destination; in others a screaming
voice using a foreign language has been superimposed, rendering
the original words unintelligible!

The book calls his bluff. He is only prince and ruler of this
world by God's permission. And that has only been given
temporarily.

DIVINE

opinion is consistently positive. It is the only book in the Bible to which divine sanctions of reward and punishment have been directly attached. On the one hand, a special blessing will rest upon those who read it aloud, both to themselves and others (1:3) and who 'keep the words', by meditation and application (22:7). On the other, a special curse will rest on those who tamper with its text. If this is done by addition, by insertions, the plagues described in the book will be added to the culprit's experience. If it is done by subtraction, by deletions, the culprit's share of eternal life in the new Jerusalem will be taken away.

Such a blessing and curse tell us how seriously God regards the facts and truths revealed here. He could hardly have made its importance clearer.

From these opinions about the book, we turn to look at the book itself.

Consider first its position in the Bible. Just as Genesis could be nowhere else but at the beginning, Revelation could be nowhere else but at the end. In so many ways it completes the 'story'.

If the Bible is simply regarded as the history of our world, Revelation is needed to round it off. Of course, biblical history is different from all other such publications. It starts earlier, before there were any observers to record events. It finishes later, by predicting events that cannot yet be observed and recorded.

This, of course, raises the question as to whether we are dealing with works of human imagination or divine inspiration. The answer depends on faith. It is a simple choice: to believe or not to believe. While going beyond reason, faith is not contrary to reason. The biblical accounts of the origin and destiny of our universe can be shown to be the best explanation of its present state. To know how it will end is of profound significance to the way we live now.

But the interest of the Bible is in the human race rather than the environment and in God's chosen people in particular. With them he has a 'covenant' relationship, analogous to marriage. From one point of view, the Bible is the story of a romance, a heavenly Father seeking an earthly bride for his Son. Like every good romance, they 'get married and live happily ever after'. But this climax is only reached in the book of Revelation, without which we would never know whether the engagement (or 'betrothal'; 2 Cor 11:2) ever came to anything or was broken off!

Indeed, it is quite difficult to imagine what it would be like to have a Bible without the book of Revelation, even if we don't use it much. Imagine a New Testament that closed with the little letter of Jude addressed to a second-generation church that was being corrupted in its creed, conduct, character and conversation. So is that how it will all end? What a depressing anticlimax!

So most Christians are glad that the book of Revelation is there, even if they are not very well acquainted with it. They can usually cope with the first few chapters and the last few, but feel out of their depth in the central bulk of it (chapters 6–18). That is largely because this portion is so unlike anything else. It is difficult because it is different. Just what makes it so?

CHAPTER FOUR

Nature of Apocalyptic

Revelation is not only different from other New Testament books in content. It is also unique in origin.

All the others were intended to be written. Each author decided to put pen to paper, either himself or through an 'amanuensis' (i.e. a secretary; e.g. Rom 16:22). He considered what he wanted to say before it was put down. The result bore the marks of his own temperament, character, outlook and experience – even though he was 'inspired' by the Holy Spirit, prompting his thoughts and feelings.

Scholars have noted many differences between Revelation and the other writings of the apostle John (one Gospel and three Epistles). The style, grammar and vocabulary are so unusual for him that they have concluded that it must come from another 'John'. They have actually found a somewhat vague reference to an obscure elder of that name in Ephesus to fit the bill. But the man who wrote Revelation simply introduces himself as 'I, John' (1:9), which indicates that he was well and widely known.

There is a simpler explanation for the contrast, even apart from the obvious difference of subject. He never intended to write Revelation. He never even thought about it. It came to him as a totally unexpected 'revelation' in verbal and visual form. As he 'heard' and 'saw' this astonishing series of voices and visions, he was repeatedly told to 'write' it all down (1:11,19; 2:1,8,12,18; 3:1; 7:14; 14:13; 19:9; 21:5). The reiterated command suggests that he became so absorbed in what was happening to him that he forgot to record it from time to time.

This explains the 'inferior Greek', compared to his normal

fluency. It was written hurriedly in very distracting circumstances. Imagine watching a film and being told to 'get it all
down on paper', while it was being shown. College students
will understand the 'scrappy' style by looking at their lecture
notes. Why, then, did John not write it up afterwards from his
scribbled précis, so that its permanent form might be rather more
polished? He was hardly likely to when the last dictated words
contained a curse on anyone who tampered with what he had
written!

All this means that John was not the author of Revelation. He
was merely the 'amanuensis' who took it down. So who was the
'author'? The message was often communicated to him by angels.
But it was also what the Spirit was saying to the churches; and
it was the revelation of Jesus Christ. But it was given to Jesus
by God. So a complex chain of communication was involved
– God, Jesus, Spirit, angels, John. More than once, poor John
was confused about who should get the glory for what he was
experiencing (19:10; 22:8–9). Only the first two links in the
chain are worshipped in this book.

More directly than any other book in the New Testament, this
deserves the name of 'Revelation'. The Greek word so translated
in the first sentence is *apokalypsis*, from which came the noun
'Apocalypse' and the adjective 'apocalyptic', which is now more
widely used of other literature similar in style and content. The
root word means 'unveiling'.

It is the pulling back of a curtain to reveal what has been
hidden (as in the unveiling of a picture or plaque).

In the context of scripture, it is the unveiling of that which is
hidden from man, but is known to God. There are some things
which man cannot know unless God chooses to inform him. In
particular, he cannot know what it happening in heaven and he
cannot know what will happen in the future. His recording and
interpreting of events is therefore strictly limited in both time
and space. It can only be, at best, a partial account of the flow
of history.

When God writes history, he gives a total picture, not least because he orders as well as observes the events. History is his story. He 'makes known the end from the beginning, from ancient times, what is still to come' (Isa 46:10). Past, present and future are interrelated in him.

So are heaven and earth. There is an interaction between what goes on up there and what goes on down here. One of the disturbing features in Revelation is the constant shift of scene from earth to heaven and back again. That is because of the connection between events above and below (e.g. war in heaven leads to war on earth; 12:7; 13:7).

'Apocalyptic' is history written from God's point of view. It gives the total picture. It enlarges our understanding of world events by seeing them in the light of what is above and beyond our limited perception. This gives us both insight and foresight, enlarging our comprehension of what is going on around us, far beyond that of the normal historian.

Patterns and purposes emerge to which he is blind. History is not just a haphazard accumulation of happenings. Coincidence gives way to providence. History is going somewhere.

Time is eternally significant. Time and eternity are interrelated. God is not outside time, as Greek philosophy imagined. He is inside time; or rather, time is inside God. He is the God who was, is and is to come. Even God himself cannot change the past, once it has happened! The death and resurrection of Jesus can never be changed or cancelled.

God is working out his plans and purposes within time (the classic book on this is *Christ and Time* by Oscar Cullmann, SCM Press, 1950). He is the Lord of history. But it is his pattern, which can only be discerned when he has revealed the missing pieces of the jigsaw. Things hidden from human observation and which God reveals are called 'mysteries' in the New Testament.

The direction of events in the past and present becomes apparent in the light of the future. The shape of history cannot be seen in the short-term, only in the long-term. For time is relative as well as real to God. 'A thousand years are like a day' to him (Ps 90:4, quoted in 2 Pet 3:8). His amazing patience with us makes him appear 'slow' to us (2 Pet 3:9).

The Bible contains a 'philosophy of history' quite different from those which man's unaided reason has adopted. The contrast is clear when we compare it with the four most commonly held ideas:

i. *Cyclic* 'History repeats itself'. It simply goes round in endless circles, or cycles. Sometimes the world gets better, then worse, then better, then worse again . . . and so on. This was the Greek idea.

ii. *Rhythmic* This is a variation on the cyclic. The world still alternates between better and worse, but never repeats itself in exactly the same way. It is always moving on, but whether it will end on an 'up' or a 'down' is anyone's guess!

iii. *Optimistic* The world is getting better and better. As one British Prime Minister said at the beginning of the twentieth century: 'up and up and up and on and on and on'. The word on everyone's lips then was 'progress'. History was an ascending escalator.

iv. *Pessimistic* The word on everyone's lips at the end of the twentieth century is 'survival'. The 'doom and gloom' experts believe we are on a descending escalator. It might be slowed down, but cannot be stopped. The world will get worse until

life becomes impossible (current estimates
are around 2040!).

The biblical pattern is quite different from all of these, com-
bining both pessimism and optimism in a realism based on all
the facts.

 v. *Apocalyptic*. The world will get steadily
worse, then suddenly better than it has
ever been – and will stay that way.

This last belief is shared by Jews, Christians and Communists.
They all got it from the same source: the Hebrew prophets (Karl
Marx had a Jewish mother and a Lutheran father). The basic
difference between them is what they believe will bring about
the sharp change of direction. Communists believe it will be by
human revolution. Jews believe it will be by divine intervention.
Christians believe it will be by the return of the God-man Jesus
to planet earth.

Those who have read through the book of Revelation will
now realise that it is actually structured on this very basis.
After dealing with the present in its earlier chapters, it turns
to the future course of history, which gets steadily worse
(in chapters 6–18). then suddenly better (in chapters 20–22),
the change coinciding with the second coming of Christ (in
chapter 19).

There are two more characteristics of 'apocalyptic' history that
we must talk about before moving on.

The first feature is that the pattern is basically *moral*. Since
history is ordered by God and he is perfectly good and all-
powerful, we would expect to see his justice administered in the
encouragement of good and the punishment of evil.

But this does not seem to be the case, either in international or individual experience. Life seems to be terribly unjust. History seems indifferent to morality. The righteous suffer and the wicked prosper. The constant cry is: 'Why does a good God allow such things to go on?' The Bible is honest enough to record the bewilderment of Job, David (Ps 73:1–4), Jesus himself (Mark 15:34, the words of Ps 22:1) and the Christians who were martyred for him (Rev 6:10).

All such doubts spring from a short-term view focused mainly on the present and partly on the past. A long-term view takes the future, the ultimate outcome, into account. This can totally change the understanding (Job 42; Ps 73:15–28; Heb 12:2; Rev 20:4; Paul sums it up in Rom 8:18).

'Apocalyptic' portions of the Bible all encourage this long-term view which reveals that history does uphold morality (Dan 7–12, with which Revelation has much in common, is an excellent example). We do live in a moral universe. The good God is still on the throne. He will bring it all to the right conclusion. He will punish the wicked and reward the righteous. He will put the world right again and give it to those who have been willing to be put right themselves. There will be a 'happy ever after' ending to the story.

'Apocalyptic' literature, including Revelation, therefore concentrates on such themes as reward, retribution and restoration. Above all, it pictures God reigning on a throne, in perfect control of world affairs. Notice that word 'pictures', which introduces the other quality.

The second feature is that the presentation is often *symbolical*. It has to be, since the unfamiliar is being communicated. As every teacher knows, the unknown has somehow to be related to the known, usually by analogy ('well, it's like this'). Most of Jesus' parables about the kingdom of heaven use earthly situations to assist understanding ('the kingdom of heaven is like . . .').

Helping people to comprehend something involves imagination as much as information. If they can 'picture' it in their mind, it will be much easier to grasp. Significantly, the response is usually: 'Now I see'.

Revelation is full of pictorial language. Through the constant use of 'symbols' we can visualise what would otherwise be incomprehensible. It cannot be too strongly emphasised that this is intended to help our understanding, not hinder it. Too many have used the 'highly symbolic' nature of the book to ignore or even dismiss its teaching, as if the symbols are too obscure to convey a clear message. That is simply not the case, as is apparent when they are listed in four categories:

Some are *obvious* in their meaning. The 'dragon' or 'serpent' is the devil. The 'lake of fire' is hell. The 'great white throne' is the Lord's judgement seat.

Some are *explained* in the context. The 'stars' are angels. The 'lampstands' are churches. The 'seals', 'trumpets' and 'bowls' are disasters. The 'incense' represents prayers ascending. The 'ten horns' are kings.

Some are *paralleled* elsewhere in scripture. In the Old Testament may be found the tree of life, the rainbow, the morning star, the rod of iron, horsemen, tyrannical regimes pictured as wild 'beasts'. It may safely be assumed that these emblems have retained their original meaning.

Some are *obscure*, but very few. One example is the 'white stone', for which scholars have offered an amazing number of interpretations. A declaration of innocence? A sign of approval? A badge of excellence? Maybe we won't know what it signifies until we receive one!

Numbers are also used as symbols. There are many 'sevens' in Revelation – stars, lampstands, lamps, seals, trumpets, bowls. It is the 'round' number of the Bible, the complete, the perfect figure. 'Twelve' is associated with the old people of God (their tribes) and the new (their apostles); 'twenty-four' brings them together. 'One thousand' is the largest number. 'Twelve thousand' from each tribe of Israel brings the total to 'one hundred and forty-four thousand'.

'666' is the one that captures attention. It is made up of sixes, a figure which always points to the human failure to reach the seven of 'complete perfection'. It is used here as a clue to the

identity of the last world dictator before Jesus reigns for a
thousand years (in Latin, a 'millennium'). Is it significant that
'666' is the total of all the Roman numerals (I=1 + V=5 +
X=10 + L=50 + C=100 + D = 500) except one (M=1000)?
But all attempts to name him from this figure will fail until his
appearing makes it perfectly clear.

There is so much in Revelation that is quite clear that we can
cope with a few obscurities now, believing that they will be
clarified by future events when the information is really needed.
Meanwhile, we can thank God that he has told us so much.

Of course, he speaks through human voices, through the
mouths of his 'prophets'. John realised that the message he
delivered was not his. He calls his writing 'this prophecy' (1:3;
22:7, 10, 18, 19). He is therefore a prophet as well as an apostle.
This is the only 'prophetic' book in the New Testament.

Prophecy is both 'forthtelling' (a word of God about the
present) and 'foretelling' (a word of God about the future).
Revelation is both, the greater part being predictions of events
yet to happen.

When will they be fulfilled? Have they happened already? Are
they happening right now? Or have they still to happen? We
must now consider the various answers being given to these
questions.

CHAPTER FIVE

Schools of Interpretation

Nearly one third of the verses in the book of Revelation contain a prediction. Between them, some fifty-six separate events are foretold. Exactly half of these are in plain language and the other half are in symbolic picture form.

Most of them occur after chapter 4, which opens with a marked change in perspective – from earth to heaven and from present to future ('come up here and I will show you what must take place after this'; 4:1).

Clearly, this refers to happenings that are future to the original writer and readers in the first century AD. But how far ahead of them did the forecast stretch? Are the predicted events past, present or future to us who live nineteen centuries later? Do we look behind, around or ahead for their fulfilment?

This is where the differences begin. Over the intervening years between then and now, four major opinions have arisen, leading to four 'schools of interpretation'. Most commentaries are written from only one point of view. It is important to look at them all before assuming that one is right. It is too easy and risky to follow the first that has been heard or read about.

The four are now so well-established, they have been given familiar labels: preterist, historicist (of which there are two distinct varieties), futurist and idealist. Don't be put off by this rather technical jargon. It is important to be able to identify the very different approaches you may encounter.

1. PRETERIST

This school regards the predictions as fulfilled during the decline
and fall of the Roman Empire, when the church was under the
pressures of imperial persecutions. It was written for Christians
of the first century, to prepare them for what would happen
in the second and third. The 'great city' of Babylon, sitting on
'seven hills' (17:9) is identified as Rome (Peter seems to make the
same comparison; 1 Pet 5:13).

Though the bulk of Revelation is thus 'past' to us, that does
not mean it is of limited value. We can learn lessons from all the
historical narrative in scripture. Indeed, it constitutes the major
part of the Bible. We can draw inspiration and instruction from
what has gone before.

The strength of this view is that all Bible study should begin
with the original context of writer and readers. What did this
mean to them? What the writer intended and what the readers
would understand in their situation are vital steps towards a true
interpretation and application.

But there are a number of weaknesses. For one thing, very
few if any of the specific predictions actually came true in the
Roman Empire. Only a few general trends can be identified
but no particular correspondence (some have tried to distil
'666' from the letters of 'Nero Caesar', though Revelation was
probably written thirty years after his death!). It also means
that after Rome fell, the major part of the book lost its direct
relevance and really said little to the later church. Since nearly
all scholars accept that the last few chapters cover the end of the
world, which is still future to us, a huge gap is left between the
beginning and end of church history, with no direct guidance
for the many intervening centuries. This deficiency is met by the
second approach.

2. HISTORICIST

This school believes the predictions cover the entire 'church age' between the first and second comings of Christ. It is a coded history of 'anno domini' in symbolic form, covering the major phases and crises of the entire period. So the fulfilment is past, present and future to us. We are right in there and from what has already come to pass we can know what is next on the programme.

One scholar produced a cross-reference index between every section of Revelation and the many volumes of the *Cambridge Ancient and Modern History*. It is generally held that we are living somewhere in chapter 16 or 17!

At least this theory has made the book relevant to every generation of Christians. It has also stimulated interest. But this is more than outweighed by its drawbacks.

One is that many details are rather forced to fit known events, which appears somewhat artificial. But the main problem is that no two 'historicists' seem to agree on the correlation of scripture and history! Were they using the right method, there would surely be a greater degree of unanimity in their conclusions. And they still finish up with many unfulfilled details.

So far we have only considered one type of 'historicism'. We will call it *linear*, because it believes that the central part of Revelation goes in one straight line of events from the first to the second advent of Christ.

There is another type, which we will call the *cyclical*, which believes that it covers the whole of church history more than once, constantly returning to the beginning and 'recapitulating' the events from another angle. One popular volume (*More than Conquerors* by William Hendiksen, Baker, 1960) claims to have discovered seven such cycles, each covering the whole church age (in chapters 1–3, 4–7, 8–11, 12–14, 15–16, 17–19, 20–22)! This enables him to place the 'millennium' (in ch. 20) before the second coming (ch. 19) and therefore hold the 'post-millennial' view (see pages 252–258). But this 'progressive parallelism', as it is called, seems to be forced onto the text, rather than found within it. In particular, the radical separation of chapters 19 and 20 is totally unwarranted.

The historicist interpretation is probably the least satisfactory and the least convincing, in either linear or cyclical form.

3. FUTURIST

This school believes that the central block of predictions applies to the last few years leading up to the second coming. It is therefore still future to us today, hence the label. It concerns the climax of evil control in the world, which will be the 'Great Tribulation' for the people of God (Rev 7:14; also referred to by Jesus in Matt 24:12–22).

All the events will be compressed into quite a short time – three and a half years, to be exact (explicitly referred to as 'a time, times and half a time' or 'forty-two months' or 'one thousand, two hundred and sixty days'; 11:2–3; 12:6 and 12:14, quoting Dan 12:7).

Since the events are still future, the predictions tend to be taken more literally, as an accurate description of what will happen. There is no longer any need to tailor them to fit past history. Certainly, the series of disasters seems to lead straight into the end of the world.

What, then, is the message for the church through the ages? Most of the book would only be relevant to the very last generation of believers in this case. Surprisingly, many futurists also believe that the church will be 'raptured' to heaven before the troubles start (see page 182), so even the last Christians don't need to know these things either!

A further weakness is that futurists are prone to treat Revelation as an 'almanac', leading to an excessive interest in charts, schedules of the future. The fact that they do not always agree suggests that Revelation was not primarily written for such speculative purposes.

4. IDEALIST

This approach removes all specific time references and discourages correlation with particular events. Revelation pictures the 'eternal' struggle between good and evil and the 'truths' contained in its narratives can be applied to any century. The battle between God and Satan is ongoing, but the divine victory can be experienced by an 'overcoming' church at any time. The 'essential message' can be universally applied throughout time and space.

The main and perhaps only merit of this view is that the message of the book becomes directly relevant to all who read it. They are in the struggle that is described and are assured that 'the one who is in you is greater than the one who is in the world' (1 John 4:4). It is possible to be 'more than conquerors' (Rom 8:37).

This, however, is to treat Revelation as 'myth'. It is spiritually true, but not historically true. These are fictional events, but the stories contain truths – as in Aesop's fables or *Pilgrim's Progress*. The truths must be dug out of the narrative before being applied. The cost of this 'demythologising' process is to jettison a great deal of material, dismissing it as poetic licence which belongs to the package rather than the content.

Behind all this is the Greek philosophy which separated spiritual and physical, sacred and secular, eternity and time. God, they said, is timeless. So truth is timeless, though it is also therefore timely. But it is not in 'the times'. Their notion of history as cyclical cut out the concept of the 'end-time', the idea that time would reach a climax or conclusion.

This has serious consequences for 'eschatology' (the study of 'the last things', from the Greek word *eschatos* = 'end' or 'last'). Events like the second coming and the day of judgement are transferred from the future to the present, from then to now. Eschatology becomes 'existential' (i.e. concerned with the present moment of existence, or it is said to be 'realised' (as in 'realising' investments – having the money to spend now).

Of course, radical changes have to be made to the 'predictions' to make them fit the present – usually by 'spiritualising' them (a 'Platonic' way of thinking). For example, the 'new Jerusalem' (in ch. 21) becomes the description of a people rather than a place, an 'idealised' (note the word) picture of the church, the architectural details conveniently forgotten!

It is time to summarise this survey. There are four different answers to the question: what period of time does Revelation cover?

The preterist replies: the first few centuries AD.

The historicist replies: all the centuries AD from the first to the second advent.

The futurist replies: the last years of the last century AD.

The idealist replies: any century AD, none in particular.

So which is right? There are pros and cons for each. Do we have to choose between them? Could they all be right? Could they all be wrong?

The following observations may help the reader to reach a conclusion.

First, it seems obvious that no one key unlocks the whole book. Each 'school' has seen some truths, but none has released all. When only one approach is used there is always some manipulation of the text.

Second, there is no reason why more than one may not be used. Texts have different meanings and applications. But some control is needed to avoid the arbitrary use of different approaches to bolster an opinion already decided upon before studying the scripture. This restraint is provided by the context and by constantly asking the question: was this the meaning intended by the divine author and the human writer?

Third, parts of each of the four methods can help understanding. Some elements from all four are compatible and can be used in conjunction with each other, though it must be added that other elements are quite incompatible and cannot be combined.

Fourth, the emphasis may change in different sections of the book. At each stage, the most appropriate method or methods of interpretation must be chosen and used. In the remainder of this chapter we shall illustrate this in practical terms by considering the three major divisions of the book:

A. The Beginning (chs. 1–3)

This section is not very controversial, so is more frequently and confidently expounded than the rest (see, for example, *What Christ thinks of the Church* by John Stott, Lutterworth Press, 1958). Most are comfortable with the traditional interpretation (though uncomfortable with the application!). The problem with this section is that we *do* understand it, only too well. There are a few problems with details (the angels) and symbols (white stones and hidden manna). But the letters to the seven churches in Asia are not unlike other New Testament epistles. So which 'school' is appropriate?

The 'preterist' is surely right in directing our attention to the first century. Any true exegesis must *begin* with what this meant to them then. But need it end there?

The 'historicist' believes that the seven churches represent the whole church in *time*, seven consecutive epochs in church history. Ephesus covers the early church, Smyrna the Roman persecutions, Pergamum the time of Constantine, Thyatira the Middle Ages, Sardis the Reformation, Philadelphia the world-wide missionary movement and Laodicea the twentieth century. But the parallels are forced (Western churches may look 'Laodicean', but the 'third world' ones are anything but!). This scheme simply doesn't fit.

The 'futurist' is even more bizarre, believing that the seven churches will be re-established in the very same cities of Asia just before Jesus returns, based on the mistaken assumption that 'I will come' (2:5,16; 3:4) refers to the second advent. Actually, these churches have long since disappeared, their 'lampstands removed'.

The 'idealist' usually shares the 'preterist' view of this section, but adds the belief that the seven historical churches represent the whole church in *space*. Ephesus represents the orthodox but loveless fellowships, Smyrna the suffering, Pergamum the enduring, Thyatira the corrupt, Sardis the dead, Philadelphia the feeble but evangelistic, Laodicea the lukewarm.

Whether they cover the entire range of church character between them is debatable. But the comfort and challenge of their example can be applied anywhere and any time.

So the preterist with a dash of idealist seems the right mixture for the first section.

B. The Middle (chs. 4–18)

This is where the differences are most acute. The opening vision of God's throne presents few problems and has inspired worship through the ages. It is when Jesus the Lion/Lamb releases disasters on the world and suffering on the church that the debate begins. When does this happen? It must be sometime between the second century (which was 'hereafter' to the seven churches; 4:1) and the second coming (in ch. 19).

The 'preterist' limits this section to the 'decline and fall of the Roman Empire'. But the fact remains that most predicted events, particularly the 'natural' catastrophes, simply did not happen during that period. Much of the text has to be treated as 'poetic licence', rather vaguely hinting at what might happen.

The 'historicist' has much the same problem when attempting to fit the whole of church history into these chapters, either as one continuous narrative or in repeated 'recapitulations'. The details will not fit.

The 'futurist' is, of course, free to believe in the literal fulfilment of the detailed forecast, since none of it has happened yet. Two features seem to confirm that this is nearer the correct application. First, the 'troubles' are clearly worse than anything the world has yet seen (as Jesus predicted in Matt 24:21). Second, they seem to lead directly into the events at the end of history. But is that all? Has this section no relevance before then?

The 'idealist' is wrong to 'demythologise' this section, divorcing it from time altogether. But it is right to look for a message that can apply to any phase of church history. The clue lies in scripture itself, which clearly teaches that future events cast their shadows ahead in time. Jesus is 'foreshadowed' in many ways in the Old Testament (as the letter to the Hebrews explains). The coming Antichrist is preceded by 'many antichrists' (1 John 2:18); the coming False Prophet by many false prophets (Matt 24:11). The coming universal persecution is already experienced in many local regions. The 'Great Tribulation' is only different in scale from the 'much tribulation' which is normal at all times (John 16:33; Acts 14:22). So these chapters can help us to understand current trends as well as their ultimate climax.

So the futurist and a measure of idealist open up this section in the best way.

3. The End (chs. 19–22)

Revelation seems to get clearer towards the end, but there are still some areas of controversy. Most take these chapters to refer to the ultimate future, the very 'last things' to happen, beginning with the return of Christ (in ch. 19).

The 'preterist' drops out here. Very few attempt to fit these chapters into the days of the early church.

The 'historicist' school divides sharply in two. The 'linear' variety invariably see this section as the 'end-times', following the 'church age'. But the 'cyclical' find 'recapitulations' even here. Some see the 'millennium' in chapter 20 as a description of the church before the second coming in chapter 19! Others see the 'new Jerusalem' in chapter 21 as a description of the millennium before the final judgement in chapter 20! Such radical dislocation of events are not justified by the text itself and suggest manipulation in the interests of theological systems and dogma.

The 'futurist' has few opponents in this section. The second coming, day of judgement, new heaven and earth have clearly not yet arrived.

The 'idealist' has few proponents in this section. These tend to overlook the new earth altogether and talk about 'heaven' as the timeless sphere into which believers are transferred at death. The 'new Jerusalem' pictures this eternal realm (the 'heavenly Zion' of Heb 12:22), which is never expected to come 'down out of heaven' (in spite of Rev 21:2,10!).

So the futurist can be given a monopoly in handling this section.

In a later chapter we shall be sharing an 'introduction' to the text of Revelation itself, using the tools we have considered appropriate (which do not include the historicist). However, before we do that, there is one other important matter to consider.

The four 'schools' of interpretation share one common assumption: that the most important question is – WHEN? That is, when are the predictions fulfilled in time?

This is to start with the supposition that Revelation is primarily concerned with forecasting the future, to satisfy our curiosity or reduce our anxiety by revealing what is going to happen, both in the immediate and ultimate future.

But this is highly questionable. The New Testament never indulges in idle speculation, even warns against it. Every 'unveiling' of what lies ahead has a practical, indeed a moral purpose. The future is only revealed so that the present may be influenced by it.

So the fundamental question is not 'when?' but WHY? Why was Revelation written? Why was it revealed to John? Why was he told to pass it on? Why do we need to read and 'keep' these words?

Not just to tell us what is going to happen but to get us *ready* for what is going to happen. How do we arrive at that answer?

CHAPTER SIX

Sense of Purpose

Why was the book of Revelation written? The answer is readily accessible by asking another question: for whom was it written?

It was never intended to be a university textbook for theological staff or students. It is often they who have made it appear so complex that simple folk have been intimidated. Let one of them confess this:

> We boldly affirm that the study of this book would present absolutely no possibility of error if the inconceivable, often ridiculous, prejudice of theologians in all ages had not so trammelled it and made it bristle with difficulties, that most readers shrink from it in alarm. Apart from these preconceptions, the Revelation would be the most simple, most transparent book that prophet ever penned (*Reuss*, in 1884, quoted in *The Prophecy Handbook*, World Bible Publishers 1991.

The situation has hardly improved since then, as a recent comment reveals:

> It is one of the misfortunes of our expertise-oriented culture that when anything seems difficult it is sent off to the university to be figured out (Eugene Paterson, writing on Revelation in '*Reversed Thunder*', Harper Collins, 1988, p. 200.

This has led to a widespread notion that this book will not be understood by the 'layman' (whether that label is used in its ecclesiastical or educational sense).

ORDINARY READERS

It cannot be too strongly emphasised that Revelation was written for very ordinary people. It was addressed to the members of seven churches at a time when 'not many were wise by human standards; not many were influential; not many were of noble birth' (1 Cor 1:26).

It was said of Jesus that 'the common people heard him gladly' (Mark 12:37; Authorised Version). This was a tribute to them as well as to him. They recognised that he 'spoke with authority', that he knew what he was talking about. It is much easier to fool the highly educated!

The book of Revelation yields its treasures to those who read it with a simple faith, an open mind and a tender heart.

A story has circulated in America which highlights the point, though it sounds like an apocryphal preacher's tale (as the pastor's little boy said: 'Daddy, was that story true, or was you just preaching?')! Apparently some theological students were tired and confused by lectures on 'apocalyptic' so decided to have a game of basketball in the campus gymnasium. While playing, they noticed the black janitor reading his Bible while waiting to lock up. They asked which part he was studying and were surprised to find he was going through Revelation. 'You don't understand that, do you?' 'Sure do'. 'What's it about, then?' With eyes lit up and a broad smile came the reply: 'Simple! Jesus wins!!'

Of course, there's more to be said than that. But it's not a bad summary of the message. Plenty have studied the contents and missed the message. Common sense is a basic requirement. No one takes the whole book literally. No one takes it all symbolically. But where is the line to be drawn between the literal and the symbolical? This will have a profound effect on interpretation. Common sense will be a great help. The four horsemen are symbols, but the wars, bloodshed, famine and disease they represent clearly literal. The 'lake of fire' is a symbol of hell, but the unending 'torment' in it is literal (Rev 20:10).

The rules of common speech may be usefully employed. Words should be taken in their plainest, simplest sense, unless clearly indicated otherwise. It should be assumed that speakers (including Jesus) and writers (including John) mean what they say. Their communications should be taken at 'face value'.

Another such rule is that the same word in the same context is presumed to have the same meaning, again unless clearly indicated otherwise. To change the meaning of a word suddenly and without warning would be as confusing as changing the pronunciation or spelling. This rule directly affects the two 'resurrections' in Revelation 20.

Having said all this, we must add the necessary qualification that Revelation was written for ordinary folk in a very different time and place from ours. It is not surprising if some things obvious to them are obscure to us two thousand years later and a similar number of miles away.

They were Gentiles of mixed race who lived in a Roman province, spoke Greek, read Jewish scriptures and were held together by a shared Christian faith. So we need to use as much knowledge of their background, culture and language as we can. The object of the exercise is to discover what *they* would have understood when they heard Revelation read aloud to them, perhaps at one sitting. That could be quite different from what we perceive as we read it silently, a short portion each day.

But the book is clearly for us in our day as well, or it would not be in the New Testament. The Lord must have intended this when he gave it to John. So we can assume that our distance in time and space is not an insuperable handicap.

A much more important factor than the cultural gap is the difference of circumstances. It is vital to ask what situation required the writing of this book. This is the master key required to unlock the whole volume. Behind every other book in the New Testament there is a reason for its being written, a need which it is designed to meet. Revelation is no exception.

PRACTICAL REASONS

We have already said that its primary purpose was not to reveal a schedule of future events but to prepare people for what would happen. So what is coming for which, without this book, they would not be ready? The answer comes on the first page (1:9–10).

John, the writer, is already suffering for his faith. He is in prison, but not for any crime. He is a 'political' prisoner on the island of Patmos in the Aegean Sea (the modern equivalent would be Alcatraz or Robben Island). He has been arrested and exiled for religious reasons. His exclusive devotion to 'the word of God and the testimony of Jesus' is seen as treason by the authorities, a threat to the 'pax Romana' based on polytheistic tolerance and an imperial cult. Citizens were expected to believe in many gods and the Emperor was one of them.

Towards the end of the first century, this situation came to a head, creating a crisis of conscience for Christians. Julius Caesar had been the first to proclaim himself divine. His successor, Augustus, had encouraged the building of temples in his honour; a number of these had been erected in Asia (now western Turkey). While Nero had begun the persecution of Christians (daubing them with pitch and burning them alive as torches for his nightly garden parties or sewing them in the skins of wild animals to be hunted by dogs), this was limited in duration and location.

It was the advent of Domitian in the last decade of the first century that inaugurated the fiercest attacks on Christians which would continue intermittently for two hundred years. He demanded universal worship of himself, on pain of death. Once a year incense had to be thrown on an altar fire before his bust with an acclamation: 'Caesar is Lord'. The appointed day on which this had to be done was designated 'the Lord's Day'.

This was the very day on which Revelation began to be written. Modern readers may be forgiven for thinking it was a Sunday. Actually, it could have been, but Sunday was called 'the first day of the week' in the early church. Two elements in the Greek text indicate the annual imperial festival. One is the definite article (on '*the* Lord's day' not 'a Lord's day'). The other is the fact that 'Lord' is in the form of an adjective, not a noun ('the Lordy or Lordly day'), the very name given to it by Domitian, who also claimed the title: 'Lord and our God'.

Tough times lay ahead. For those who refused to say anything but 'Jesus is Lord', it would be a matter of life and death. The word 'witness' (in Greek: *martur*) would take on a new, deadly meaning. The church was facing its fiercest test so far. How many would remain loyal under such pressure?

After all, John was the only one of the twelve apostles left. All the others had already suffered a martyr's death. Christian tradition records that Andrew died on an X-shaped cross in Patras of Achaia, Bartholomew (Nathaniel) was flayed alive in Armenia, James (brother of John) was beheaded by Herod Agrippa in Jerusalem, James (son of Cleopas and Mary) was thrown from the pinnacle of the temple and stoned, Jude (Thaddeus) was shot with arrows in Armenia, Matthew was slain by the sword in Parthia, Peter was crucified upside down in Rome, Philip was hanged on a pillar in Hieropalis in Phrygia, Simon (Zelotes) was crucified in Persia, Thomas was slain with a spear in India, Matthias was stoned and beheaded. Paul also had been beheaded in Rome. So the writer of Revelation was only too aware of the cost of loyalty to Jesus. He did not then know that he would be the only apostle to die a natural death.

Revelation is a 'manual for martyrdom'. It calls believers to 'be faithful, even to the point of death' (2:10). Martyrs figure largely in its pages.

Believers are encouraged to 'stick it out'. One frequent exhortation is to 'endure', a passive attitude. Right in the middle of the biggest trouble comes the plea: 'This calls for patient endurance on the part of the saints who obey God's commandments and remain faithful to Jesus' (14:12). This may be said to be the key verse in the whole book.

But there is also a call to an active attitude in suffering for Jesus: to 'overcome'. This verb is used even more frequently than 'endure' and may be said to be the key word in the whole book.

Each letter to the seven churches concludes with a call to each member to be an 'overcomer', that is, to overcome all temptations and pressures, both inside and outside the church. To lapse from truly Christian belief and behaviour is to be unfaithful to Jesus.

The message is not just that Christ wins, but that Christians must also win through. They are to follow the Lord who said: 'Take heart! I have overcome the world' (John 16:33) and who now says in Revelation: 'You also must overcome the world'.

Of course, that is why this book becomes so much more meaningful to Christians under persecution. Maybe this is also why Western Christians in comfortable churches fail to find it relevant. It has to be read through tears.

The book offers two incentives to encourage the persecuted to 'overcome'. One is positive: *reward*. Many prizes are offered to those who persevere – the right to eat of the tree of life in the paradise of God; never to be hurt by the second death; to eat the hidden manna and be given a white stone with a secret new name on it; to have authority to rule the nations; to sit with Jesus on his throne; to be dressed in white and made a pillar in the temple of God bearing his name and never to leave it. Above all, and beyond all the suffering, the overcoming believer is promised a place in the new heaven and earth, enjoying God's presence for ever and ever. The prospect is glorious.

But there is a negative motivation as well: *punishment*. What is the fate of believers who are unfaithful under pressure? In a word, they will have none of the above blessings. Worse than that, they will share the fate of unbelievers in the 'lake of fire'. Two verses alone, taken from first and last sections, confirm this awful possibility.

'He who overcomes . . . I will never erase his name from the book of life' (3:5). If language means anything at all, it means that those who do not overcome are in danger of having their names erased (literally, 'scraped off' the parchment with a knife). The 'book of life' appears in four books of the Bible (Exod 32:32; Ps 69:28; Phil 4:3; Rev 3:5). Three of these contexts mention names of the people of God being blotted out after they have sinned against the Lord. To read the verse in Revelation as if it could include 'he who doesn't overcome' in the promise as well is to make the reward meaningless.

'He who overcomes will inherit all this [the new heaven and earth, with the new Jerusalem] and I will be his God and he will be my son. But the cowardly, the faithless, the immoral . . . their place will be in the fiery lake of burning sulphur. This is the second death' (21:7–8). It needs to be remembered that the whole of Revelation is directed to believers, not unbelievers. Throughout, it is addressed to 'the saints' and 'his servants'. The reference here is to cowardly and faithless believers. This is confirmed by the word 'but', directly contrasting those deserving such a fate with the believers who 'overcome'.

In other words, Revelation sets two destinies before *Christians*. They will either be raised with Christ and share his reign, ending up in the new universe. Or they will lose their inheritance in the kingdom and end up in hell.

This alternative is confirmed elsewhere in the New Testament. The Gospel of Matthew is a 'manual for discipleship' containing five major discourses addressed to 'sons of the kingdom'. Yet most of Jesus' teaching on hell is to be found here and all but two of his warnings are addressed to his disciples. The Sermon on the Mount (in chs. 5–7), which blesses those who are persecuted because of Jesus, goes on to speak of hell and concludes with a reminder that there are two destinies. The missionary commissioning (in ch. 10) includes the charge: 'Do not be afraid of those who kill the body but cannot kill the soul. Rather be afraid of the one who can destroy both body and soul in hell' (verse 28) and 'whoever disowns me before men, I will disown him before my Father in heaven' (verse 33). The Olivet discourse (in chs. 24–25) condemns slothful and careless servants of the master to being 'assigned a place with the hypocrites' (24:51) and 'thrown outside into the darkness, where there will be weeping and gnashing of teeth' (25:30).

Paul takes the same line when reminding Timothy of a 'trustworthy saying':

> If we died with him,
>   we will also live with him;
> If we endure,
>   we will also reign with him.
> If we disown him,
>   He will also disown us ... (2 Tim 2:11–12)

Many Christians deny the implications of all this. Certainly there is more to be said (the author intends to deal more fully with this vital question in a later volume entitled: *Once Saved, Always Saved*?). Meanwhile, the position in Revelation seems very clear. It is even possible for believers to lose their 'share in the tree of life and in the holy city' simply by tampering with the text of the book (22:19), thus changing its message.

We could summarise the aim of Revelation by saying it was written to exhort Christians facing immense pressures to 'endure' and 'overcome' and thus avoid the 'second death' by keeping their names in the 'book of life'. We shall find that every chapter and verse fit easily into this overall purpose, as we look at the shape or structure of the whole book.

CHAPTER SEVEN

Analysis of Structure

If we have been right in defining the purpose of Revelation as the preparation of believers to face persecution and even martyrdom, it should be possible to relate this to every part of the book. Moreover, the overall structure should reveal a development of this theme.

We shall construct a number of outlines by analysing the contents from different perspectives and for different purposes, starting with the simplest. The most obvious division occurs at 4:1, with the radical shift in viewpoint from earth to heaven and from the present situation to the future prospects:

1–3 PRESENT
4–22 FUTURE

The larger second part also divides neatly between the bad news and the good news. The change from one to the other comes in 19. So now we have:

1–3 PRESENT
4–22 FUTURE
   4–18 *Bad news*
  20–22 *Good news*

Now we consider how each section relates to the main purpose of the book. That is, how does each section prepare believers for the coming 'Big Trouble'? We can expand the outline thus:

1–3	PRESENT
	Things must be put right now.
4–22	FUTURE
4–18	*Bad news*: things will get much worse before they get better.
20–22	*Good news*: things will get much better after they get worse.

Only one more item remains to be added, namely, 19. What occurs in this chapter to change the whole situation? The second coming of Jesus to planet earth! This is really the framework of the whole book, according to the prologue and epilogue (1:7 and 22:20). We can now insert '19 Jesus returns' between the bad and good news (rather than repeat the outline unnecessarily, readers are invited to write it themselves in the gap left above).

If this simple outline is kept in mind when reading through the book, many things will become clearer. Above all, the unity of the whole book will become apparent. Its objective is achieved in three phases.

First, Jesus tells the churches that they must deal with internal problems if they are to face external pressures. Compromise in belief or behaviour, tolerance of idolatry or immorality, weaken the church from within.

Second, Jesus, who was always noted for his honesty, shows them the worst that can happen to them. They will never have to go through anything worse! And the very worst time ahead will be at most only a few years.

Third, Jesus reveals the wonders that will follow. To throw away such eternal prospects for the sake of avoiding temporary troubles would be the greatest tragedy of all.

In all three ways, Jesus is encouraging his followers to 'endure' and 'overcome' until he gets back. One verse sums it all up: 'Only hold on to what you have until I come' (2:25). Then he can say: 'Come and share your master's happiness' (Matt 25:21).

Of course, there are other ways of analysing the book. A 'topical' outline is more like an index of subjects and will assist us to 'find our way around' the book.

Such an outline will ignore the switch from earth to heaven and back again. We can work with three periods of time:

A. What is already happening in the present (1–5)
B. What will happen in the nearer future (6–19)
C. What will happen in the distant future (20–22)

We will then note the main features of each period and seek to list these in a way that can easily be memorised. Here is one example of such a 'catalogue' of events:

A. THE PRESENT
   1–3   One ascended Lord
          Seven assorted lampstands
   4–5   Creator and creatures
          Lion and lamb

B. THE NEAR FUTURE
   6–16   Seals, trumpets, bowls
          Devil, antichrist, false prophet
   17–19 Babylon – last capital
          Armageddon – last battle

C. THE FAR FUTURE
   20   Millennial reign
          Judgement day
   21–22 New heaven and earth
          New Jerusalem

Note that chapters 4–5 are now in the first division. That is because the 'action' leading to the 'Big Trouble' actually begins with chapter 6. Chapter 19 is now in the second division because the 'Big Trouble' ends here, with Christ defeating the 'unholy trinity'.

This kind of outline is easily memorised and provides a useful 'ready reference' when looking up particular subjects.

It is important to do this kind of exercise before getting down to a closer look at the several sections. There is an over-used proverb about 'not being able to see the wood for the trees'! Revelation is one of the easiest books in which to get so interested in the details that the overall thrust is lost sight of.

However, it is now time to exchange the telescope for a microscope – or at least for a magnifying glass!

CHAPTER EIGHT

Digest of Contents

In a book this size it is impossible to include a full commentary. What we intend to do is give an introduction to each section that will enable the Bible student to 'read, mark, learn and inwardly digest the same', as the Book of Common Prayer puts it.

We shall highlight the major features, tackle some of the problems and generally help the reader to keep on course through some of the hazards. Many questions will have to be left unanswered, but these can be followed up in some of the published commentaries (George Eldon Ladd's is one of the best; Eerdmans, 1972).

The suggestion is that each part of Revelation is read before and after the relevant section in this chapter.

CHAPTERS 1–3: CHURCH ON EARTH

This is by far the most straightforward, easy to read and understand. It is like paddling at the edge of the sea, after which you may find yourself out of your depth and in the grip of an undertow, swirling around in a panic!

Though frequently describing itself as a 'prophecy', Revelation is actually in the form of a letter (compare 1:4–6 with the opening 'address' of other epistles). However, it is sent to seven churches rather than one. While containing a particular message for each, it is clearly intended that all should hear each other's.

After the usual Christian greeting ('grace and peace'), the main theme is announced: 'he is coming', an event which will cause unhappiness to the world but joy to the church. This event is absolutely certain ('Amen').

The 'sender' of the letter is God himself, the Lord of time, who is, was and is to come, the Alpha and Omega (the first and the last letters of the Greek alphabet, symbolising the beginning and end of everything). The same titles will be given to Jesus, by himself (1:17; 22:13), proof that he believed in his own deity.

The 'secretary' who writes the letter down is the apostle John, exiled to the eight-miles-by-four island of Patmos in the 'Dodecanese' of the Aegean Sea, a political prisoner for religious reasons.

The contents were given in verbal and visual form. Note that he 'heard' something before he 'saw' anything. The voice commanding him to write was followed by an overwhelming vision of Jesus as John had never seen him before: snow-white hair, blazing eyes, thundering voice, sharp tongue, glowing feet. Even on the Mount of Transfiguration, he had never looked like this. No wonder John swooned, until he heard some very familiar words: 'Don't be afraid'.

Every other great figure of history was alive and is dead. Jesus alone was dead and is alive, 'for ever and ever' (1:18; literally: 'to the ages of the ages').

John is told to write 'what is now' (chs. 1–3) and 'what will take place later' (chs. 4–22). The word for the present is the state of the seven churches of Asia, each of which has a 'guardian angel' and for which Jesus has oversight (as well as insight and foresight!). They were represented in the original vision by seven stars (the angels) and seven lampstands (the churches). Note that Jesus characteristically 'walks' around them, as John must have done when he was free. In the Gospels, most of Jesus' messages were delivered and miracles were done as he walked 'in the way', both before his death and after his resurrection.

The seven letters to the seven churches are best studied together and compared with each other. It is very illuminating when they are written out side by side, which emphasises both their similarities and differences.

It becomes immediately obvious that their form is identical, comprising seven elements (yet another 'seven'):

1. ADDRESS:
   'To the angel of the church in . . .'
2. ATTRIBUTE:
   'These are the words of him who . . .'
3. APPROVAL:
   'I know your deeds . . .'
4. ACCUSATION:
   'Yet I hold this against you'
5. ADVICE:
   '. . . or else I will come and . . .'
6. ASSURANCE:
   'To him who overcomes, I will . . .'
7. APPEAL:
   '. . . let him hear what the Spirit says . . .'

The only variation from this order is in the last four letters, where the final two items are reversed (the reason for this is not apparent). We shall now compare and contrast the letters.

The *address*
This is exactly the same in all seven, except for the named destination. The cities are on a circular route, starting in the major port of Ephesus (a church of which we have more information than any other in those days), heading north up the coast, then inland to the east and finally south to the rich valley of the river Meander.

The only point of debate is whether the word *angelos* (literally 'messenger') refers to a heavenly or human person. Since everywhere else in Revelation it is rightly translated as angel, the strong presumption is that it is the same here. Angels are very much involved with churches (even noting hairstyles of worshippers! 1 Cor 11:10). Since John is totally isolated, heavenly 'messengers' would have to deliver the letters. It is only modern scepticism about the existence of angels that has led to the translation: 'minister' (presumably with the title: 'Rev.'!).

The *attribute*

It is noticeable that Jesus never refers to himself by name, only by titles, many of them quite new. In fact, he has over *two hundred and fifty* titles, the largest number of any historical personage (it is a useful devotional exercise to list them). In each letter, the title of Jesus is carefully chosen to describe an aspect of his character which that church has tended to forget or needs to remember. Some are to be found in John's original vision of him. All are very significant. The 'key of David' points to his fulfilment of the messianic hopes of Israel. 'Ruler of God's creation' signifies his universal authority (Matt 28:18).

The *approval*

This opens the most intimate part of each letter, switching from the third person ('him') to the first ('I'). Is this the same person? The 'him' certainly refers to Christ, but the 'I' could be the Spirit, the 'Spirit of Christ', of course. Later comments (e.g. 'I have received authority from my Father' in 2:27) favour the former.

'I know' is a claim to be totally aware, both of their internal state and external situation. His knowledge, and therefore his understanding, is total. His judgement is accurate, his opinion crucial and his honesty transparent.

Above all, he knows their 'works', that is, their deeds, their actions. This emphasis on works runs right through Revelation. That is because its theme is judgement. Jesus is coming again – to judge the living and the dead. We are justified by faith, but we shall be judged by works (2 Cor 5:10). Jesus approves good works and encourages their continuance.

When the letters are viewed side by side, it is immediately apparent that Jesus has nothing good to say about two of them, Sardis and Laodicea. Yet these are both 'successful' to human eyes. Jesus' opinion may be very different from ours.

Large congregations, big collections and full programmes are not necessarily signs of spiritual health.

Five of the churches are commended: Ephesus for effort, patience, persistence and discernment (rejecting false apostles); Smyrna for its courage in the face of opposition and deprivation (though adjacent to a 'synagogue of Satan', possibly an occult form of Judaism); Pergamum for not denying the faith under pressure, even when one member was martyred (though under the shadow of the 'throne of Satan', a gigantic temple now re-erected in an East Berlin museum); Thyatira for its love, faith, patience and progress; Philadelphia for its costly fidelity (with another 'synagogue of Satan' nearby).

In passing we note that Jesus frequently speaks of Satan, who is behind all hostility towards the churches. He is also responsible for the looming crisis they will face, 'the hour of trial that is going to come upon the whole world to test those who live on the earth' (3:10).

Finally, how characteristic of Jesus to commend before he criticises, an example followed by the apostles. Paul thanked God that the Corinthians had all the 'spiritual gifts' (1 Cor 1:4–7) before he corrected their abuse of them. Of course, he also encountered church situations where this was not possible, as in Galatia. But the principle is one to be emulated by all Christians.

The *accusation*

Again, two are exempt from criticism, Smyrna and Philadelphia. What a relief they must have felt when their letters were read out! They are weaker than the others and already suffering, but they have remained faithful, which pleases Jesus more than anything else (Matt 25:21, 23).

What was wrong with the others? Ephesus had forsaken its 'first love' (for the Lord, each other or lost sinners? Probably all three, since they are interconnected); Pergamum was into idolatry and immorality (syncretism and permissiveness are the modern counterparts); Thyatira was guilty of the same things (as a result of listening to 'Jezebel', a false prophetess); Sardis was for ever starting new ventures, giving it the reputation of being a 'live' church, but they were not kept up or seen through to the finish (does that strike a chord?); Laodicea was sick, but didn't know it.

This last letter is perhaps the best known and most striking. They prided themselves on being a warm fellowship, with a warm welcome for the many visitors. But 'lukewarm' churches make Jesus feel sick. He can handle icy cold or piping hot ones more easily! This is a reference to the salty hot springs covering a hillside outside the city (the 'white castle' of Pamukkale is still a popular 'spa' for health seekers); by the time the stream reached Laodicea it was 'lukewarm' and acted as an emetic, causing vomiting when drunk.

Jesus has stopped attending services here! He cannot be found inside – but stands just outside. Verse 20 is probably the most abused text in scripture and has been almost universally used as an evangelistic invitation and in counselling enquirers. It has nothing to do with becoming a Christian. Indeed, it gives quite a wrong impression when used in this way (actually, it is the sinner who is on the outside needing to knock and enter the kingdom, of which Jesus is the door; Luke 11:5–10; John 3:5; 10:7). The 'door' in 3:20 is the church door in Laodicea. The verse is a prophetic message to a church which has lost Christ and it is full of hope. It only takes one member who wants to sit at his table with him to get Christ back inside! For a fuller treatment of this verse and the New Testament way to become a Christian, see my book: *The Normal Christian Birth* (Hodder and Stoughton, 1989).

Before we leave this section, it needs to be pointed out that these accusations stem from the love of Jesus for the churches. He says this himself: 'as many as I love I reprove and chasten' (3:19). In fact, the absence of such discipline could be a sign of not belonging to his family at all (Heb 12:7–8)!

He is not wanting to put them down, but lift them up. Above all, he seeks to get them ready for pending pressure, which will 'test' them (3:10). If they compromise now, they will surrender then. That could cost them their inheritance.

The *advice*
There is a word of counsel for all seven churches. Even the two of which he thoroughly approves are exhorted to keep up the good work, to 'hold on to what you have until I come' (2:25).

The other five are cautioned with two words: remember and repent. They are to call to mind what they once were and what they ought to be. And true repentance involves much more than regret or remorse; it requires confession and correction.

He warns those that spurn his appeal that he 'will come' and deal with them. There will be a time when it will be too late to put things right. Sometimes this refers to his second coming, when the 'crown of life' will be given to those who have been 'faithful, even to the point of death' (2:10; cf. 2 Tim 4:6–8), but those who are not ready will hear the dreadful words: 'I don't know you' (Matt 25:12).

Usually, 'I will come' refers to an earlier 'visitation' to a single church, to remove its 'lampstand' (2:5). Jesus has a ministry of closing churches down! A compromised church that is not willing to be corrected is worse than useless to the kingdom of God. It is better to remove such a poor advertisement for the gospel altogether.

We could summarise this part of the letters: 'put it right, keep it up or I will close it down'.

The *assurance*
It is noticeable that the call to 'overcome' is not addressed to a church as a whole, but to each individual member. Judgement is always individual, whether for the purpose of reward or punishment, never corporate (note 'each one' in 2 Cor 5:10). There is no suggestion of leaving a corrupt church and catching a chariot to a better one down the road! Neither is a person excused compromise because their whole church is slipping. The wrong trends in a fellowship are not to be followed. In other words,

a Christian may have to learn to resist pressures in the church first before facing them in the world. If we cannot 'overcome' the former, we are unlikely to 'overcome' the latter.

Jesus has no hesitation in offering rewards as incentives (5:12). He himself endured the cross, scorning its shame, 'for the joy set before him' (Heb 12:2). In each of the letters he encourages 'overcomers' to think of the prizes awaiting those who 'press on toward the goal' (Phil 3:14).

Just as his title in each letter is taken from the first chapter, the rewards he offers are taken from the last chapters. They will come in the ultimate future rather than the immediate present. Only those who have faith that he keeps his promises will be motivated by distant compensations.

Once again, we must realise that the joys of the new heaven and earth are not for all believers, but only for those who overcome the pressures of temptation and persecution (21:7–8 makes this abundantly clear). It is those who remain obedient and faithful 'to the end' (2:26) who will be saved (cf. Matt 10:22; 24:13; Mark 13:13; Luke 21:19).

The *appeal*

The final call: 'he that has an ear, let him hear' is a familiar conclusion to Jesus' words (Matt 13:9, for example). Its meaning becomes clear in the light of one of the most frequently quoted texts from the Old Testament in the New: 'You will be ever hearing, but never understanding . . . they hardly hear with their ears . . . otherwise they might . . . hear with their ears, understand with their hearts and turn, and I would heal them' (Isa 6:9–10, quoted in Matt 13:13–15; Mark 4:12; Luke 8:10; Acts 28:26–27).

Jesus knew that this would be the general response from the Jews. Now he is challenging Christians not to have the same reaction. He is highlighting the difference between hearing and heeding a message. It is a question of how much notice is taken of what he says. His words in Revelation will only be a blessing if they are read and 'kept', that is, not just taken into the ear but 'taken to heart' (1:3). A parent whose child has ignored the order to 'put that down' will say: 'Did you hear what I said?', knowing full well that it was heard, but was not heeded.

Quite simply, the closing remark in each of the letters to the seven churches means that Jesus expects a reply, in the form of a positive response of obedience. He has the right to expect this. He is Lord.

CHAPTERS 4–5: GOD IN HEAVEN

This section is relatively straightforward and needs little introduction. In particular, chapter 4 is probably familiar in the context of worship; it is often read to stimulate praise and has provided the content for many hymns and choruses. It gives a glimpse of that heavenly adoration of which all earthly worship is an echo.

John has been invited to 'come up here' (4:1) and see what heaven looks like, a privilege shared by few during their lifetime (Paul had a similar experience; 2 Cor 12:1–6). It is the place where God reigns and from which he rules. 'Throne' is the keyword and it occurs sixteen times. Notice the emphasis on 'sitting' (4:2,9,10; 5:1). This is the control centre of the 'kingdom of heaven'.

The scene is breathtakingly beautiful, almost defying description. Green rainbows(!), golden crowns, thunder and lightning, blazing lamps – one can almost imagine John's eyes darting from one striking feature to another as he gazes in awe and wonder. In trying to describe what he can see of God himself, he can only compare this with two of the most brilliant gemstones he has ever seen before (jasper and carnelian).

Above all, there is a peaceful aspect to the whole scene, expressed as a 'sea of glass', stretching to the horizon. The sharp contrast with profound disturbances on earth (from ch. 6 onwards) is clearly intentional. God reigns supreme above all the battles between good and evil. He does not have to struggle; even Satan has to ask his permission before he can touch a human being (Job 1). He is not even surprised by anything. He knows exactly how to deal with whatever arises, since that also can only be what he allows.

He is God, not man. He is therefore worthy of worship (the word derives from 'worth-ship', telling someone how much they are worth to you). The Creator receives non-stop praise from the creatures he has made. The four 'living' ones are only 'like' a lion, ox, man and eagle; together they may represent all creatures from the four corners of the earth (though there are twenty other interpretations!). Their praise is vaguely 'trinitarian': 'holy' three times and God in three dimensions of time – past, present and future.

Twenty-four elders comprise the 'council' of heaven (Jer 23:18). Almost certainly they represent the two covenant peoples of God, Israel and the Church (notice the twenty-four names on the new Jerusalem's gates and foundations; 21:12–14). They have 'crowns' and 'thrones', but only delegated authority.

There is no action in chapter 4, other than unceasing worship. It is a permanent scene with no time reference. With chapter 5 the action begins – with the search for someone 'in heaven and earth', someone 'worthy to break the seals and open the scroll'.

The significance of the scroll becomes apparent in the light of events. On it must be written the programme which will bring to an end the age of earthly history in which we live. Breaking its seals begins the countdown.

Until this happens, the world must continue in its present state. The 'present evil age' must be closed before the 'age to come' can open. There must be a decisive termination of the 'kingdoms of the world' if the 'kingdom of God' is to be universally established on the earth. That is why John 'wept and wept' in frustration and grief when no one was found 'worthy' to set this in motion.

But why was this a problem? God himself had released many judgements on the earth through history. Why not the final ones? Either he does not choose to do so or does not feel he is qualified to do so! This last thought is not so bizarre or even blasphemous as some might think, in the light of what is said about the one person who is found to be 'worthy'.

Who is it? Someone who is both a 'lion' and a 'lamb'! Actually, the contrast between the two is not as great as many assume. The lamb is male and fully mature, as was every lamb used in sacrifice ('one year old'; Exod 12:5). In this case, the 'Ram', as we should really say, has seven horns (one more than Jacob sheep), signifying perfect power and seven eyes, signifying perfect oversight. Yet it has been 'slain' as a sacrifice.

The lion is king of the jungle, but here of the tribe of Judah and rooted in the Davidic dynasty. So we have a unique combination of the sovereign lion and the sacrificial lamb, which corresponds to the coming king and suffering servant predicted by the Hebrew prophets (e.g. Isa 9–11 and 42–53).

But it is not just what he is, but what he has done, that fits him to release the troubles that will bring the world to an end, for 'end' can mean two things: termination or consummation. He will bring it to the latter.

He has prepared a people to take over the government of the world. He has purchased them, at the price of his own blood, out of every ethnic group in the human race. He has trained them in royal and priestly duties in God's service and thus prepared them for the responsibility of *reigning on the earth* (this is fully developed in Rev 20:4–6).

Only someone who has done all this is able to begin the series of disasters that will bring all other regimes down. To destroy a bad system without having a good one ready to replace it can only lead to anarchy.

And he himself is a worthy sovereign over the government he has prepared, precisely because he was willing to give his all to make it possible. It was because he became 'obedient to death – even death on a cross!' that 'God exalted him to the highest place' (Phil 2:8–9).

No wonder thousands of angels agree, in musical acclamation, that it is only right to give him power, wealth, wisdom, strength, honour, glory and praise. Then all the creatures in the universe join the choir's anthem, though with one significant addition. The power, honour, glory and praise should be shared between the one sitting on the throne and the one standing in the centre in front of him, the Father and the Son together. For it was a joint effort. They were both involved. They both suffered to make it all possible, though in very different ways.

Nothing reveals more clearly the divinity of our Lord Jesus Christ as the offering of unqualified praise and worship to both him and God together.

CHAPTERS 6–16: SATAN ON EARTH

This section is the heart of the book and the most difficult to understand and apply.

We are into the bad news. Things will get much worse before they get better. At least there is the comfort of knowing that the situation cannot ever be worse than that foretold in these chapters. But that's bad enough!

There are three major problems for interpreters.

First, what is the *order* of events? It is quite difficult to put them all on a time chart, as those who attempt this soon discover.

Second, what do all the *symbols* mean? Some are clear. Some are explained. But some are a problem (the 'pregnant woman' in ch.12 is a case in point).

Third, when is the *fulfilment* of the predictions? In our past, our present or our future? Have they already happened, are they happening right now or are they yet to happen? Since we have already discussed this (in the chapter on 'Schools of Interpretation') we don't need to cover the same ground here.

So we shall concentrate on the order of events, which is far from clear at the first reading, looking at the symbols as we come to them. The task is complicated by the insertion of three features which are out of order, scattered seemingly at random through these chapters.

First, there are *digressions*. In the form of 'interludes' or parentheses, these deal with subjects that seem to be outside the main stream of events.

Second, there are *recapitulations*. From time to time the narrative seems to go back on its track, recalling events already mentioned.

Third, there are *anticipations*. Events are mentioned without explanation until later in the story (for example, 'Armageddon' first appears in 16:16, but does not happen until ch. 19).

These have led to misunderstanding and speculation, notably in the 'cyclical historicist' interpretation already discussed (on page 99). We shall follow a simpler route, working from the obvious to the obscure.

Reading through these chapters at one sitting, the most striking features are the three sequences of seals, trumpets and bowls. The symbolism in these is comparatively easy to decode.

Seals:
1. White horse – military aggression
2. Red horse – bloodshed
3. Black horse – famine
4. Green horse – disease, epidemics

*   *   *

5. Persecution and prayer
6. Tremor and terror

*   *   *

7. Silence in heaven, listening to prayers which are then answered in a final catastrophe: severe earthquake.

Trumpets:
1. Scorched earth
2. Polluted sea
3. Contaminated water
4. Reduced sunlight

*   *   *

5. Insects and plague (5 months)

6. Oriental invasion (200 million)

*   *   *

7. Kingdom comes, world taken over by God
   and Christ after severe earthquake

Bowls: 1. Boils on the skin
             2. Blood in the sea
             3. Blood from the springs
             4. Burning by the sun

*   *   *

5. Darkness
6. Armageddon

*   *   *

7. Hailstorm and severe earthquake, leading to
   international collapse

As soon as they are laid out like this a number of things
become clear:

The events are not totally unfamiliar. They are vaguely
reminiscent of the plagues in Egypt when Moses confronted
Pharaoh, even down to frogs and locusts (Exod 7–11). They are
also happening today on a local or regional scale. For example,
the sequence of four horses can be observed in many parts of the
world, each a result of the previous one. The major novelty is
the universal scale on which they happen here, as if the troubles
have spread worldwide.

Each series divides into three parts. The first four belong
together, the most notable example being the 'four horsemen
of the Apocalypse' as they have become known since the artist
Albrecht Dürer portrayed them. The next two are not quite so
closely related and the last one stands on its own. The last three
in each are labelled 'woes', a word indicating curses.

Looking at the three series together, there appears to be an *intensification* in the severity of events. While a quarter of mankind perish in the 'seals', one third of the remainder fail to survive the 'trumpets'. Furthermore, there is a progression in the causes of disaster. The 'seals' are of human origin; the 'trumpets' seem to be a natural deterioration of the environment; the 'bowls' are directly poured out by angelic agents.

There is also an *acceleration* of events. The 'seals' seem quite spread out in time, but the later series appear to be measured in months or even days.

All this suggests a progression in the three series, which brings us to the question of the relation between them. The most obvious answer is that they are *successive*, which may be represented thus:

Seals: 1234567, then trumpets: 1234567, then bowls: 1234567.
In other words, the series simply follow each other.

But it is not quite as simple as this! A careful study reveals that the seventh in each case seems to refer to the same event (a severe earthquake on a world scale is the common factor; 8:5; 11:19; 16:18). This has led to an alternative theory, beloved by the 'cyclical historicist' school, which believes the series are *simultaneous*, thus:

Seals: 1 2 3 4 5 6 7
Trumpets: 1 2 3 4 5 6 7
Bowls: 1 2 3 4 5 6 7

In other words, they cover the same period (usually held to be the whole time between the first and second advents) from different angles.

A more convincing, but more complicated pattern combines these two insights, treating the first six as successive and the seventh as simultaneous:

Seals: 1 2 3 4 5 6 7   7
Trumpets: 1 2 3 4 5 6   7
Bowls: 1 2 3 4 5 6 7

In other words, each series advances on the previous one but all climax in the same catastrophic end. This seems to best fit the evidence and is mainly held by the 'futurist' school who believe all three series still lie ahead in history.

All three concentrate on what will happen to the world. In passing, the reaction of human beings should be noted. While recognising that these terrible tragedies are evidence of the wrath of God (and the Lamb's!), the human response is one of terror (6:15–17) and curses on God (16:21) rather than repentance (9:20–21), even though the gospel of forgiveness is still available (14:6). It is a sad comment on the hardness of the human heart, but it is true to life. In disasters we either turn towards God or against him (the last words of crashing airline pilots often curse God; they are usually edited out of the 'black box' recording before it is played at the enquiry).

It is time to look at the chapters inserted between the three series of seals, trumpets and bowls – or rather, within them, as we shall see. There are three such insertions: chapter 7, chapters 10–11 and chapters 12–14. The first two sections are put between the sixth and seventh seals and trumpets, but the third is put before the first bowl, as if there is no time-scale for it between the sixth and seventh bowls. We can put this in diagram form, using the previous illustration:

Seals:	1 2 3 4 5 6	(ch. 7)		7
Trumpets:		1 2 3 4 5 6 (chs. 10–11)		7
Bowls:		(chs. 12–14)	1 2 3 4 5 6 7	

We now have a complete outline of chapters 6–16.

Whereas the three series of seals, trumpets and bowls are primarily concerned with what will happen to the *world*, the three insertions deal with what will happen to the *church*. Here we are given information about God's people during this terrible upheaval. How will they be affected? Since Revelation aims to prepare the 'saints' for what is to come, these insertions are more relevant and important for them.

Chapter 7: the *two groups*. Between the sixth and seventh seals, we catch a glimpse of two distinct kinds of people in two very different places.

On the one hand, *a limited number of Jews are protected on earth* (verses 1–8). God has not rejected Israel (Rom 11:1, 11). He made an unconditional promise that they would survive as long as the universe lasted (Jer 31:35–37). He will keep his word. They have a future.

The numbers seem somewhat arbitrary, even artificial. Perhaps they are 'round' numbers or maybe symbolic in some way. What is clear is that it will be a very limited proportion of a nation now numbered in millions. And the total will be equally divided between the twelve tribes, without favouring any. This means that the ten tribes taken to Assyria were not 'lost' to God and that he will preserve the survivors of each tribe that are known to him. There is one lost tribe, Dan, which rebelled against God's will for it and was replaced – in much the same way as Judas Iscariot among the twelve apostles. Both are warnings against taking our place in God's purposes for granted.

On the other hand, *an uncountable number of Christians are protected in heaven* (verses 8–17). The international crowd stand in an honoured place before the King, joining with the elders and living creatures in their songs of praise. But they add one new note of praise: for their 'salvation'.

John does not realise their significance and confesses ignorance of their qualifications for such honour. One of the elders enlightens him: 'These are they who are coming out of the Great Tribulation' (verse 14; the tense of the verb clearly indicates a continuing procession of individuals and groups through the whole time of trouble). How are they escaping? Not by one sudden and secret 'rapture' (see the third section of this volume), but by death, most by martyrdom, which figures so prominently in these very chapters (we have already heard the cries of their 'souls' for vengeance; 6:9–11).

But it is the shedding of the Lamb's blood rather than their own that has rescued them. It was his suffering, not theirs, a

sacrifice that atoned for their sins and made them clean enough
to stand in God's presence and offer their service.

But God is mindful of what they have suffered for his Son's
sake and he will make sure that they will 'never again' experience
such pain. The scorching sun will not burn them (16:8–9). They
will be looked after by the 'good shepherd' (Ps 23; John 10).
They will be refreshed with water, 'living' (fizzy!) rather than
'still' (John 4:14; 7:38; Rev 21:6; 22:1, 17). And God, like every
parent with a weeping child, will 'wipe away every tear from
their eyes' (21:4). Note that being in heaven now is a foretaste
of life on the new earth.

Chapters 10–11: the *two witnesses*. Between the sixth and
seventh trumpets, attention is focused on the human channels
through which the divine revelations are communicated. The
keyword in both chapters is 'prophesy' (10:11; 11:3,6). At the
beginning of the church age, John in Patmos is the prophet; at
the end there will be two 'witnesses' who will prophesy in the
city of Jerusalem.

There is a sense of impending disaster in the spectacular
appearance of two 'mighty' angels. The terrible truths uttered
by the first in a thunderous voice are for John alone and must
not be communicated to anyone else (cf. 2 Cor 12:4). The second
announces that there will be no more delay in the build up of
events – the seventh trumpet will be the climax (confirming our
conclusion that the seventh seal, trumpet and bowl all refer to
the same 'end').

The last and worst part of the 'bad news' is about to be given.
It is on a 'little scroll' (an expanded, more detailed, version of
part of the larger one already opened?). John is told to 'eat it'
(we would say: 'digest it'). It will taste 'sweet and sour', sweet
at first but sour when it begins to sink in (a reaction that many
have to the whole book of Revelation when they begin to grasp
its message).

John is told to 'prophesy again', to continue his work of
foretelling the future of the world. Then he is 'shown' around
the city of Jerusalem and its temple. He measures its courts but

not the outermost one for Gentile worshippers since they will be coming to 'trample' on the city rather than pray in it. They will, however, encounter two extraordinary persons who will preach to them about the God they despise.

The result will be death for preachers and hearers alike! The two witnesses will have miraculous power, to stop the rain (like Elijah; 1 Kgs 17:1; Jas 5:17) and to bring fire upon their enemies (like Moses; Lev 10:1–3). But they will be killed when their testimony is concluded. Their bodies will lie in the streets for just over three days, while the multinational crowd, 'tormented' in conscience by their words, gloat over and celebrate their removal. The relief will turn to terror when the two are resurrected in full view of all. A loud voice from heaven 'Come up here' will result in their ascension. At the moment of their departure, a severe earthquake will destroy one tenth of the city's buildings and seven thousand of its population.

The similarity between the fate of the two witnesses and '*the prophet*' Jesus is striking. It will be impossible not to recall his crucifixion, resurrection and ascension in this very same city. Of course, there are differences: in his case, the earthquake coincided with his death (Matt 27:51) and neither his resurrection after three days nor his ascension were witnessed by the general public. But it will still be a vivid reminder, especially to the Jewish inhabitants, of those far-off days. It will result in fear of, and glory to, God.

Who these two witnesses are, we are not told. All attempts to identify them are sheer speculation. There is no suggestion that they are 'reincarnate' figures from previous times, so they are not Moses and Elijah, even though they are like them in some ways, any more than they are two Jesus's, though they are like him in others. We must 'wait and see' who they are, but it obviously does not really matter. What they do and what is done to them are the important things.

Before leaving this section, two 'anticipations' need to be noted.

For one thing, there is the first mention of a time period of

1,260 days, which is forty-two months, which is three and a half
years. We shall come across this figure in succeeding chapters,
where it seems to indicate the duration of the 'Big Trouble'. Many
link it with the 'half week' predicted by Daniel (Dan 9:27; the
New International Version rightly translates 'week' as 'seven').
It is quite a brief time and recalls Jesus' own prediction that it
would be kept short (Matt 24:22).

For another thing, this is the first mention of the 'beast',
who figures so largely in the next parenthesis in the ongoing
narrative.

Chapters 12–14: the *two beasts*. To follow the literary pattern
so far, this section should have come between the sixth and
seventh bowls, but these follow each other so closely that there
is neither time nor space between them for other events. So these
three chapters are inserted before the seven bowls are poured out
as the final expression of God's wrath on a rebellious world (see
the diagram on page 134).

Six seals and six trumpets are over. The very last series of
disasters is about to happen. It will be the worst for the world –
and the toughest for the church. Evil powers will gain a tighter
grip on society than they have ever had before, though their hold
is about to be broken.

The section introduces three persons who form an alliance to
rule the world themselves. One is angelic in origin and nature: a
'great dragon' and 'ancient serpent', otherwise known as 'Satan',
or 'the devil' (12:9). The other two are human in origin and
nature: 'beasts', otherwise known as 'the Antichrist' (1 John
2:18; also 'the man of lawlessness' in 2 Thess 2:3) and 'the false
prophet' (16:13; 19:20; 20:10). Together they form a kind of
'unholy trinity' in a ghastly mimicry of God, Christ and the
Holy Spirit.

Satan is introduced into the 'troubles' for the first time. He
has not been mentioned in Revelation since the letters to the
seven churches (2:9,13,24; 3:9). Seals and trumpets have loosed
their burdens on the earth, while Satan has been in heaven. As
an angel he has access to 'the heavenly realms' (Eph 6:12; cf.

Job 1:6-7). That is where the real battle between good and evil is being fought out, as anyone entering these realms through prayer will discover.

This battle, between good and bad angels in heaven, will not last for ever. For one thing, the forces are unequal in number. The devil's side comprises one third of the heavenly host (12:4); the two thirds are led by the archangel Michael, who will lead his forces to victory (a sculpture portraying this conquest adorns the east wall of Coventry cathedral).

The devil will be 'hurled' down to the earth. Later he will again be defeated and thrown into the 'abyss' (20:3). Meanwhile, in the few years he has left, his fury and frustration are concentrated on our planet. Unable to challenge God directly in heaven any more, he declares war on God's people below. It is a rearguard action, undertaken in the hope of retaining his kingdom on earth, through puppet rulers, one political and the other religious.

So far the message of chapter 12 is quite clear, even if it stretches the imagination. But we have overlooked (deliberately) the other major figure in the drama – a pregnant woman, bathed in sunshine, standing on the moon and wearing a crown of twelve stars on her head.

Who is she? Is she an individual person at all, or perhaps a 'personification' of a place or a people (as are the other 'women' in Revelation, for example, the 'prostitute' representing Babylon in chs. 17–18)?

Certainly, this figure has been the source of much debate and many differences among Bible students. For some, the matter is settled by the fact that the devil wanted to 'devour her child the moment it was born' (verse 4) and the statement that 'she gave birth to a son, a male child, who will rule all the nations with an iron sceptre' (verse 5). Surely, they say, this is an unmistakable reference to the birth of Jesus and Herod's immediate but abortive attempt to destroy him. The woman is therefore his mother, Mary (the usual Catholic interpretation); or a personification of Israel, from whom the Messiah came (a common Protestant interpretation to exclude Mary).

But it is not quite so simple as this. Why should there be a sudden and unexpected return to the very beginning of the Christian era in the middle of a passage describing the end-times? Why bring Mary into the picture (after Acts 1 she disappears from the New Testament, her work completed). Of course, the 'cyclical historicists' see this as proof of yet another 'recapitulation' of the entire cycle of church history, this time starting with the nativity, Satan being defeated and exiled from heaven at that time.

There are still problems. Apparently the child is 'snatched up to God and to his throne' almost immediately after his birth. This could be a 'telescoping' of the incarnation and ascension, but the absence of any reference to the ministry, death and resurrection of Jesus in between is at least striking. And if the woman is his mother, who are 'the rest of her offspring' to whom the frustrated dragon turns his attention (verse 17)? We know she had other children, including four boys and some girls (Mark 6:3), but they are unlikely candidates. Nor is it certain that 'ruling the nations with an iron sceptre' necessarily points to Jesus; it is applied to him (19:15, in fulfilment of Ps 2:9), but it is also promised to his faithful followers (2:27). Then there is the preservation of the woman in 'the desert' for 1260 days (12:6), a period which has already emerged as the duration of greatest distress at the end of the church age.

The interpretation which best fits all this data sees the woman as a personification representing the church in the end-times, preserved outside urban areas during the worst troubles. Her man-child is also a personification, representing the martyred believers at this time, safe in heaven, out of Satan's reach. They will return to the earth one day and rule it with Christ (20:4 emphatically declares this). The 'rest of her offspring' are those who survive the holocaust, yet 'obey God's commandments and hold to the testimony of Jesus' (verse 17; cf. 1:9; 14:12). There are still some tensions with the text in this view, but far fewer than with any other explanation.

Once again, there seems to be an implied comparison between the experience of Christ at the beginning of the Christian era and his followers at the end of it (as we saw in the previous chapter). In particular, as he 'overcame' (John 16:33) his followers will 'overcome', not 'loving their lives so much as to shrink from death' (12:11). Their victory demonstrates 'the kingdom of our God, and the authority of his Christ' (12:10; cf. 11:15 and Acts 28:31).

The two 'beasts' arrive in chapter 13. The first and foremost is a political figure, a world dictator wielding a totalitarian regime over all known ethnic groupings. He is 'the Antichrist' (1 John 2:18; note that 'anti-' in Greek means 'instead of' rather than 'against', indicating a counterfeit rather than a competitor), 'the man of lawlessness' (2 Thess 2:3-4) acknowledging no higher law than his own will and therefore claiming divinity and demanding worship. The beast is a human individual who accepts the satanic offer which Jesus refused (Matt 4:8-9; had he accepted he would have become Jesus Antichrist!).

But he is also 'anti-christian' in the other sense of that prefix. He has the power to 'make war against the saints and to *overcome* them' (13:7; he overcomes them temporarily, but they overcome him eternally, 12:11).

His characteristics are those of other fierce beasts – leopard, bear and lion. He seems to arise from a federation of political rulers, gaining the attention of the world through an astonishing recovery from a fatal wound, presumably in an attempted assassination. His blasphemous egotism is broadcast for forty-two months.

His position is bolstered by the second beast, a religious colleague with supernatural power who focuses the world's worship on his superior. His miracles will deceive the nations as he commands fire to fall down from the sky and images of the dictator to speak.

His appearance will be 'like a lamb', a young sheep with only 'two horns'. This would seem to indicate mildness rather than Christlikeness, since it is contrasted with his dragon-like speech.

His master-stroke will not be his display of miracles but his domination of markets. Only those bearing a special number on a visible part of their body (hand or forehead) will be allowed to trade and the number will only be marked on those who engage in imperial idolatry. Jews and Christians will therefore be excluded from all commerce, even to the purchase of bare necessities of life.

The number '666' is the coded name of the dictator. We have already discussed its meaning (see pages 95–96). Until he arrives, when his identity with this figure will be only too obvious, all attempts to decode it are useless speculation. One thing is clear, he will fall short of perfection (7) in every regard.

Chapter 14 seems to compensate for these horrific scenes by turning our attention to a group of people standing (literally) in sharp contrast to those who have allowed themselves to be entrapped in the system. Instead of the cryptic name of the beast, they carry the Lamb's Father's name on their foreheads (another feature picked up in 22:4). Instead of the arrogant lies, they are known for integrity of speech, as well as pure sexual relations.

There is a little uncertainty about their location, whether in heaven or on earth, but the context favours the former, because of the songs of praise from living creatures and elders (14:3 seems to repeat 4:4–11), songs which only the redeemed can 'learn', much less sing. The number (144,000) is puzzling. It is not to be confused with the same number in chapter 7. There it referred to Jews on earth, here to Christians in heaven. There it was made up from twelve tribes, here it is not. Neither can it be equated with the 'great multitude that no one could count' in that same chapter. Again, it may be a 'round' number. But the clue probably lies in their being 'purchased from among men and offered as *firstfruits* to God and the Lamb' (verse 4). They are only the small foretaste of a very large harvest. So the point may be that what is the total number of Jews preserved on earth is only a partial number of Christians praising in heaven.

The rest of the chapter has a procession of angels bringing various messages from God to men:

The first calls for the fear and worship of God, with a reminder that the gospel is still available to save anyone from the 'coming wrath' (Luke 3:7).

The second announces the fall of Babylon. Here is another 'anticipation', since this is the first time such a place has been mentioned. All will be made clear in the next section (chs. 16–17).

The third warns believers of the terrible consequences of giving in to the pressures of the final totalitarian system. The language is that of hell: unceasing 'torment' (the same word describing the experience of the devil, the antichrist and the false prophet in the 'lake of fire'; 20:10). In other words, they will share the fate of those to whom they have surrendered. The fact that 'saints' could find themselves in this dreadful destiny is underlined by a call to 'patient endurance' immediately after the warning (verse 12, which repeats 13:10). Both contexts recognise that some will pay for their loyalty with their lives. For them a special beatitude is written: 'Blessed are the dead who die in [the sense is almost 'for'] the Lord from now on' (verse 13). The blessing is twofold: they can now rest from travail and, since the record of their loyalty has been kept, look forward to a reward. Even those who die of natural causes at that time will enjoy this blessing. But this verse should not yet be used at funerals; the promise is qualified by 'from now on', which refers to the reign of the 'beast'.

The fourth shouts to someone 'like a son of man on the clouds' (a clear reference to Dan 7:13), telling him it is high time for harvest time. Whether this is to gather tares for burning or wheat for storing (Matt 13:40–43) is not immediately clear.

The fifth simply appears with a sickle in his hand.

The sixth directs the sickle to 'grapes' which are to be trampled on in the 'great winepress of God's wrath', which is 'outside the city'. That this refers to a mass slaughter of human beings is indicated by the massive pool of blood (a metre deep over 180 square miles, surely a touch of hyperbole?). This is probably an anticipation of the battle of Armageddon, where vultures will clean up the corpses (19:17–21). In passing, we note this link between blood, wine and God's wrath, which occurs quite frequently. This throws a flood of light on the cross and particularly on his agonising prayer in Gethsemane, which means 'crushing'. The metaphorical use of 'cup' in scripture invariably refers to God's wrath (Isa 51:21–22; Mark 14:36; Rev 16:19).

These six angels are followed by seven more who act out rather than speak about the outpoured wrath of God. They carry seven bowls, not just cups, of wrath to tip on the earth. This is accompanied by a song of triumph from the martyrs in heaven, consciously echoing the rejoicing of Moses after the Egyptian forces were drowned in the Red Sea (15:2–4). The theme is the justice and righteousness of God, expressed in great and marvellous deeds which vindicate his holiness by punishing the oppressors. The 'King of the Ages' may take his time to judge the guilty, but judgement is certain to come – and at last has come.

* * * * *

Before we leave this major middle section of Revelation, two further observations must be made.

The first concerns the *order* of events. An attempt has been made to fit the seals, trumpets and bowls, together with the inserted parentheses, into some kind of consecutive schedule. Whether this has been successful must be judged by the reader, who may have already worked out a different scheme.

The fact is that it is extremely difficult, if not impossible, to fit all the predicted events into a coherent pattern. But Jesus is too good a teacher to hide his essential message in such a complex narrative. What does this tell us?

Simply this: *the order is not the primary thrust* in this section. It is far more concerned with what will happen than with when anything will happen. The purpose of it all is not to enable us to become accurate soothsayers, able to forecast the future, but to be faithful servants of the Lord, ready to face the worst that can happen to us. But will it happen to us?

The second concerns the *fulfilment* of predictions. If the 'Big

Trouble' only covers the last few years, it may be that we shall not have to face it in our lifetime. So could it be a waste of time for all but the last generation of saints to prepare for it?

One answer is that the current trend and speed of world events makes it an increasing possibility in the near future.

But the main response to this kind of thinking must be the reminder that future events cast their shadows before them. 'Dear children, this is the last hour; and as you have heard that the Antichrist is coming, even now many antichrists have come' (1 John 2:18). The false prophet is coming, but even now many false prophets have come (Matt 24:11; Acts 13:6; Rev 2:20).

In other words, what will one day be experienced by the whole church on a universal scale ('hated by all nations'; Matt 24:9) is already happening in local and regional settings. Any Christian can go through much tribulation before all go through the 'Great Tribulation'. We must all be ready for the kind of troubles that reach a climax then, but can come now (see the wise words of Corrie Ten Boom on page 199).

This section (chapters 6–16) is therefore directly relevant to all believers, whatever their contemporary situation. The church is already under pressure in the majority of countries and the number of those where this is not the case diminishes annually.

And beyond all this lies the return of the Lord Jesus Christ, for which every believer needs to be ready. The main motive for preparing to be faithful under pressure is to be able to face him without shame. Perhaps that explains the following reminder inserted between the sixth and seventh bowls of wrath (incidentally, confirming that some Christians will still be on earth at that time): 'Behold, I come like a thief! Blessed is he who stays awake and keeps his clothes with him, so that he may not go naked and be shamefully exposed' (16:15; note the same emphasis on attire in Matt 22:11; Luke 12:35 and Rev 19:7–8).

CHAPTERS 17–18: MAN ON EARTH

This section is still part of the 'Big Trouble', but only just. It concerns the very end, at the time of the severe earthquake in the seventh seal, trumpet and bowl (see 16:17–19).

World history is hastening to an end. The final denouement is at hand. In spite of all the warnings, whether in divine word or deed, human beings still refuse to repent and curse God for all their troubles (16:9,11,21).

The remainder of Revelation is dominated by two female figures, one a filthy prostitute and the other a pure bride. Neither is a person; both are personifications. They represent cities.

We could use the title: 'A tale of two cities'. They are Babylon and Jerusalem, the city of man and the city of God. In this section we consider the former, which has been mentioned already (14:8; 16:19).

Cities are generally regarded as bad places in the Bible. The first mention (which is usually significant) associates them with the line of Lamech and the manufacture of weapons for mass destruction. They concentrate people, therefore sinners, therefore sin. With less community and more anonymity, vice and crime flourish. There is more lust (prostitution) and anger (violence) in urban than rural communities.

The two sins that are singled out here are greed and pride. Both are related to the idolatry of money. Since it is impossible to worship both God and Mammon (Luke 16:13), it is easier to forget the Maker of heaven and earth in a prosperous city. Self-made men worship their own creator! Arrogance shows in architecture; buildings are often monuments to human ambition and achievement.

Such was the tower of Babel by the Euphrates river, sitting on the route between Asia, Africa and Europe. Founded by Nimrod the mighty hunter (of animals) and warrior (among men), it was founded on the belief that might is right, that the fittest survive.

Typically, the tower was to be the tallest man-made structure in the world, as an impressive statement both to men and God. The expressed intention to 'make a name for ourselves' (Gen 11:4) marks the beginning of humanism, man's self-deification. God judged this presumption by granting its inhabitants the gift of tongues! But the simultaneous removal of their common speech brought unintelligible bedlam, from which we derive the verb 'babble' (note that at Pentecost this did not happen, for the same gift brought unity; Acts 2:44).

This city later became the capital of a large and powerful empire, especially under Nebuchadnezzar, a ruthless tyrant who destroyed babies, animals and even trees when conquering new territory (Hab 2:17; 3:17).

Meanwhile, King David of Israel had established Jerusalem as his capital. By contrast, it was not in a strategic position for trade, since it was not by the sea, a major river or a main road. It was, however, the 'city of God', the place where he put his name and chose to live among his people – at first in the tent Moses assembled, later in the temple Solomon built.

Babylon became the greatest threat to Jerusalem. Nebuchadnezzar ultimately destroyed the holy city, with its temple, transporting its treasures and deporting its people into seventy years of exile. God allowed this to happen because the inhabitants had made it an 'unholy' city like all others.

But this was a temporary chastisement rather than a permanent punishment. Through the prophets God promised both the restoration of Jerusalem and the ruin of Babylon (for example, Isa 13:19–20 and Jer 51:6–9, 45–48). Sure enough, that evil city became a desolate heap of rubble, totally uninhabited, except by wild creatures of the desert, exactly as foretold.

It is no coincidence that there are profound similarities between the books of Daniel and Revelation. Both contain visions of the end-times that are in remarkable agreement. Yet the revelations were given to Daniel during the time of Nebuchadnezzar (he had been a young man in the first of three deportations). He had 'seen' the future course of world empires right up to the time of

Christ and then beyond, to the very end of history, the reign of antichrist, the millennial rule, the resurrection of the dead and the day of judgement.

Both books talk about a city called 'Babylon'. But are they talking about the same place?

If so, it will have to be rebuilt. Those who take the Revelation 'Babylon' as the very same are quite excited that parts of it have already been rebuilt by the present President of Iraq, Saddam Hussein. But he seems to have no intention of restoring it as a living city; it is more a showcase for his own prestige (laser lights project his profile, alongside Nebuchadnezzar's, on to the clouds!). It is highly unlikely that ancient Babylon, even fully rebuilt, could ever become a strategic centre again.

The 'preterist' school of interpretation applies 'Babylon' to the metropolis of Rome. There is some ground for doing so, not least because this was probably the way original readers of Revelation would take it. One of Peter's letters, written for a very similar purpose (to prepare saints for suffering), may already have made this coded link (1 Pet 5:13). And the reference to 'seven hills' would probably clinch it (17:9, though note that the 'hills' represent kings).

Rome's decadent character would also fit the description in Revelation. Her seductive attraction of goods and finance in return for favours rendered and her domination of petty kings fit the picture well.

Yet it is doubtful if this is the total fulfilment. Rome was certainly *a* Babylon. But it was only a foreshadowing of *the* Babylon which dominates the end of history, which is where Revelation firmly places it.

Some have resolved the problem by postulating a revived Roman Empire. Their pulses quickened when ten nations (17:12) signed the 'Treaty of Rome' as the basis for a new superpower, the European Community. Interest has subsided with the addition of other states; there are now too many 'horns'!

The reluctance to let go of Rome as the main candidate is also apparent in the 'historicist' school of interpretation.

Taking Revelation as an overview of the whole of church history, Protestants invariably fastened on the papacy and the Vatican, with their claims to political as well as religious power, as the 'scarlet woman' of Babylon (this identification has created havoc in the 'troubles' of Northern Ireland). Catholics returned the compliment and regarded the Protestant Reformers in a similar light!

Actually, there is no hint in Revelation that 'Babylon' is in any way a religious centre. The emphasis is on business and pleasure as the primary occupations of its inhabitants.

The 'futurist' school seems to be nearer the truth in seeing the city as a new metropolis rising to dominate others during the 'end-time'. Since it is designated as a 'mystery' (i.e. a secret now revealed), it would appear to be a fresh creation of man rather than the re-establishment of a former city (whether ancient Babylon or Rome).

It is clearly going to be a, even the, centre of commerce, a place for getting and spending money (note how the traders are affected by its downfall; 18:11–16). Culture will not be neglected (note the music in 18:22).

But it will be corrupt and corrupting, characterised by materialism without morality, pleasure without purity, wealth without wisdom, lust without love. The simile of the harlot is peculiarly appropriate, giving anyone what they want in exchange for money.

So far we have only considered the 'woman', but she rides a 'beast' with seven heads and ten horns, which clearly represent a federation of political figures. We are not told who they are, nor are we given many details about them. They are powerful men but without territory to rule. Their authority derives from the 'beast', presumably the antichrist, to whom they will devote absolute allegiance. Above all, they will be blatantly anti-Christian, making 'war against the Lamb' and those 'with him' (17:14), presumably because their consciences will be pricked.

But Babylon is doomed. She and they will fall. Their days will be numbered. The astonishing way in which this is brought about is entirely credible in the modern world.

The woman rides the beast. A queen is riding on the backs of kings (a reversal of gender contrary to creation). It is another way of saying that economics will rule politics, that the power of money will override other authority. Since by the year AD 2000 the bulk of the world's business will be in the hands of three hundred colossal corporations, this scenario is not difficult to imagine.

Ambitious politicians, hungry for power, resent this financial clout. They are even prepared to bring about economic disaster if that will enable them to take over. One thinks of Hitler's treatment of the Jews, who controlled many banks in Germany.

The 'kings' will be jealous of the 'woman' who rides them and will resolve to destroy her. The city will be razed by fire. It will be the biggest economic disaster the world will have seen. Many, many people will 'weep and mourn' over the ruins.

God will have caused the catastrophe, but not by any physical action. He will have 'put it into their hearts to accomplish his purpose' (17:17). He will have encouraged them to make an alliance with the beast against the city. The antichrist will have political control and the false prophet religious control; the 'kings' will now offer them economic control in return for delegated powers for themselves. But their enjoyment of such privileges will be extremely brief ('one hour'; 17:12).

So sure is Babylon's downfall that it is pictured in Revelation as already having happened. Christians can be absolutely certain of this. But there are practical reasons why they are being told about it. What is the relation between God's people and this last 'Babylon'? Three guidelines are given:

First, there will be many martyrs in the city. The whore is 'drunk with the blood of the saints, the blood of those who bore testimony to Jesus'. This last phrase again indicates the presence of Christians and occurs throughout Revelation (1:9; 12:17; 14:12; 17:6; 19:10; 20:4). There is no place for holy people in a city devoted to immorality. The community does not want a conscience.

Second, the Christians are told to 'come out of her, my people, so that you will not share in her sins, so that you will not receive any of her plagues, for her sins are piled up to heaven, and God has remembered her crimes' (18:4–5). This is almost identical to Jeremiah's plea to Jews in ancient Babylon (Jer 51:6). Note that they have to 'come out'; the Lord does not take them out. Clearly, not all believers will be martyred; some will escape with their lives, though they may have to leave their money and possessions behind.

Third, when Babylon falls, a celebration is commanded: 'Rejoice over her, O heaven! Rejoice, saints and apostles and prophets! God has judged her for the way she treated you' (18:20). This is done in 19:1–5. Very few realise that the famous 'Hallelujah' chorus in Handel's *Messiah* oratorio is a celebration of the collapse of the world economy, the closure of stock exchanges, the bankruptcy of banks and the disruption of trade and commerce! Only God's people will be singing 'Hallelujah' (which means: 'Praise the Lord') on that day!

The prostitute disappears and the bride appears. The 'wedding supper of the Lamb' is about to take place. Jesus is going to get married – rather, he's coming to get married (Matt 25:1–13). The bride has 'made herself ready' by acquiring a dress of pure white linen (note the 'clothes' reference again); this is explained as a symbol of 'the righteous acts of the saints' (19:8). The guest list is completed and 'blessed' are those on it.

We have already strayed into chapter 19, which leads into the next section, while rounding off this one. But then the chapter divisions were not part of the original text and often come in the wrong places, putting asunder what God has joined together, never more so than in the penultimate section of Revelation.

CHAPTERS 19–20: CHRIST ON EARTH

This series of events brings history, as we know it, to a close. Our world is brought to an end at last. We are now dealing with the ultimate future.

Alas, this section has given rise to more controversy than any other in the whole book, mainly centred on the 'millennium', the repeated mention of a 'thousand years'. This is such an important issue that it will be dealt with as a separate subject (see pages 203–269). That treatment will include an exhaustive exegesis of the text, so no more than a summary will be given here.

It is vital to note the change from verbal to visual revelations. Throughout the previous section John says: 'I heard' (18:4; 19:1,6). Then the phrase becomes a repeated: 'I saw', until it changes back to 'I heard' again (in 21:3).

When the visual part is analysed, a series of seven visions is clearly discerned. But for the unwarranted intrusion of chapter divisions ('20' and '21'), this sevenfold revelation would have been noticed by most readers. As it is, few have marked it. Yet it is the final 'seven' in Revelation. As with previous sevens, the first four belong together, the next two are less closely related and the last stands on its own (we shall postpone study of it until we look at chapters 21–22). They may be listed as follows:

i.   PAROUSIA (19:11–16)
         King of kings, Lord of lords (and 'logos' = word)
         White horses, blood-stained robes

ii.   SUPPER (19:17–18)
         Angelic invitation to birds . . .
         . . . to gorge on corpses.

iii. ARMAGEDDON (19:19–21)
         Kings and armies destroyed (by 'word' = logos)
         Two beasts thrown into lake of fire

iv.   SATAN (20:1–3)

Bound and banished to 'abyss'
But for limited time

*   *   *   *   *

v. MILLENNIUM (20:4–10)
   Saints and martyrs reign (first resurrection)
   Satan released and thrown into lake of fire

vi. JUDGEMENT (20:11–15)
   General resurrection of 'the rest'
   Books and 'book of life' opened

*   *   *   *   *

vii. RE-CREATION (21:1–2)
   New heaven and earth
   New Jerusalem

Clearly this indicates a consecutive series of events, beginning
with the second coming and ending with the new creation. This
is confirmed by internal cross-references (e.g. 20:10 refers back
to 19:20). Unfortunately, commentators have tried to disrupt the
sequence in the interests of a theological system (by claiming that
ch. 20 precedes ch. 19, for example). But the order in these last
chapters is far clearer than the middle of Revelation – and it is
very significant.

For example, the enemies of the people of God are expelled
from the scene in reverse order to their introduction. Satan
appears in chapter 12, the two 'beasts' in chapter 13 and
Babylon in chapter 17. Babylon disappears in chapter 18, the
two 'beasts' in chapter 19 and Satan in chapter 20. The city falls
before the return of Christ, but he is needed on earth to deal
with the 'unholy trinity' of devil, antichrist and false prophet.

The opening vision is acknowledged to be a picture of the
second coming by almost all scholars (only a few, for vested

theological interests, say it refers to his first). But Jesus' return to earth will cause consternation in the powers-that-be. Shocked by his reappearance, they will plan a second assassination. But this time a small platoon of guards will be totally inadequate, since millions of his devoted followers will have met him in Jerusalem (1 Thess 4:14–17). A huge military force will gather some miles north in the valley of Esdraelon at the foot of the 'mountain of Megiddo' (in Hebrew, Har-mageddon): it is the crossroads of the world, overlooked by Nazareth. Many battles have been fought here; many kings have died here (Saul and Josiah among them).

Jesus only needs a 'word' to raise the dead or kill the living. It is more a sentence than a struggle. Vultures deal with the bodies, too many to bury.

At this point, there are a number of surprising developments. The two 'beasts' are not killed but 'thrown alive' into hell, the first human beings to go there. The devil is not sent there, but taken into custody – to be released again later!

Above all, Jesus does not then bring this world to an end, but takes over the government himself, filling the political vacuum left by the 'unholy trinity' with his own faithful followers, especially the martyrs. They will, of course, have to be raised from the dead to fulfil this responsibility. This 'kingdom' will last for a thousand years but come to an end when a paroled devil deceives the nations into a final but abortive rebellion, put down by fire from heaven.

This interim between Jesus' return and the day of judgement is widely rejected in the church today, yet it was the accepted view of the early church. The reasons for this change and the many questions it raises are fully discussed in the section on 'The Millennium Muddle' (pages 203 to 267).

There is widespread agreement on what follows. A final day of reckoning is clearly taught throughout the New Testament.

It is heralded by two remarkable portents. The earth and sky disappear. We know (from 2 Pet 3:10) that both will be 'razed' by fire. The dead, including those lost at sea, reappear. This is the second, or 'general' resurrection (20:5) and confirms that the wicked as well as the righteous will be re-embodied before entering their eternal destiny (Dan 12:2; John 5:29; Acts 24:15). Both 'soul and body' will be thrown into the lake of fire (Matt 10:28; Rev 19:20). The 'torment' will be physical as well as mental (Luke 16:23–24). Therefore, both 'death', which separates body from spirit, and 'hades', the abode of disembodied spirits, are now abolished (20:14). The 'second death', which neither separates body and soul nor annihilates either, takes over from then on.

All that is now visible are the judge sitting on a throne, the judged standing before it and an enormous pile of books. The throne is large and white, representing absolute power and purity. It is probably not the same throne as the one John saw in heaven (4:2–4). That was not described as 'great' or 'white'. Furthermore, it is most unlikely that the resurrected wicked would be allowed anywhere near heaven. Indeed, there is no hint that the scene in chapter 20 has shifted back to heaven; it is more likely to be located where the earth has been, the earth having disappeared leaving only its past and present inhabitants. Above all, the person sitting on this throne is not identified as God (as in 4:8–11). It is, in fact, not God. From other scriptures, we know that he has delegated the task of judging the human race to his Son, Jesus: 'For he has set a day when he will judge the world with justice by the man he has appointed' (Acts 17:31; cf. Matt 25:31–32; 2 Cor 5:10). Human beings will be judged by a human being.

This will be no long drawn-out trial. All the evidence has already been gathered and examined by the judge. It is contained in 'books', volumes truly deserving the title: 'This is Your Life'! They will not be a selection of the commendable occasions for a television presentation, but a complete record of the deeds (and words; Matt 5:22; 12:36) of a whole lifetime, from birth to death. We may be justified by faith, but we shall be judged by works.

If this was all the evidence to be considered, it would damn us all to the 'second death'. What hope would there be for any?

Thank God, one other book will be opened on that terrible day. It is the record of the judge's own life on earth, both absolving him and qualifying him to judge others. It is the 'Lamb's book of life' (21:27). But it contains other names besides his. Those who are 'in Christ' are listed there, those who have lived and died in him, those who have been joined to and have remained in this 'true vine' (John 15:1–8). They have thus borne the fruit that attests their continuing union with him (Phil 4:3; contrast Matt 7:16–20). The fruitfulness is proof of their faithfulness.

Their names have been put into this book when they came to be in Christ, when they repented and believed (the phrase 'from the creation of the world' in 17:8 refers to those whose names are *not* written in the book and simply means 'through the whole of human history'; likewise in 13:8 though the phrase there may be linked to the slaying of the Lamb). Their names have not been 'erased' from the book of life because they have 'overcome' (3:5).

Only those whose names are still in this book escape the 'second death' in the 'lake of fire'. In other words, outside of Christ there is no hope whatsoever, since 'all have sinned and fall short of the glory of God' (Rom 3:23). The gospel is therefore *exclusive*: 'Salvation is found in no-one else, for there is no other name [except 'Jesus'] under heaven given to men by which we must be saved' (Acts 4:12). But it must also therefore be *inclusive*: 'Go into all the world and preach the good news to all creation' (Mark 16:15; cf, Matt 28:19; Luke 24:47).

The human race will then be permanently divided into two groups (Matt 13:41–43, 47–50; 25:32–33). For one, their destination has already been 'prepared' (Matt 25:41). The lake (or 'sea') of fire has been in existence for at least a thousand years (19:20). For the other, a new metropolis has been 'prepared' (John 14:2), but there is no earth on which it may be sited, much less a sky above it. A new universe is needed.

CHAPTERS 21-22: HEAVEN ON EARTH

It is with great relief that we enter this final section. The atmosphere has changed dramatically. The dark clouds have rolled away and the sun is shining again – except that the sun has also disappeared, to be replaced by the much more brilliant glory of God (21:23).

This is the final act of redemption, bringing salvation to the entire universe. This is the 'cosmic' work of Christ (Matt 19:28; Acts 3:21; Rom 8:18–25; Col 1:20; Heb 2:8), the renewal of heaven and earth (note that 'heaven' means 'sky', what we call 'space'; it is the same word in 20:11 and 21:1). Christians have already received new bodies, when Jesus came back to the old earth. Now they are to be given a new environment corresponding to their new bodies.

The first two verses cover the last vision in the sequence of seven which John 'saw' (19:11 to 21:2), the climax to the final events of history. There is more than a new universe here. Within the 'general' creation is a 'special' creation. Just as within the first universe God 'planted a garden' (Gen 2:8), so here he has designed and built a 'garden city', which even Abraham knew about and looked forward to (Heb 11:10).

Just as the new 'heaven and earth' are recognisably similar enough to the old to bear the same names, this city is given the same name as David's capital. Jerusalem has a place in the New Testament as well as the Old. Jesus called it 'the city of the Great King' (Matt 5:35; cf. Ps 48:2). It was just 'outside a city wall' that he died, rose again and ascended to heaven. It is to this city that he will return to sit on the throne of David. In the millennium it will be 'the camp of God's people, the city he loves' (20:9).

Of course, the earthly city was in a sense a temporary replica of 'the heavenly Jerusalem, the city of the living God', of which all believers in Jesus are already citizens, together with Hebrew saints and angels (Heb 12:22–23). But that does not mean that the original is somehow less real than the copy, that one is material and the other 'spiritual'. The main difference between them is one of location. And that will change.

The heavenly city will come 'down out of heaven' and be sited on the new earth. It will be a real city, a material construction, though of rather different materials! Unfortunately, ever since Augustine's Platonic separation of the physical and spiritual realms, the church has had real difficulties in accepting the concept of a new earth, never mind a new city on it. The equation of 'spiritual' and 'intangible' has done immense damage to Christian hopes for the future. This new universe and its metropolis will not be less 'material' than the old.

Verses 3–8 are an explanatory comment on this final vision. The attention is immediately diverted from the new creation to its Creator. Note the transition from what John 'saw' to what he 'heard'. But whose 'loud voice' did he hear? It speaks of God in the third person, then in the first. This is surely Christ speaking (cf. 1:15). The phrase 'seated on' the throne is the same as in the previous chapter (cf. 20:11 with 21:5). In both contexts judgement is expressed and the 'lake of fire' mentioned (cf. 20:15 with 21:8). Above all, the identical claim is made by this 'voice' as Jesus makes in the epilogue (cf. 21:6 with 22:13). However, the 'throne of God and of the Lamb' are later seen as one (22:1).

Three startling statements follow:

The first is the most remarkable revelation about the future in the whole book. God himself is changing his residence from heaven to earth! He will come to live with human beings at their address, no longer 'our Father in heaven' (Matt 6:9), but 'our Father on earth', leading to the most intimate relationship ever between human and divine persons. Since all death, sorrow and pain are contrary to his nature, they will have no place. There will be no more separation, no more tears. In passing, we recall the only other mention of God on earth in the Bible: his evening stroll in the garden of Eden (Gen 3:8). Once again, the Bible has come full circle.

The second is the announcement that 'I am making everything

new' (21:5). Here the carpenter of Nazareth claims to be the Creator of the new universe, as he was of the old (John 1:3; Heb 1:2).
His work is not limited to regenerating people, though that also is
'the new creation' (2 Cor 5:17). He is restoring all things as well.

There is considerable debate about the word 'new'. How new
is 'new'? Is this 'new' universe simply the old one 'renovated'
or a brand new manufacture? There certainly are two Greek
words for 'new' (*kainos* and *eos*), but they are somewhat
synonymous and the use of the former here does not settle the
issue. References to the old universe as being 'destroyed by fire'
(2 Pet 3:10) and having 'passed away' (21:1) suggest eradication
rather than transformation. But the process has already begun
– with the resurrection of Jesus. His 'old' body dissolved inside
the graveclothes and he came from death with a new 'glorious'
body (Phil 3:21); see also my book: *Explaining the Resurrection*
(Sovereign World, 1993). The exact 'connection' between the two
bodies is hidden in the darkness of the tomb, but what happened
there will one day happen on a universal scale.

The third spells out the practical implications of this new
creation for the readers of Revelation (note that John has had
to be reminded to keep writing down what he is hearing because
'these words are trustworthy and true'; 21:5). On the positive side
is the promise to satisfy the thirst of those seeking 'the water of
life' (21:6; 22:1,17). But this must lead on to an 'overcoming'
life, in order to inherit a place in the new earth and enjoy the
family relationship with God in it.

On the negative side is the warning that those who do not
overcome, but are cowardly, faithless, immoral and deceitful,
will never be part of all this, but end up in 'the fiery lake of
burning sulphur. This is the second death' (21:8). It needs to be
pointed out that this warning is given to wayward believers, not
unbelievers, as is the whole book. Most of Jesus' earlier warnings
about hell were addressed, not to sinners, but to his own disciples.
(see my book *The Road to Hell*, Hodder and Stoughton, 1992).

*   *   *   *   *

At this point an angel takes John on a conducted tour of the new Jerusalem and its life (the idea that what follows is actually a 'recapitulation' of the 'old' Jerusalem in the millennium is so bizarre we shall not consider it; verse 10 clearly expands verse 2). The description is breathtaking, straining vocabulary to the limit, which raises a fundamental question: how much is literal and how much is symbolical?

On the one hand, taking it entirely literally seems wrong. Clearly, John is describing the indescribable (Paul had the same difficulty when shown heavenly realities; 2 Cor 12:4). Notice how often he can only use a comparison ('like' or 'as' in 21:11, 18, 21; 22:1), yet all analogies are only approximate and ultimately inadequate. But the realities imperfectly portrayed here must be more wonderful than this, not less.

On the other hand, taking it entirely symbolically also seems wrong. Taken to this extreme, the whole picture dissolves into 'spiritual' unreality, which fails to do justice to the 'new earth' as the clear location.

To highlight the problem, we may ask the question: does the 'new Jerusalem' represent a place or a people? The question arises because she is called a 'bride', which previously indicated a people, the church (in 19:7–8). At first, this is only an analogy (in 21:3; *as* a bride') and anyone who has seen a Semitic wedding will understand the likeness of the highly coloured clothes bedecked with jewellery. Later, however, the city is specifically designated 'the bride, the wife of the Lamb' (21:9). The angel, promising to *show* 'the bride' to John, *shows* him the city (21:10), though the vision moves on to reveal the life of its inhabitants (21:24–22:5).

The answer to the dilemma is much more obvious to a Jew than a Christian. 'Israel', the bride of Yahweh, was always a people *and* a place, inextricably involved with each other, hence all the prophetic promises of the ultimate restoration of the people to their own land. By comparison, Christians are a people without a place here, strangers, pilgrims, sojourners passing through, the new 'diaspora' or dispersed and exiled people of God (Jas 1:1;

1 Pet 1:1). Heaven is our 'home'. But heaven is coming down to earth at the last. Jew and Gentile will together be the people with a place. That is why the names on the city are the twelve tribes and the twelve apostles (21:12–14).

This dual unifying of Jew and Gentile, heaven and earth, is fundamental to God's eternal purpose 'to bring all things . . . together under one head, even Christ' (Eph 1:10; Col 1:20). So the 'bride', who becomes one both in herself and with her husband, is a people and a place. And what a place!

The measurements are clearly important, all multiples of twelve. The *size* is enormous: over two thousand kilometres in each of three dimensions; the city would cover most of Europe or just fit into the moon if it were hollow. In other words, big enough to accommodate all God's people. The *shape* is also significant, more like a cube than a pyramid, indicating a 'holy' city like the cubed 'holy of holies' in tabernacle and temple. The walls define the outside rather than defend the inside, since the gates are always open. There is no threatened danger so its inhabitants can freely leave and return at any time.

The materials used in its construction are already known to us, but only as rare and precious gemstones which give us a tiny glimpse of heaven. The list here is one of the most remarkable proofs of the divine inspiration of this book. Now that we can produce 'purer' light (polarised and laser), a hitherto unknown quality of precious stones has been revealed. When thin sections are exposed to cross-polarised light (as when two lenses from sun-glasses are superimposed at right angles), they fall into two very distinct categories. 'Isotropic' stones lose all their colour, for they depend on random rays for their brilliance (e.g. diamonds, rubies and garnets). 'Anisotropic' stones produce all the colours of the rainbow in dazzling patterns, whatever their original colour. *All* the stones in the 'new Jerusalem' belong to this latter category! No one could possibly have known this when Revelation was written – except God himself!

Another striking feature of this description is that in just thirty-two verses there are over fifty allusions to the Old

Testament (mainly from Genesis, Psalms, Isaiah, Ezekiel and Zechariah). Every major feature is, in fact, the fulfilment of Jewish hopes expressed in prophecy. This also indicates that Old and New Testament prophecies all spring from the same source (1 Pet 1:11; 2 Pet 1:21). Revelation is the climax and conclusion to the whole Bible.

When the angelic demonstration moves on to the life enjoyed by the inhabitants of the city, there are some surprises. Perhaps the biggest contrast to the 'old' Jerusalem is the absence of a dominating temple to focus worship at a particular place (or at a particular time?). The whole city *is* his temple, in which the redeemed 'serve him day and night' (7:15), which suggests that work and worship have been blended together again, as they were for Adam (Gen 2:15; Adam was not told to have one day in seven for worship).

The city will be enriched with international culture (21:24,26). It will never be polluted with immoral behaviour (21:27). That is why compromised believers are in danger of having their names erased from 'the Lamb's book of life' (3:5; 21:7–8).

The river and tree of life will ensure continuous health. As at the beginning, the diet will be fruit rather than meat (Gen 1:29), though there is no obligation to be vegetarian before then (Gen 9:3; Rom 14:2; 1 Tim 4:3).

Above all, the saints will live in the presence of God. They will actually see his face, a privilege given to few before (Gen 32:30; Exod 33:11) but then to all (1 Cor 13:12). They will reflect him in their own faces, his name on their foreheads, as once others bore the number of the 'beast' (13:16). They will 'reign for ever and ever', presumably over the new creation rather than each other, as was originally intended (Gen 1:28). In this way they will 'serve' the Creator.

Once again, it needs to be emphasised that human beings have not gone to heaven to be with the Lord for ever; he has come to earth to be with them for ever. The 'new Jerusalem' is at once the eternal divine and human 'dwelling-place', their permanent residence.

As before, John has to be reminded to write it all down. His distraction from the task is understandable!

*   *   *   *   *

The 'epilogue' (22:7–21) has much in common with the 'prologue' (1:1–8). The same title is applied to God in one and Christ in the other (1:8; 22:13). This concluding exhortation is thoroughly trinitarian: God, the Lamb and the Spirit are all present.

There is a strong emphasis on the fact that time is short. Jesus is coming 'soon' (22:7,12,20). The fact that many centuries have elapsed since this was said and written should not lead to complacency; we must be much nearer 'the things that must soon take place' (22:6).

The day of opportunity is still here. The thirsty may still drink the water of life as a free gift (22:17). But choices must be made now. The time is coming when the moral direction of our lives will be fixed for ever (22:11). Pharaoh hardened his heart against the Lord seven times, so then God hardened it for him three times (Exod 7–11; Rom 9:17–18). There will come a point when this happens to all who defy and disobey his will.

There are only two categories of people in the end: those who 'go on washing their robes' (22:17; cf. 7:14) and thus enter the city – and those kept outside it (22:15), like the wild curs of the Middle East today. This is now the third time a list of disqualifying offences has been included in this sublime finale (21:8,27; 22:15), as if the readers must never be allowed to forget that the glories of the future will not come to them automatically because they have believed in Jesus and belong to a church, but to those who 'press on towards the goal to win the prize for which God has called us heavenwards in Christ Jesus' (Phil 3:14) and who 'make every effort . . . to be holy, for without holiness no one will see the Lord' (Heb 12:14).

Another way in which believers can forfeit the future is by tampering with this book of Revelation, either by addition or

subtraction. Since it is a 'prophecy', God speaking through his
servant, to alter it in any way is to commit sacrilege, incurring
the severest penalty. It is unlikely that unbelievers would even
bother to do this. It is much more likely to be done by those who
take upon themselves the task of explaining and interpreting it
to others. May God have mercy on this poor author if he has
offended in this way!

But the final note is positive, not negative, and is summed up
in one word: 'Come!'

On the one hand, this invitation on the lips of the church is
addressed to the world, to 'whoever' will respond to the gospel
(22:17; cf. John 3:16). On the other hand, it is addressed to the
Lord: 'Amen. Come, Lord Jesus' (22:20).

This dual plea is characteristic of the true bride who is moved
by the Spirit (22:17) and is experiencing the grace of the Lord
Jesus (22:21). All the saints cry: 'Come!' to the renegade world
and its returning Lord.

CHAPTER NINE

Centrality of Christ

This last book of the Bible is 'the revelation of Jesus Christ' (1:1). The genitive ('of') can be understood in two ways: It is *from* him or *about* him. Perhaps the double meaning is intended. Either way he is central to its message.

If the theme is the end of the world, he is 'the end', as he was 'the beginning' (22:13). God's plan is 'to bring all things in heaven and on earth together under one head, even Christ' (Eph 1:10).

The prologue and epilogue both focus on his return to planet earth (1:7; 22:20). The hinge on which future history swings from getting worse to getting better is that coming (19:11–16).

It is 'this same Jesus' (Acts 1:11) who will return. He is the Lamb of God who came the first time to take away 'the sin of the world' (John 1:29). Throughout Revelation the Lamb looks 'as if it had been slain' (5:6). Presumably the scars will still be visible on his head, side, back, hands and feet (John 20:25–27). There are frequent reminders that he shed his blood to redeem human beings of every type (5:9; 7:14; 12:11).

Yet the Jesus of Revelation is also very different from the man of Galilee. His first appearance to John was so awesome that this disciple who had been closest to him (John 21:20) fell in a dead faint. We have already mentioned his snow-white hair, blazing eyes, sharp tongue, shining face and burnished feet.

Though there are brief glimpses of the angry Jesus in the Gospels (Mark 3:5; 10:14; 11:15), his sustained 'wrath' in Revelation strikes terror in the hearts of all kinds of people, who would rather be crushed by falling rocks than look into his eyes (6:16–17). This is no 'Gentle Jesus, meek and mild'. Though that would be a doubtful description of him at any time, it is particularly inappropriate here.

Many believe Jesus preached and practised pacificism, despite his assertion to the contrary: 'Do not suppose that I have come to bring peace to the earth. I did not come to bring peace, but a sword' (Matt 10:34; Luke 12:51). Of course, his words can be 'spiritualised', but it is far less easy to explain them away in Revelation, where the most natural understanding of the final conflict is physical.

Jesus rides down from heaven on a horse of war rather than a donkey of peace (Zech 9:9; Rev 19:11; cf. 6:2). His robe is 'dipped in blood' (19:13), but not his own. Though the only 'sword' he wields is his tongue, the effect of using it is to slaughter thousands of kings, generals and mighty men (both volunteering and conscripted), as once that same tongue dealt death to a fig-tree (Mark 11:20–21).

Jesus is clearly depicted here as a mass killer, the vultures cleaning up the mess afterwards! This graphic portrayal comes as a shock to respectable worshippers used to seeing him gazing benignly from stained glass windows. It will be an even greater surprise to those who use the weeks of 'Advent' in the church calendar to present him in nativity plays as a helpless baby. He will never be that again.

Has Jesus changed? We know that old age mellows some but others become cantankerous and even malicious. Has this happened to him during the intervening centuries. God forbid!

It is not his character or personality that have changed, but his mission. His first visit was 'to seek and save what was lost' (Luke 19:10). He did not come 'into the world to condemn the world, but to save the world' (John 3:17). He came to give human beings the opportunity to be separated from their sins before all sin has to be destroyed. His second visit is for the opposite purpose – to destroy rather than to save, to punish sin rather than pardon it, 'to judge the quick [living] and the dead', as the Apostles' and the Nicene creed put it.

It has become a cliché that Jesus 'loves the sinner but hates the sin'. The former was clearly seen in his first coming; the latter will be just as apparent at his second. Those who cling to their sins must face the consequences. At that time 'the Son of man will send out his angels and they will weed out of his kingdom everything that causes sin and all who do evil' (Matt 10:41). This 'weeding' will be as thorough as it will be fair.   But if it is to be totally fair, it must be applied to believers as well as unbelievers (as Paul clearly teaches in Rom 2:1–11, concluding that 'God does not show favouritism').

Once again, we need to remember that the book of Revelation is addressed exclusively to 'born-again' believers. The descriptions of his fierce opposition to sinning are intended to induce a wholesome fear in 'saints' as an incentive to 'obey God's commandments and remain faithful to Jesus' (14:12).

It is all too easy for those who have experienced the grace of our Lord Jesus Christ, to forget that he will still be their Judge (2 Cor 5:10). Those who have known him as friend and brother (John 15:15; Heb 2:11) are apt to overlook his more challenging attributes. At the least, he is worthy of 'praise and honour and glory and power, for ever and ever' (5:13).

Of the 250 names and titles given to Jesus in scripture, a considerable number are used in this book and some are unique to it, found nowhere else. He is the first and the last, the beginning and the end, the Alpha and the Omega. He is the ruler of God's creation. That is *his relation to our universe*. He was involved in its creation, is responsible for its continuation and will bring it to its consummation (John 1:3; Col 1:15–17; Heb 1:1–2).

He is the lion of the tribe of Judah, the root (and offspring) of David. That is *his relation to God's chosen people Israel*. He was, is and always will be, the Jewish Messiah.

He is holy and true, faithful and true, the faithful and true witness. He is the living one, who was dead and is alive for evermore, who holds the keys of death and Hades. That is *his relation to the church*. They need to remember his passion for truth, which means for reality and integrity, as opposed to hypocrisy.

He is King of kings and Lord of lords. He is the bright morning star, the one still shining when all others (pop and film stars included!) have disappeared. That is *his relation to the world*. One day his authority will be universally recognised.

So many of these titles are introduced with a formula familiar from the Gospel of John: 'I am'. This is not just a personal claim. The phrase sounds so much like the name by which God revealed himself that using it directly led to assassination attempts and ultimate execution for Jesus (John 8:58–59; Mark 14:62–63). That it was intended to indicate shared divinity and equality with God is confirmed in Revelation by Father and Son claiming exactly the same titles: for example, 'Alpha and Omega' (1:8 and 22:13).

The world is coming to an end, but that end is personal rather than impersonal. In fact, the end is a person. Jesus is the end.

To study Revelation primarily to discover *what* the world is coming to is to miss the point. The essential message is about *who* the world is coming to or, rather, who is coming to the world.

Christians are really the only ones who are longing for 'the end' to come, every generation hoping that this will happen during their lifetime. For them 'the end' is not an event, but a person. They are eagerly awaiting 'him', not 'it'.

The penultimate verse (22:20) contains a very personal summary of the whole book: 'He who testifies to these things says, "Yes, I am coming soon"'. There can only be one response from those who have understood: 'Amen. Come, Lord Jesus'.

CHAPTER TEN

Rewards of Study

We have already noted that Revelation is the only biblical book to carry both a blessing on those who read it and a curse on those who tamper with it (1:3; 22:18–19). By way of summary, we shall now list ten benefits that result from mastering its message, all of which assist authentic Christian living.

1. COMPLETION OF BIBLE

The student will begin to share God's knowledge of 'the end from the beginning' (Isa 46:10). The story is complete. The happy ending is revealed. The romance ends in the wedding and the real relationship begins. Without this, the Bible would be incomplete. It would have to be known as the 'Amputated Version'! The striking resemblances between the first and last pages of holy scripture (e.g. the tree of life) make sense of all that lies between.

2. DEFENCE AGAINST HERESY

So often the cults and sects, whose representatives come knocking at our doors, major on Revelation. Their apparent knowledge of it deeply impresses churchgoers who have never grasped it, largely through lack of teaching (and lack of teachers who know it). They are unable to challenge the interpretation offered, which can be quite bizarre. The only real defence is a superior knowledge.

3. INTERPRETATION OF HISTORY

A superficial awareness of current affairs can leave anyone baffled as to any discernible direction. Since future events cast their shadows before them, the student of Revelation will find an astonishing correspondence with world events, as they clearly head towards a world government and a world economy. Any preacher who systematically expounds the book is likely to be given many relevant newspaper cuttings by his hearers.

4. GROUND FOR HOPE

Everything is going according to plan, God's plan. He is still on the throne, directing affairs towards the end, Jesus. Revelation assures us that good will triumph over evil, Christ will conquer Satan and the saints will one day rule the world. Our planet will be cleared of all pollution, physical and moral. Even the universe will be recycled. The hope of all this is 'an anchor for the soul' in the storms of life (Heb 6:19). Paganism, secularism and humanism only appear to gain ground. Their days are numbered.

5. MOTIVE FOR EVANGELISM

There is no clearer presentation of the alternative destinies placed before the human race – the new heaven and earth or the lake of fire, everlasting joy or everlasting torment. The opportunity to choose will not last indefinitely. The day of judgement must come, with every member of the human race accountable. But the day of salvation is still here: 'Whoever is thirsty, let him come; and whoever wishes, let him take the free gift of the water of life' (22:17). The invitation to 'Come!' is issued jointly by the 'Spirit and the bride [i.e. the church]'.

6. STIMULUS TO WORSHIP

Revelation is full of worship, sung and shouted by many voices. There are eleven major songs, which have inspired many other hymns down the ages, from Handel's *Messiah* to the 'Battle Hymn of the Republic' ('Mine eyes have seen the glory of the coming of the Lord'). Worship is directed towards God and the Lamb, not the Spirit; and never to the angels. 'Therefore, with angels and archangels, we laud and magnify your holy name . . .'

7. ANTIDOTE TO WORLDLINESS

It is so easy to be 'earthly-minded'. As William Wordsworth reminds us: 'The world is too much with us, late and soon, getting and spending, we lay waste our powers, little we see in Nature that is ours'. Revelation teaches us to think more about our eternal heavenly home than a temporary 'Ideal Home', more about our new resurrection body than our old ageing frame.

8. INCENTIVE TO GODLINESS

God's will for us is holiness here and happiness hereafter, not vice versa, as many would wish. Holiness is essential if we are going to survive present troubles, overcoming internal temptation and external persecution. Revelation shakes us out of slackness, complacency and indifference by reminding us that God is 'holy, holy, holy' (4:8) and that only 'holy' people will share in the first resurrection when Jesus returns (20:6). The whole book, but especially the seven letters at the beginning, confirms the principle that 'without holiness no-one will see the Lord' (Heb 12:14).

9. PREPARATION FOR PERSECUTION

This, of course, is the fundamental purpose for Revelation being
written. Its message comes across loud and clear to Christians
who are suffering for their faith, encouraging them to 'endure'
and 'overcome', thus keeping their names in the book of life and
their inheritance in the new creation. Jesus predicted universal
hatred of his followers before the end (Matt 24:9). So we all need
to be prepared.

Reader, if this is not already happening in your country, it will
certainly come. And so will Jesus, before whom cowards will be
'shamefully exposed' (16:15) and condemned to hell (22:8).

10. UNDERSTANDING OF CHRIST

With Revelation, the picture of our Lord and Saviour is completed. Without it, the portrait is unbalanced, even distorted. If
the Gospels present him in his role as prophet and the Epistles
cover his role as priest, Revelation clarifies his role as King, the
King of kings and the Lord of lords. Here is the Christ the world
has never seen, yet will one day see; the Christ the Christian sees
now by faith and will one day meet in the flesh.

*   *   *   *   *

After studying Revelation, no one can ever be quite the same
again. Yet its message can be forgotten. That is why its blessing
is not just for those who read it, even aloud to others, but for
those who 'keep' what is written. This means that we 'take it to
heart' (1:3; New International Version) as well as mind, but also
that we put it into practice. 'Do not merely listen to the word,
and so deceive yourselves. Do what it says' (Jas 1:22).

C. THE RAPTURE RATIONALE

CHAPTER ELEVEN

The Novel Doctrine

Early in the nineteenth century, a radically new understanding of the second coming appeared and has now spread to all parts of the globe. It is probably to be found in the majority of contemporary books on the subject.

In a word, the return of Jesus to planet earth was divided in two, into a 'second' and 'third' coming, though these would only be separated by a few years, in contrast to the centuries between the first and second.

The 'second' would be invisible to the world, a private event. It would be a fleeting visit, for one purpose only – to take all true believers to heaven *before* the 'Big Trouble' (or 'Great Tribulation') of the last few years, dominated by Satan, antichrist and the false prophet.

This taking away of the church will only be noticed by the world because of the sudden disappearance of a considerable proportion of the population and the resulting chaos. Sensational sermons and films have envisaged crashes resulting from driverless cars and pilotless planes!

More significant, especially for believers, is that it will occur without any preceding signs. Since all unfulfilled prophecies in scripture (about 150 out of over 700, according to the *Encyclopedia of Biblical Prophecy* by J. Barton Payne, Hodder and Stoughton, 1973) refer to the Great Tribulation and beyond, the 'secret' coming of Jesus to take his church to heaven is the next event on God's calendar. It could therefore occur at 'any moment', a favourite phrase of adherents to this view; others talk about its 'imminence'. This lack of any warning provides, of course, a powerful motive for being constantly 'ready'.

The 'third' coming is very public and corresponds to the church's traditional expectation. Jesus will descend from the clouds 'in the same way' as he ascended into them (Acts 1:11). The major difference is that he will not only be accompanied by his angels, but also by the church which he will have taken to heaven some years earlier. The two 'comings' are therefore commonly distinguished by the phrases: '*for* his saints', then '*with* his saints'.

The earlier visit is often described as 'the secret rapture' or more usually simply 'The Rapture'. This has nothing to do with emotional exuberation, though undoubtedly that would be a side-effect! It comes from the old Latin Vulgate translation of the Bible which uses the word *raptura* for the Greek *arpagesometha* in 1 Thessalonians 4:17, both of which mean to be 'snatched up'. Even in archaic English, 'rapture' meant 'to be transported from one place to another'. The word 'transport' also has the same double meaning, physical and emotional ('mechanised transport' and 'transport of delight').

It must be understood that there is *no* disagreement about the 'rapture' itself. The Scripture quoted above clearly teaches that living believers, as opposed to 'dead' believers who will 'rise first' (1 Thess 4:16), will be '*caught up* with them in the clouds to meet the Lord in the air'. The point at issue is *when* this will take place, on a private and invisible occasion or at the public and visible return. Significantly, this passage contains no answer – or even any awareness of the question!

At this point we need to introduce some technical terms usually used in this debate to describe the different beliefs about the timing of this great event, to which all Bible-believing Christians look forward. The view we have been describing so far is known as 'the *pre*-tribulation rapture', since it believes that Christians will be removed from the scene before the worst troubles, from which they will escape. The older view is then called 'the *post*-tribulation rapture' because it believes that Christians will only meet Christ in the air after those troubles, through which they will have to pass. More recently a third view has emerged, called 'the *mid*-tribulation rapture', which believes that Christians will experience the first of the troubles but be taken away before the worst. We shall say more about this third view later, but it has never attracted a majority and is essentially only a variation on the 'pre-' position. The main debate is between 'pre-' and 'post-' tribulation. We return to our consideration of the former.

Having outlined this novel teaching, it may be enlightening to trace its history, which begins with an Englishman, an Irishman and a Scotsman! As already stated, there is no trace of it at all before 1830, which makes one wonder why, if it is clearly to be found in scripture.

The origin is shrouded in mystery, though some claim it lies in a 'prophecy' given by one Margaret Macdonald in Port Glasgow, Scotland (see a number of books by Dave MacPherson; for example, *The Great Rapture Hoax*, New Puritan Library, 1983).

It clearly emerged in the teaching of the Rev. Edward Irvine (who left a church in Scotland to found the Catholic Apostolic church whose empty 'cathedral' still stands in Albury near Guildford in Surrey); Dr Henry Drummond (owner of Albury Court, in the library of which were held prophetic conferences, to which came the following); the Rev. John Nelson Darby (who left the Anglican church in Dublin to found the 'Brethren').

It was this last man who did more than any other to popularise the novel doctrine. Though some of his colleagues in the movement (such as George Müller, of Bristol orphanage fame) never accepted the idea of a 'secret rapture', it became the 'orthodox' teaching from which few later dared to deviate.

Crossing the Atlantic, Darby persuaded a lawyer, Dr C. I. Scofield, to adopt this concept. He in turn incorporated it into the 'Scofield' Bible, which combined interpretive comments and the inspired text in such a way that readers were hardly able to distinguish between the two. They found the secret rapture in the 'Bible'! This version was a bestseller and was probably the biggest factor in the astonishing spread of the idea.

It is now taught in Bible colleges (Dallas, Texas, is one of the most well-known) and widely read in popular writings (Hal Lindsay, who wrote the popular *The Late Great Planet Earth*, is a former student of Dallas).

At this point, it should be made clear that this doctrine rarely stands by itself. It is invariably presented as part of a whole theological package, usually referred to as 'dispensationalism' (which is dealt with in chapter 18 in the section 'The Millennium Muddle'; see pages 262–269).

This sprang from the framework of J.N. Darby's biblical studies. He emphasised strongly the need to 'rightly *divide*' the word of truth (Authorised Version of 2 Tim 2:15; the New International Version more accurately substitutes 'correctly handles'). This method of 'dividing' scripture was taken too far in three directions.

First, he divided Bible history into seven separate eras or 'dispensations' (which gave the label to his scheme). These were:

1. Innocence (Adam)
   THE FALL
2. Self-determination (Cain to Enoch)
   THE FLOOD
3. Human government (Noah to Terah)
4. Patriarchs (Abraham to Joseph)
5. Law (Moses to Malachi)
   THE FIRST COMING
6. Grace (the church)
   THE SECOND COMING
7. The millennium (Israel)

As a summary of the phases of the unfolding story, it is unexceptional. But a crucial principle was added to the analysis – that God 'dispensed' his relationship with human beings on an entirely different basis in each of these epochs. For each he made a distinct covenant and the scriptures of that era must be interpreted in the light of its terms.

Second, he divided the future destiny of the church (God's heavenly people) from that of Israel (God's 'earthly' people). The Christian 'church age' and the Jewish millennium became disconnected. In eternity the Christians will be in heaven and the Jews on earth. The so-called 'secret rapture' marks the inauguration of this permanent separation. Israel will take over the church's calling both to suffer for and propagate the gospel on earth.

Third, in line with all this, he divided the second coming into two visits, some years apart, as outlined above.

It is therefore quite rare to find belief in the 'secret' rapture in isolation from its context in this dispensational scheme. The whole bundle is either accepted or rejected.

That it has been widely accepted is very understandable. Apart from the 'biblical case' that is presented for it (which we shall look at in the next section and critique in the following one), it is very welcome news.

On the one hand, it is an immense *comfort*. It is very gratifying to be told that Christians will be taken away before the 'Big Trouble' (as spelled out in Revelation 6–18). There is no need to prepare for such dreadful times. We won't be around when things get really bad. Eschatology gives way to escapology!

On the other hand, it is an immense *challenge*. The teaching that Jesus can return without warning and at any moment to take his followers away is a great pressure on unbelievers to join them before it is too late. Many children in 'Brethren' assemblies have turned to Christ in fear that their parents might disappear during the night (there is an absence of this kind of pressure in New Testament evangelism). After conversion, the teaching is a powerful incentive to press on to faithfulness and holiness (this can be found in the New Testament, though it is not the timing of Jesus's return, but the accountability then called for, that is the main thrust).

So, in practice, this teaching has achieved considerable results in the lives of sinners and saints alike. But is it the truth? Is it a true interpretation of the biblical references to the second coming? Its adherents and proponents claim that it is.

CHAPTER TWELVE

The Biblical Case

The fact is that there is not one single clear statement in the New Testament that there will be a 'secret rapture' of the church before the 'Great Tribulation'. Many claim 1 Thessalonians 4 as a proof-text. While it does speak of a 'rapture', there is nothing to suggest it is secret nor is there any hint of its timing, other than 'at his coming', as if there is only one such.

In the absence of any explicit mention, advocates appeal to implicit inferences, which can be deduced from various passages. When doctrine is built upon inference rather than clear statements, there is a much greater risk of reading into scripture (*eis*egesis) what is not actually there, rather than reading out of scripture (*ex*egesis) what is actually there.

However, let us first consider the case that is made, reserving criticism for the next chapter. There are seven main strands in the argument, though some of these tend to overlap. Remember that all are thought to support the idea of an any-moment secret rapture of the church before the worst trouble.

1. Statements about the *speed* of his coming. The repeated phrase that he is 'coming soon' (Rev 22:7,12,20; translated 'quickly' in the Authorised Version) implies an imminent event. Other statements such as 'he is standing at the door' (Jas 5:9; cf. Matt 24:33) suggest that his next step will bring him through. So in both temporal and spatial terms, we are led to believe his coming is very near.

2. Statements about the *surprise* of his coming. There is the use of the phrase 'thief in the night' by both Jesus and Paul (now the title of a sensational film propagating the theory). There are the

statements of Jesus to his disciples that no one knows when he will return, 'not even the angels in heaven, nor the Son, but only the Father' (Matt 24:36), followed by the exhortation: 'Therefore keep watch, because you do not know on what day your Lord will come' (Matt 24:42). There is a repeated emphasis on the unexpectedness of his reappearance.

3. The different *language* used to describe his return. In Greek three nouns are used: *parousia*, *epiphaneia* and *apokalupsis* (for a definition of their meaning, see pages 16–17). He is described as coming 'for' and 'with' his saints. Sometimes the occasion is described as 'the day of Christ' and sometimes as 'the day of the Lord'. It is said that behind this variety of expression lies a distinction between two visits, one secret and one public. The terms are not synonymous and each refers only to one or other of the two events.

4. The *expectation* of the early church. An appeal for constant readiness runs throughout the New Testament. This appears to have been based on some remarks of Jesus that 'some who are standing here will not taste death before they see the kingdom of God come with power' (Mark 9:1) and 'I tell you the truth, this generation will certainly not pass away until all these things have happened' (Matt 24:34). If the early church expected him 'at any moment', how much more should we, all this while later?

5. The absence of the word '*church*' in the 'tribulation' passages (such as Matt 24). Though frequent in Revelation 1–3, it disappears through the whole middle section (chs. 4–18), which describes the dreadful final years before the return of Christ (ch. 19). The words 'elect' and 'saints', which do occur in these chapters, are familiar terms in the Old Testament and must refer to the Jews left on earth during the Big Trouble (Rev 7:1–8), while the church enjoys relief in heaven (Rev 7:9–17). It is even thought that the invitation to John in Patmos to 'come up here' to heaven (Rev 4:1) also indicates the point at which the church is taken up, escaping all that follows.

6. The 'tribulation' is an outpouring of *wrath*. After the 'seals' and 'trumpets', seven 'bowls' of wrath are emptied on the earth,

intensifying its sufferings and sorrows (Rev 14:10, 19; 15:7; 16:1). Christians cannot share in this for the wrath of God has been turned away from them through Christ's atoning death on the cross (Rom 5:9). 'For God did not appoint us to wrath' (1 Thess 5:9; note that this occurs in a passage directly dealing with the second coming). This seems to be clinched by the promise in Revelation 3:10 to those who 'endure patiently, I will keep you from the hour of trial that is going to come upon the whole world to test those who live on the earth'.

7. The emphasis on *comfort* and encouragement. This is the reason Paul gives for his revelation of the 'rapture' (1 Thess 4:13, 18). What real comfort can there be in this if believers have to suffer terrible things first? But if the 'rapture' removes us from the earthly scene before they even start, that is indeed 'balm to our souls'. The good news is not so much that Jesus is coming back as that he is coming back for us, to take us out of the trials and troubles to come.

These, then, are the 'grounds' for believing in the 'secret rapture'. It is usually admitted that no one of these inferences is sufficient to be decisive in itself, but the cumulative effect is thought to be conclusive.

CHAPTER THIRTEEN

The Doubtful Claim

Since the case is cumulative, it is seriously weakened if any of its components is found to be faulty. The number surviving scrutiny will decide how convincing it is.

Let us go through the seven items again, examining them in the light of all the biblical data.

SPEED

What are we to make of 'soon' and 'quickly', especially after a delay of nearly two millennia? It is very obvious that the terms must be relative. But relative to what? Or perhaps more appropriately, to whom? The answer is: to God himself, to whom 'a day is like a thousand years and a thousand years is like a day' (Ps 90:4).

This very verse is quoted in the New Testament (2 Pet 3:8) to answer the question before us: 'Where is this "coming" he promised? Ever since our fathers died, everything goes on as it has since the beginning of creation' (2 Pet 3:4). The writer is pointing out that for God it has only been a couple of days since he sent his Son on his first visit, so he cannot be accused of being 'slow'. But the delay which seems so long to us has an explanation: God's incredible patience and his longing to have as many of us as possible in his family, to which repentance is the admission. This is why he had to send his Son, to make forgiveness possible by suffering the wrath of God against our sins on the cross the first time the Father has ever been separated from his Son, a day that must have seemed like a thousand years!

Of course, this delay is irksome to those who 'love his appearing' (2 Tim 4:8). Bernard of Clairvaux cried out: 'Dost thou call that a little while in which I will not see thee? O this little while is a long little while!'

We need to balance the 'soon' and 'quickly' with other strands in the New Testament which clearly indicate a lengthy period between the first and second advent. Note the delay in each of Jesus' parables about his return (Matt 24:48; 25:5,19 – in each case 'a long time'). There is also the frequent parallel with the time of harvest (Matt 13:30,40–41). This does not happen a short time after the seed has been sown, which is why James, the brother of Jesus, exhorts his readers to 'be patient, then, brothers, until the Lord's coming. See how the farmer waits for the land to yield its valuable crop and how patient he is for the autumn and spring rains. You, too, be patient and stand firm, because the Lord's coming is near' (Jas 5:7–8).

Note that in this last quotation there is a remarkable call to patient waiting for an event that is 'near'. This reflects a paradox running through the whole New Testament. The second coming is both a 'long time' ahead and yet 'soon'. Both notes need to be sounded, even together. From our perspective we can understand the 'long time', but we have difficulty with the 'soon'.

If it is only 'soon' from God's viewpoint, why has he left such a time reference in scripture, which could be misleading to us? Perhaps partly because he wants us to learn to think his way and take the longer-term view of things. But the word can be helpful to us, even when we take it in a human sense. It keeps us on our toes, by bringing the future to bear on the present and by reminding us that when he comes, we shall be accountable for what we are doing right now.

What 'soon' does not do is provide proof that he could come at any moment. It is a relative term in both human and divine measurement of time.

SURPRISE

While it is true that both Jesus and Paul said his coming would be as unexpected as a burglary ('as a thief in the night'; Matt 24:43; 1 Thess 5:2), at an 'hour' which is neither known nor expected, it does not follow that it will be without any warning or could be at 'any moment'.

A clear distinction is drawn between unbelievers and believers in relation to this. To the former, it will come as a complete surprise, even a sudden shock. An analogy is drawn from the first contractions felt by a pregnant woman (1 Thess 5:3). This is further emphasised by the stress on 'night' and 'darkness', the time when things are less difficult to discern and most people are asleep anyway. Even the word 'thief' is significant to the world for the arrival of Christ will mean the loss of so many opportunities of selfish pleasure and indulgence.

To the latter, it will not come as a surprise, for believers live in the light and stay 'awake' and 'alert' to what is happening around them (1 Thess 5:5–7). The householder who stays up and keeps a sharp look out will see the burglar's approach *before* he reaches the house (Matt 24:43). Presumably, he acts this way because of receiving prior information that 'a prowler is in the neighbourhood'!

The word 'watch' is a key, often linked with 'pray' in connection with Jesus' counsel to be ready for his coming. He might just have meant us to 'watch' ourselves and our lifestyle to make sure we can welcome him without embarrassment, but this is unlikely. He surely cannot have meant us to be studying the sky whenever it is cloudy (Acts 1:11). That would be a rather dangerous habit in the modern world. And, in any case, it would only be relevant in the Jerusalem area.

The various contexts of 'watch' clearly indicate that he meant looking for the *signs* of his coming, in the events of time rather than the reaches of space. When the disciples asked him what these would be, he gave a clear list in his answer (Matt. 24;

see the explanation of this chapter on pages 22–28). Not until
'all these things' have happened and been clearly seen by his
followers can they expect his return.

The final signal will be unmistakable: 'the sun will be darkened, and the moon will not give its light; the stars will fall
from the sky, and the heavenly bodies will be shaken' (Matt
24:29, putting together Isa 13:10 and 34:4). It is at that time
they will see the Son of Man coming in a cloud with power
and great glory. 'When these things begin to take place, stand
up and lift up your heads, because your redemption is drawing
near' (Luke 21:27–28).

But there is always the possibility of some believers becoming
spiritually sleepy, less alert to what is going on, even losing their
self-controlled attention through befuddled intoxication more
characteristic of the world (1 Thess 5:6–7). They, too, will be
'caught out' when the Bridegroom comes (that is the message
of the parable of the ten virgins in Matt 25:1–13; half of them
end up 'shut out' of the wedding).

Once again, there is no ground here for an 'any-moment,
no-warning' return. But there is a clear need for all believers
to 'keep their eyes open' lest they be as surprised as the world
will be.

LANGUAGE

There is no case for dividing the words and phrases used to
describe the second coming between two quite separate events,
with some years between. Assuming for a moment that the theory
is true, that there is a 'secret rapture' of the church some time
before Christ's public appearance, is there a distinct demarcation
between the language used of one and the other?

It is impossible to find this. Such Greek words as *parousia*,
epiphaneia and *apokalypsis*, while describing different aspects
of his coming are clearly synonymous for the *same event*. 'The
day of Christ' and the 'day of the Lord' are used interchangeably.

The notion of his people being 'gathered' is used of both their meeting with the Lord in the air and their accompanying him to earth (cf. Mark 13:27 with 2 Thess 2:1).

The supposed separation of his coming 'for his saints' and 'with his saints' requires a little more comment. On the one hand, 'saints' is a translation of a Greek word (hagioi), which literally means 'holy ones'. As such, it is used freely of both angels and believers in the New Testament. It is not always easy to know which group is being referred to and it often has to be determined by the context. So the resolution of the problem of 'for' and 'with' need not be the hypothesis of two separate events. The relevant passages may simply be saying: Jesus will return with his angels for the believers. While there are scriptures which clearly state he will bring angels with him (Matt 24:31, 25:31; 1 Thess 3:13; 2 Thess 1:7; Jude 14), this may be too neat a solution, since some contexts do seem to suggest that the 'holy ones' coming with him do include believers.

On the other hand, this still need not imply two separate comings. The clue lies in the most popular word describing his advent: parousia (from the Greek words for 'beside' and 'to be', it came to mean 'arrival'). One of its common uses was to describe the visit of a king to a city in his domain, a peculiarly appropriate application to the second coming. The royal visitor would be met some distance out of town by a select group of dignitaries and any close relatives, who would then accompany him in procession through the city gates to be seen by the resident population (much as the Queen would be met at an airport today before driving through the crowds).

This, surely, is what the New Testament indicates will happen. Believers, both those who have died and those still living (the 'quick') will 'meet the Lord in the air' (1 Thess 4:17) and accompany him on the last part of his journey back to earth. There is no hint of any time lag between these two phases and certainly no ascension to heaven for some years in any interval.

In any case, this meeting with the Lord is not inaudible.

1 Thess 4:16 has been called 'the noisiest verse in the Bible' – hardly a 'secret' rapture!

We must conclude that there is no basis for two separate 'comings' during the second advent in the words or terms used to describe it. Though we have given few references, any reader can check our conclusion by using a concordance.

EXPECTATION

It is frequently claimed that the New Testament church universally expected the Lord Jesus to reappear at any time and lived in daily expectation of seeing him again. What can be established is that they hoped it would be in their lifetime. The apostle Paul clearly shared this longing (2 Cor 5:2–3; note also 'we who are still alive' in 1 Thess 4:15), though later he realised this was not to be (2 Tim 4:6).

Jesus himself allowed them to have this hope. This is borne out by a fascinating exchange between Peter and his Lord on the shores of Galilee after the resurrection (recorded in John 21:18–25). Jesus had predicted Peter's death by crucifixion, which apparently did not greatly disturb him, perhaps because it would not happen until he was 'old'. He was far more interested in what would happen to John, Jesus' 'beloved' disciple (was Peter a tiny bit jealous of his special relationship, wanting to know if, because of that, he would be spared such a painful and humiliating end?). The reply told him to mind his own business, which was to follow his Lord, even to a cross. He was also reminded that John's fate was Jesus' responsibility: 'If I want him to remain alive until I return, what is that to you?'

This last remark became the source of a widely spread rumour that John would still be alive when Jesus returned, that this would occur during his lifetime, if no one else's. Certainly he outlived the other apostles; and he was the only one, so far as we know, to die a natural death. But he did die, before Jesus came back. Writing his Gospel, towards the end of his life (possibly AD 85–90), he was at pains to point out that the rumour had overlooked the crucial word 'if' in Jesus' statement (John 21:23).

We can assume from this that Jesus allowed for the possibility of his return within the lifetime of an apostle (he had already confessed that he had no idea when it would be; Matt 24:36, though some early manuscripts omit the phrase: 'nor the Son'). But we cannot use it as evidence that all the apostles expected him back at any time. Indeed, it points in the opposite direction. Peter knew he would die first and only when he was 'old' (John 21:18).

Consistent with the thought that many years would intervene between the two advents are the commands to 'make disciples of all nations' (Matt 28:19), to 'preach the good news to all creation' (Mark 16:15), and to be 'witnesses . . . to the ends of the earth' (Acts 1:8). All this would take a great deal of time. Could it even have been accomplished within one generation? One thinks of Paul's ambition to evangelise Spain, the western 'end' of the then known world, which he may or may not have fulfilled (Rom 15:24).

Another line of argument against the 'any-moment' expectation of the early church is the prediction of preceding events. For example, Jesus clearly foresaw the destruction of Jerusalem and its temple after a military siege (Matt 24; Mark 13 and Luke 21). This would happen before his return, yet there was no sign of it happening for almost a whole generation.

A further example occurs in the correspondence of Paul with the believers at Thessalonica. They were persuaded, apparently through a forged letter purporting to have been written by Paul, to think that the 'day of the Lord' was already dawning (2 Thess 2:1–2); the last phrase, usually translated 'has already come' can also mean 'is imminent', as in 1 Cor 7:26 and 2 Tim 3:1). Paul points out that this cannot possibly be true because of what has to happen before that. In particular, the 'man of lawlessness' has not yet appeared (2 Thess 2:3); this is usually taken to refer to 'the antichrist' (1 John 2:18) and the 'beast coming out of the sea' (Rev 13:1). Whatever his identity, one thing is clear: the Lord's return would not be without warning and therefore could not be at any moment.

Sometimes the 'any moment' concept is justified by its influence on Christian behaviour. It is said to be a healthy corrective to ask: 'Would I want to be doing this if Jesus returned right now?' Actually, that kind of thinking could lead to an unbalanced attitude. A believer could feel guilty about taking a needed vacation, making love to a married partner or even enjoying a good meal. One poor girl known to the author was spending her spare time in a cemetery so that she was ready for the resurrection!

Whatever its psychological effects, good or bad, this motivation is almost the exact opposite of Jesus' teaching on how to apply his return to daily living. The real test of our 'faithfulness' is not how we behave if his coming is imminent but how we behave if he is a 'long time coming' (Matt 24:48; 25:5,19). He is not looking for panic action but loyal service. It is not what we are doing when he returns that matters, so much as what we have been doing all the time he has been away. The latter receives his approval: 'Well done!'

CHURCH

Much weight is put on the absence of the actual word for 'church' (in Greek *ecclesia*, which literally means 'out-called' and was used for special assemblies) in key New Testament passages. This is taken to mean that the church and its members are not involved in the events described and have thus been removed before they happen. Therefore the descriptions 'elect' and 'saints' which do occur here must refer to the Jewish people still on earth at that time.

This is probably one of the weakest arguments for a 'secret rapture'. But it must still be answered.

The first thing to say is that all these passages are directly addressed to Christian believers and not to 'the remnant of

Israel'. Matthew 24, for example, is part of a private discourse between Jesus and his disciples, who throughout are addressed in the second person plural: 'I have told *you* . . . when *you* see . . . see that no one deceives *you*'.

This raises a rather obvious question: of what value to Christian edification can such descriptions of what dreadful things will happen after they have gone possibly be? We may suppose it could increase their gratitude, but it could also produce complacency and satisfaction. And why should the sufferings be so detailed? This is in marked contrast to the rather sparse information about hell, which is just enough to communicate its horror without creating an unwholesome fascination (not all preachers have exercised the same restraint!).

The next thing is to note that both 'elect' and 'saints' are normal collective terms for Christians throughout the New Testament. The former is used fifty-five times and the latter forty-eight times. To say they just refer to Jews in Revelation 4–18 is a purely arbitrary judgement (and the game is given away by reverting to the 'Christian' understanding of 'saints' in Rev 22:21!).

There happen to be six epistles in the New Testament which also avoid using the word 'church' (2 Timothy, Titus, 1 & 2 Peter, 2 John and Jude). Does that mean they are intended for Jews after the church has been 'raptured'? That would be a ridiculous deduction! Significantly, five of these just use the term 'elect', while one (Jude) uses 'saints'.

Even more striking the word 'church' is also missing from those passages directly dealing with the 'rapture' when Christians see Jesus again (e.g. John 14; 1 Cor 15; 1 Thess 4–5). It is not even in the description of the new heaven and earth or the new Jerusalem (Rev 21–22). Does that mean that only Jews will experience the new creation?

If so, we are left without any idea where Christians will be after their acquittal on the day of judgement!

That Christians are on earth throughout the disastrous final years pictured in the central chapters of Revelation is decisively proved by an explanatory comment in chapter 14: 'This calls for patient endurance on the part of the *saints* who obey God's commands and remain faithful to Jesus' (Rev 14:12). It is also confirmed by the use of the phrase 'testimony of Jesus' in these chapters (12:17; surely the same as in 1:9 and 19:10). Even if it is claimed that this only refers to converted Jews (as a few do), why were they not raptured as part of the church? This forced interpretation creates more problems than it solves.

However, there might just be another reason why Revelation does not contain the word 'church' after chapter 3. God has not rejected the Jews, even if they have rejected him (Rom 11:1). They are not finished (Rom 11:11). God still has a love and a purpose for them. Therefore he is still committed to their preservation as a people, as he promised unconditionally (see Jer 31:35–37 for just one example).

This is clearly spelled out in the New Testament – and in the middle chapters of Revelation (7:1–8). Whatever we make of the exact figures of the survivors (12,000 from each tribe, making a total of 144,000), the thrust of the passage is that God will protect a remnant of his ancient people until the end of time (the marginal alternative translation of Matt 24:34 in the New International Version reads: 'I tell you the truth, this *race* will certainly not pass away until all these things have happened').

Thus God is dealing with two groups on earth during the 'Great Tribulation': his old covenant people, Israel, and his new covenant people, the church. Maybe the words 'elect' and 'saints' are being used to cover both. Jesus could have been doing this when he said that 'for the sake of the elect those days [of great distress, unequalled from the beginning of the world] will be shortened' (Matt 24:22).

This preserved remnant of Israel will believe in Jesus when they 'look on him whom they pierced' (Zech 12:10; significantly referred to in Rev 1:7), presumably when he returns (Rev 19:11–16). Thereafter, Jewish and Christian destinies merge into one, the new Jerusalem bearing the names of the twelve tribes and the twelve apostles (Rev 21:12–14).

This possible reason for the omission of 'church' and the substitution of 'elect' and 'saints' is speculative and therefore tentatively presented. It is by no means established. And it is not necessary to the argument here being presented. We have already seen that the non-use of 'church' is not in itself evidence for the absence of Christians.

We now turn from the weakest argument for a 'secret' rapture to what is perhaps the strongest.

WRATH

At first sight this argument is impressive, to some even conclusive. It can be simply stated: if the 'Great Tribulation' is an outpouring of God's wrath on the world, how can Christians possibly experience it since they are 'not appointed to wrath' (1 Thess 5:9)?

There is more to be said, however, and we shall need to spend some time on this point.

Perhaps this is an appropriate place to expand the latest variation: the 'mid-tribulation' rapture. Attention has been drawn to the fact that 'wrath' is used of the third sevenfold series of disasters (the 'bowls') but not of the first and second series (the 'seals' and the 'trumpets'). It is therefore suggested that Christians will go through the *first* part of the 'Great Tribulation', but not through the *worst* part, which is the direct expression of divine wrath.

Yet another variation is the 'partial rapture', the belief that only 'overcomers' will be taken out, while weaker believers remain!

It will be realised that in almost everything these proposals are in fact identical with the 'pre-tribulation rapture'. Apart from the postponement in time, there are still two comings, a secret one *for* the saints and a public one *with* them. All supporters still use the 'wrath' argument; they only differ as to how much of the final distress can be described by that word.

Actually, the word 'wrath' does appear in connection with the seals and trumpets (see Rev 6:16–17); and the 'seven bowls of God's wrath' (Rev 16:1) are only said to 'complete' the earth's experience of that wrath (Rev 15:1). So the whole sequence of disasters (Rev 6–16) is all 'wrath'. Christians will either escape all of it or go through all of it. We must think again.

Perhaps the first thing to note is that Christians and their families are not exempt from the normal tragedies that happen in a fallen world. While writing this very page, the author was asked to counsel a Christian couple whose new baby was born with spina bifida. Christians can die in famines and earthquakes. Such tragedies neither belong to the Creator's original intention nor do they reflect the spiritual state of those concerned. They belong to a corrupted creation and can happen to anyone in it.

Next, it is important to remember that disciples of Jesus are likely to suffer more than others in this world. In addition to their share of natural hazards, they will experience social hostility. Jesus was honest enough to promise his followers: 'you will have trouble in this world' (John 16:33). Paul told his converts that they 'must go through many hardships to enter the kingdom' (Acts 14:22); he thought such suffering was inevitable: 'in fact, everyone who wants to live a godly life in Christ Jesus will be persecuted' (2 Tim 3:12). The word 'tribulation' actually occurs about fifty times in the New Testament, only three of which refer to the 'Great Tribulation'.

Further, 'believers' live in a world that is *already* experiencing the wrath of God (Rom 1:18–31). As men reject the truth about God revealed in creation outside them and conscience inside them, preferring to believe lies, he removes his restraining hand from their relationships to themselves and each other. As they give God up, he gives them up – to uncontrollable lusts and unnatural liaisons, particularly of a homosexual nature. Their minds as well as their bodies are abused, leading to anti-social attitudes and activities in family and community. It is impossible for Christians to be totally untouched by such a decadent environment.

The point we are making is that Christians are *already*

inhabiting a world that is on the receiving end of divine wrath. The difference between this and the 'Great Tribulation' is one of degree rather than kind. The fact that it is universal does not make it radically different for the individual who is caught in a limited disaster of the same kind today.

But even though Christians have to live in a world that is suffering the effects of divine wrath, their attitude towards this will be different. For one thing they know that the wrath is not personally directed towards them; they will not be crying out with the fear of a guilty conscience, begging to be hidden from it under falling rock (Rev 6:16–17). They will also know that the duration of this outpoured wrath will be strictly limited. Further, they know they will never face the ultimate climax of divine anger, the 'wrath to come', which is not the Great Tribulation but the 'lake of fire' – hell itself. Above all, they will know that Jesus' return must be very near. All these factors will help to make it bearable.

What, then, is the meaning of the promise of Jesus that 'I will also keep you from the hour of trial that is going to come upon the whole world' (in Rev 3:10)? This is widely considered to be the 'proof-text' of a pre-tribulation rapture. But every text must be seen in its context, or it will be used as a pretext!

This reassurance is to be found in the letter to the church in Philadelphia, one of the two of the seven in Asia about which Jesus makes no criticism and expresses only approval. The promise to keep them is *only* given to this fellowship and not to the other six or even to the other one which Jesus approves. It is specifically directed to this faithful congregation. This is confirmed by the fact that the promise is made in that part of the letter that pertains to the specific local situation, rather than the general ones addressed to individuals who 'overcome', which are to be found at the end of each letter and are applied later in the book to *all* believers.

At most, this promise could only be claimed by other churches

in the same blameless condition as the congregation in Philadelphia. It cannot be stretched to include churches needing
correction, much less to encompassing all believers.

We need also to ask whether 'the hour of trial that is going
to come upon the whole world' is a reference to the 'Great
Tribulation' at all.

The church at Philadelphia has long since disappeared altogether! Is that the way Jesus fulfilled the promise? If so, it has
nothing to do with the 'secret rapture'. If not, how can Jesus
possibly keep what doesn't exist from the 'Great Tribulation'?
It just doesn't make any sense to the original hearers to whom
the promise was given.

But it does make sense if the 'hour of trial' is understood to
mean the imperial persecutions that spread thoughout the Roman
Empire during the second and third centuries. This would fit
the statement that the 'hour of trial' would 'test', rather than
punish, those living on the earth. How would Jesus keep the
Philadelphians from this? There is no hint that he would whisk
them off to heaven before it started. It is far more likely that he
would do so by preventing the wave of oppression from reaching
their city, perhaps by tenderising the hearts of its authorities,
which he was well able to do.

This is exactly what God did when he loosed the plagues on
Egypt. He said: 'On that day I will deal differently with the land
of Goshen, where my people live ... so that you will know
that I, the LORD [literally: Yahweh, his covenant name], am
in this land. I will make a distinction between my people and
your [i.e. Pharaoh's] people' (Exod 8:22–23; cf. 10:23; 11:7).
Though he was pouring out his wrath on the whole country,
God was perfectly capable of protecting his people from the
disastrous results. Maybe that is exactly what will happen in the
'Great Tribulation'. Many have noticed the similarities between
its disasters and the Egyptian plagues (even to the locusts! Exod
10:13–15; Rev 9:3). If the woman in Revelation 12 represents
the church (see pages 139–40), she is 'taken care of' in a 'place
prepared for her in the desert for a time, times and half a time',

surely the forty-two months or three and a half years of the 'Great Tribulation' (Rev 12:14). Her 'offspring' are identified as 'those who obey God's commandments and hold to the testimony of Jesus' (Rev 12:17; cf. 14:12).

We have perhaps strayed into the realm of speculation. Our starting point was the doubtful application of Revelation 3:10 to a future 'secret rapture'. It is time to return to the main issue: will Christians go through the 'Great Tribulation'?

If they do not, why on earth should the major portion of a book addressed to believers contain such a detailed description of all that will happen during that terrible time? Since the clear purpose of the whole book is to prepare them for what is to come, why tell them so much about that for which they do not need to prepare? If they will not be around to witness the events covered by chapters 6–18, that whole section is, to say the very least, a waste of paper! Its inclusion is a complete mystery.

Coupled with this is the fact already stated in another connection – that right in the middle of this section is a call to 'remain faithful to Jesus' (Rev 14:12). This can only mean that Christians are in the thick of it!

When this direct statement is set against the indirect inference, which is what the argument about 'wrath' actually is, then surely the former should be accepted, however logical the latter may seem to be.

Remembering that the evidence for a 'secret rapture' is freely admitted to be 'cumulative', we have not found a single inference yet that is substantial enough to be included. This is also true of the last one to be considered:

COMFORT

This is really concerned with the morale of believers. Surely, it is said, the early return of Christ is hardly a 'blessed hope' if it means that we have to go through the 'Great Tribulation' first!

But this is to confuse the subjective effect of 'hope' with its objective ground. There can be no lasting consolation in a lie. A sure and certain hope can only be based on the truth.

The word 'comfort' can have different connotations. It is often used of relieving pain or stress. But its deepest meaning is to strengthen and encourage. It is cousin to '*fortify*'. Real comfort comes from facing the truth, the whole truth, about the situation.

Consider the 'comforting' words of Jesus (in John 16:33): 'In this world you will have trouble' (that is the truth). 'But take heart! I have overcome the world' (that is the whole truth). When the 'Big Trouble' comes, he says: 'Now you overcome, as I have done. Take heart! I am coming soon' (this statement is not a verse in scripture, but is an accurate summary of the message of Revelation!).

Forewarned is forearmed. In the very same context in which Jesus described this last and greatest of all 'distress', he says: 'See, I have told you ahead of time' (Matt 24:25). How kind of him to prepare us in this way.

This is surely why such passages as Matthew 24 and Revelation 6–18 are in our New Testament: to get us ready for the worst that can happen. Yet even when it does, we shall be able to endure it, knowing that the 'best is yet to be' and will follow so soon afterwards.

Our study of 'the rapture' is over. The reader may not be convinced by the reasoning or conclusions presented. The writer could be wrong, but he'd rather be wrong this way than the other! It is surely better to warn believers to be ready for the 'Great Tribulation' and then discover that they will not go through it than to tell them they need not be prepared for it and then find that they should have been.

Whether the idea of a 'secret rapture' originated in a false prophecy, as some claim, or not, its extremely slender basis in scripture indicates that it is a false prophecy whenever it is communicated to others. All false predictions are danger-ous, and this one carries particular risks. Consider the fol-lowing testimony of that saintly Dutch woman, Corrie Ten

Boom, who enjoyed listening to this author's tapes during her last illness:

> I have been in countries where the saints are already suffering terrible persecution. In China the Christians were told: 'Don't worry, before the tribulation comes, you will be translated, raptured.' Then came a terrible persecution. Millions of Christians were tortured to death. Later I heard a bishop from China say, sadly: 'We have failed. We should have made the people strong for persecution rather than telling them Jesus would come first.' Turning to me, he said: 'Tell the people how to be strong in times of persecution, how to stand when the tribulation comes – to stand and not faint.' I feel I have a divine mandate to go and tell the people of this world that it is possible to be strong in the Lord Jesus Christ. We are in training for the tribulation. Since I have gone already through prison for Jesus' sake, and since I met that bishop from China, now every time I read a good Bible text I think: 'Hey, I can use that in the time of tribulation.' Then I write it down and learn it by heart.

Few could have put it better, both with her lips and in her life. She is now with the Lord, having been through her own tribulation. When we go through ours, whether that be personal, local or universal, may we be among the 'overcomers', as she was and is.

D. THE MILLENNIUM MUDDLE

CHAPTER FOURTEEN

The Common Disappointment

The world is generally disappointed with Jesus. He has failed to live up to the expectations of Jew and Gentile alike.

JEWS

were the first to feel he had let them down. When he came, many were looking for the 'kingdom' or 'rule' of God to be re-established on planet earth. They believed he would send an 'anointed' king (in Hebrew: *meschiah*), of the Davidic dynasty, to accomplish this, through his chosen people, Israel. Their hopes, therefore, had both a national and international flavour.

On the one hand, their restored monarchy would bring the political freedom they had lost five centuries before and only briefly regained in the abortive Maccabean revolt against the Greeks. Now under Roman domination the longing for liberty continued, expressed in such phrases as 'the consolation of Israel' and 'the redemption of Jerusalem'. (Luke 2:25,38).

On the other hand, they expected this liberation from other nations to give them a position of leadership to other nations, the 'tail' becoming the 'head' (Deut 28:13). Jerusalem would not just be their own capital; it would be the centre of world government (Mic 4:1–5; Isa 2:1–5). The just arbitration available in Zion would provide the proper basis for peace, leading to multilateral disarmament.

This dual dream, of national liberty and international leadership, is particularly clear in the later prophecies of Isaiah (note the interaction between 'Jerusalem' and 'nations/islands/ends of the earth' in chs. 40–66). It is typified in the words of the elderly Simeon when he caught sight of the baby Jesus in the temple courts – he told the Lord he could die happy, having seen 'a light for revelation to the Gentiles and for glory to your people Israel' (Luke 2:32).

Thirty-three years later Jesus left this earth without having accomplished either objective. Between his resurrection and ascension, the disappointed national aspiration was expressed more than once. 'We had hoped that he was the one who was going to redeem Israel' was the heartfelt cry of the two on the road to Emmaus (Luke 24:21). The very last question of the disciples was: 'Lord, are you at this time going to restore the kingdom [i.e. the monarchy] to Israel?' (Acts 1:6 – note that Jesus accepted the premises of the question, but told them the date set for that by 'the Father' was not their business).

It seems that Jesus himself had switched the focus of the kingdom from the national to the international dimension during his last six weeks on earth (Matt 28:19; Mark 16:15; Luke 24:47; Acts 1:3). Even earlier, he had announced that 'the kingdom of God will be taken away from you [i.e. Israel] and given to a people who will produce its fruit' (Matt 21:43).

This was not, as many have supposed, the cancellation of the national aspect. Too many scriptures point to a future place for Israel and Jerusalem in God's purposes to allow this conclusion (e.g. Matt 23:39; Luke 21:24; 22:29–30; Rom 11:1,11). Their part has been postponed. The order of events has been reversed. The Gentiles will receive the kingdom before the Jews (Rom 11:25–26). The first shall be last and the last first.

But has the rule of God been established among the nations, in accordance with this change of plan?

GENTILES

too, have expressed disillusionment with Jesus. It is commonly said that Christianity has been around for nearly *two thousand* years, yet the world is no better. If anything, it appears to be getting worse! The twentieth century has seen two major wars and the 'holocaust' in the 'civilised' continent of Europe. Evil seems more rampant and entrenched than ever. Yet over one third of the world's population carry the label 'Christian'.

Of course, we can say that many of the latter are only 'nominal' in their religious allegiance. Or we can claim with G.K. Chesterton that 'the Christian ideal has not been tried and found wanting; it has been found difficult and left untried'. And we could make quite a list of benefits to mankind which have sprung from Christian compassion – the emancipation of slaves and women, the care of sick and handicapped, orphaned and illiterate. A strong case can be made for the Christian origins of modern science and all its achievements.

Yet the criticism can still be made. Few would boldly claim that the world is now a safer, happier, better place to live. Fewer still would claim that this is largely due to the influence of Christ. The New Testament assessment that 'the whole world is under the control of the evil one' (1 John 5:19) seems as accurate now as it was then.

CHRISTIANS

also have their doubts. A large proportion seem to have accepted that this world will never be any different. Their hope for the future is centred on the next world. Their task is seen as the saving of as many individuals as possible from a society that is terminally sick.

Surprisingly, and perhaps in reaction to such pessimism, there is another sector of the Christian spectrum which has confidence to think that the church is well on the way to taking over national and international governments. Christians could become the majority and therefore play a decisive role in social, political and universal affairs.

Perhaps most believers are in between these two extremes, seeking realism rather than gloomy pessimism or naive optimism. In addition to evangelising, they believe they must be doing whatever they can to make this world better by working for the welfare of both individuals and communities.

Not all of these will ask about the ultimate goal of their endeavours. Many will be content with meeting some immediate needs. Even if the total scene gets worse, they will be satisfied that they have 'done their bit'. That is infinitely preferable to being so depressed about the whole trend that action is paralysed.

But the question of ultimate outcome cannot be shelved. Faith and love are not sufficient to sustain full Christian service. Hope is the vital third dimension. It is 'an anchor for the soul' (Heb 6:19), especially when experiencing discouragement and the temptation to despair. The thought of final success gives the strength to overcome all intermediate obstacles.

Jesus taught his followers to pray every day that the kingdom of God, the divine rule, would 'come on earth . . . as it is in heaven' (Matt 6:10). Clearly, this has not happened yet or we would not need to go on using this petition. But what are we praying for? What do we expect to happen when the prayer is answered? Someone has said that our whole theology can be deduced from our answers to these questions!

Will the kingdom come on earth? If so, how and when? Will it come gradually or suddenly? By human infiltration or divine intervention? Will it be purely spiritual or political as well?

To put it another way, will the Lord Jesus Christ ever rule this world in such a visible way that everyone knows that all authority has been given to him in heaven and on earth (Matt 28:18), that he is the King of kings and Lord of lords (Rev 19:16) that every knee must bow to him and every tongue confess his lordship (Phil 2:11)? Or will only Christians 'see' these things by faith?

We are already discussing the issue of 'the millennium'! For these are the very questions that lie at the heart of the debate.

Far too many dismiss the subject as an academic debate with little or no practical significance. What is the point of arguing over the interpretation of 'one obscure passage in a highly symbolic book'? The resulting differences are said to threaten the unity of the church and distract it from its mission.

But we have already seen that future expectations are the essence of the Christian virtue of hope. We are saved by faith and in hope (Rom 8:24).

Let it be stated at once that there is widespread agreement about the *next* world, that 'new heaven and new earth' (Rev 21:1) that will succeed this old universe, though it is usually referred to as 'heaven', with little or no emphasis on 'earth'. There are few arguments about the last two chapters in the Bible!

The real differences emerge when the future hopes for *this* world are discussed. How far will the divine authority given to Jesus be made manifest in this world before it comes to an end? As we have already indicated, there is a huge range of Christian opinion, which has grown wider over the centuries of church history.

The controversy, fierce at times, has centred on the twentieth chapter of the book of Revelation. This is hardly surprising, since it appears to cover the very last events of this age, leading up to the final day of judgement, which in turn ushers in the new creation.

From this chapter a simple reader could easily conclude that Christ and his followers, particularly those who have been martyred for their faith, will actually 'reign' over this world for one thousand years before it comes to an end.

It is from this repeated phrase 'a thousand years' that the word *millennium* has come (from the Latin: *mille* = thousand and *annum* = year). Hence the noun 'millennialism' describes the belief that Christ will reign on earth for this period. The doctrine is sometimes called 'chiliasm' (in Greek: *chilioi* = thousand).

As we approach the end of the twentieth century the word

'millennium' has come back into daily use, since on 1 January 2001, we shall enter the third millennium AD (Latin for *anno domini* = year of our Lord). This date on the calendar has led directly to renewed interest in the promised return of our Lord and indirectly to renewed debate about his 'millennial' reign on earth, especially among those who still believe the twenty-first century will begin the seventh millennium since creation (a kind of cosmic 'sabbath'), by assuming creation took place in 4004 BC, as a note in some old Bibles suggested.

We must not let dating attempts obscure the real issue by bringing the debate into speculative disrepute. The primary question is not when but whether. Will Christ ever rule this world for a thousand years?

Our starting point must obviously be the passage of scripture from which many have reached a positive conclusion, namely, Revelation 20. This will be studied in detail and in context. Then we shall work backwards through the New and Old Testaments to see if we find confirmation or contradiction of our findings. After that we shall work forwards through church history, noting when and why very different interpretations arose. These will be assessed for their exegetical accuracy and practical influence. Finally, I will give the reasons for my own conclusion and conviction.

The current position is much more complex than many realise. Most readers will probably be familiar with the three labels: a-millennial, pre-millennial and post-millennial. A friend of mine, when asked which described his own view, replied: 'That is *a pre-post*-erous question!' Others avoid committing themselves by saying they are pan-millennial, explaining the prefix to mean that 'things will pan out alright in the end whatever we think now'!

However, jocular evasions cannot diminish the importance of reaching some conclusion. As we shall see, our real belief will have a profound effect on our attitude to this world and our responsibility for it. So we need to be clear.

One problem is that each of the three main approaches has two quite different variations, so that in reality there are six positions from which to choose. A further complication is that most who call themselves 'a-millennial' are actually one subdivision of 'post-millennial', though this is rarely realised. Keep reading and all will be made clear!

Meanwhile, it is with some relief that we turn to scripture itself and begin our study by looking at what the Bible actually *says* before we consider what others think it *means*. As we do so, we constantly need to recall that the book of Revelation was written for ordinary believers in the seven churches of Asia (now western Turkey). It was not a complex conundrum for theological professors and biblical scholars to unravel. It is a sound principle to read scripture in its plain, simple sense unless there is a clear indication that it should be taken otherwise. We must seek to recover the message it would communicate to its original readers.

With these few guidelines we can now approach the key passage, over which there has been so much debate.

CHAPTER FIFTEEN

The Basic Passage (Revelation 20)

This is undoubtedly the clearest passage on the 'millennium' in the whole Bible. Some would say it is the only passage about it. Certainly, without this chapter it would not be an issue. Life would be much simpler if it wasn't there at all! Those who wish that were so and try to ignore it need to be reminded of the curse on those who take anything away from 'this prophecy' (Rev 22:19); they could lose their place in eternity!

Those who believe that the Bible consists of, and not just contains, the inspired words of God must take this chapter seriously. Even if it were the only mention of this part of his purpose, it would still be his word. How often does God have to say something before we believe it?

So we must let the passage speak for itself. But first we must see it in its context – not just its immediate context (chapters 19 and 21) but its wider setting.

It is in the New Testament, not the Old. It belongs to the 'new' covenant of Jesus, not the 'old' covenant of Moses. It is addressed to Christians rather than Jews. Though 'Jewish' in atmosphere (the book of Revelation contains four hundred allusions to Hebrew scriptures, though not a single quotation), it is intended for Gentile believers and does not need to be re- interpreted for them (as would the Deuteronomic laws, for example). This is written by a Christian for Christians.

This chapter is part of a unique book in the New Testament. In another section of this volume we examined Revelation in greater detail (see pages 85–172); but a brief summary is needed here.

It is basically a letter, a composite circular epistle to a group of churches – but here all similarity (e.g. to Ephesians) ends. It was never intended to be written! It is a transcription of verbal and visual reflections which came unexpectedly to a man in prison who was told by an angel to write them down and pass them on. This is probably why the letter is described as a 'prophecy', the only such in the New Testament. It is both a word for the present (forthtelling) and about the future (foretelling), with the major emphasis on the latter. Nearly two thirds of its 'verses' contain predictions, covering fifty-six separate events. Inevitably, pictorial language is used to describe the unknown and even unimaginable; but the symbolism is intended to clarify rather than conceal and is rarely obscure.

The book/prophecy/letter is intended to be read aloud (note the blessing on reader and hearers in Rev 1:3). Perhaps it is only in these circumstances that it yields its deepest meaning and makes its greatest impact.

Above all, we need constantly to remember that its purpose is intensely practical: to prepare Christian individuals and churches for tougher times ahead. Its aim is to encourage (to put courage into) believers to 'endure' suffering for their faith even to the point of martyrdom, and to 'overcome' all hostile pressures, thus keeping their names in the 'book of life' (Rev 3:5). Every part of the book is directed to this end. Of each passage and its interpretation the question must be asked: how does this help persecuted disciples?

The book divides into clear sections. The most obvious division is between the first three chapters, which deal with the readers' *present* situation, and the remainder, which unveils the *future* to them (see 4:1). The latter section goes right to the end of the world and beyond, but divides into two phases, which may be seen as 'bad news' and 'good news'. This simple threefold message may be presented as follows:

i.   Things which must be put right now (1–8).
ii. Things will get much worse before they get better (4–18).
iii. Things will get much better after they get worse (19–22).

The second section deals with the more immediate future while the third deals with the ultimate future, with the very last things. It is the return of Christ to planet earth which turns the tide in the flow of events.

Chapter 20 sits firmly in this third section. It belongs to the 'last things'. It is part of the 'good news'. It is part of that encouraging future to which the persecuted can look forward and for which they should be willing to die.

At this point it is necessary to introduce an important principle of biblical study: namely, to *ignore chapter divisions*! They were not in the original text. Though convenient for reference, they are not inspired by God and are often in the wrong place, putting asunder what God has joined together! The large figure '20' is seriously misleading (another argument for reading the book aloud). The continuity clearly apparent in the original is violently disrupted and this has enabled commentators to separate the chapter from its context, radically to revise its message and application and to relocate the millennium in history (more of that later).

When the chapter divisions are ignored and 'chapters' 18–22 are read as a continuous narrative, a remarkable pattern emerges. It could be entitled: 'A tale of two cities' (Babylon and Jerusalem) which are personified as two women, a filthy prostitute and a pure bride. The destruction of the one metropolis and the descent of the other are separated by an extraordinary series of events, revealed in a sevenfold vision.

It is instructive to note the switches from verbal to visual revelations. The fall of Babylon is told by an angel and is 'heard' by John (18:4), as is the heavenly rejoicing over it (19:1,6). John is then told to write down what he has *heard* (19:9). After these voices comes a series of visions, which John *saw* (19:11, 17, 19; 20:1, 4, 11; 21:1). Seven things are 'seen' before the next thing is 'heard' (21:3). This series of visions may be listed as follows:

1. The rider on a white horse at the open door of heaven.
2. An angel invites birds to the 'last supper' of human flesh.

3. The battle with all anti-God forces at Armageddon.
4. An angel binds, banishes and imprisons the devil.
5. The saints reign with Christ for a thousand years, at the
    end of which Satan is released, defeated and thrown into
    the lake of fire.
6. The resurrection of the dead and the final day of judge-
    ment.
7. The creation of a new heaven and a new earth; and the
    descent of the new Jerusalem.

Seven is, of course, a familiar number in this book, beginning
with the seven churches of Asia and the seven letters to them.
More significant are the three series of disasters under the figure
of seals, trumpets and bowls.

The latter clearly present a sequence of events, increasing
in intensity. Furthermore, in each series the first four belong
together (the clearest example is the four horsemen of the first
four seals in 6:1–8), the next two are related and the last or
seventh stands on its own. The same 4–2–1 pattern may be clearly
discerned in the final series of visions we are now examining (in
19:11 to 21:2).

Once the chapter numbers (20 and 21) have been removed, the
series of seven visions clearly presents a sequence of events, each
relating to the preceding one. There is internal evidence that the
visions are consecutive, in chronological order. Two examples
will suffice:

i. The devil is thrown into the lake of fire *after* the beast and
    the false prophet (compare 20:10 with 19:20).
ii. The new heaven and earth appear *after* the old have passed
    away (compare 21:1 with 20:11).

In particular, to separate chapter 20 from chapter 19 destroys
the whole sequence. This is widely done in the interests of the
a-millennial and post-millennial positions, who want to make
chapter 20 a 'recapitulation' of the whole church age and not

a sequel to the events of chapter 19. This should be seen as an artificial separation, relying heavily on the medieval chapter divisions.

The sequence belongs together. The only valid question is: what period of time does it cover?

All agree on when it *ends*. The day of judgement (vision 6) and the new heaven and earth (vision 7) take us to the very end of this age, what we know as 'history'.

But when does it *begin*? Who is the rider on the white horse and when does he come charging with the forces of heaven?

There is no argument about his identity. The titles 'Faithful and True' (applied to Jesus in 3:14); 'Word of God' (only used elsewhere in the New Testament of Jesus in John 1:1,14) and 'King of kings and Lord of lords' (identified with 'the Lamb' in 17:14) leave no room for doubt. He is the Lord Jesus Christ. (Note that this is not necessarily the case in 6:2, where the rider is not identified, uses a bow rather than a sword and the emphasis is on the colour of the horse – a general symbol of military aggression.)

There is some disagreement about his 'exit' from heaven. The choice is between his first and second advent.

The small number of scholars who claim this to be a representation of his *first* visit to earth do so in order to retain the sevenfold sequence while applying the 'millennium' to the church age. To maintain this, the details have to be heavily 'allegorised'. The white horse of conquest is a purely 'spiritual' symbol, for in actuality he rode on a donkey of peace (Matt 21:4–5, fulfilling Zech 9:9). The stained robe is only his own blood. The striking down of the nations is only metaphorical, though of what is not usually stated. But this whole attempt to maintain the sequence fails because it involves applying the decisive battle of 'Armaggedon' to the crucifixion, which means that the beast and the false prophet were 'thrown alive into the fiery lake' at Calvary! This makes nonsense of their appearance in chapter 13 among the things that 'must take place after this' (4:1). This approach creates more problems than it solves and has convinced very few.

Most are agreed that the first vision (19:11–16) refers to the *second* advent of Christ. There are many sound reasons for this conclusion. First, this 'warlike' mission is far more compatible with his second coming 'to judge the living and the dead'. Second, the enemies he destroys here are human as well as demonic, which was not the case at his first coming. Third, the preceding context is the announcement of a wedding and a 'ready' bride, which naturally leads into the coming of the Bridegroom (compare Matt 25:6). Fourth, and this seems decisive, if this is not a reference to the second advent then our Lord's return is nowhere mentioned in the main body of this prophecy, though both the prologue and epilogue indicate it as the main theme (1:7 and 22:20). It is hardly surprising that most commentaries accept this interpretation. The sequence begins at the second advent.

We may pick out four major events in the sevenfold vision:

1. The second advent (ch. 19)
2. The millennial reign (ch. 20)
3. The judgement day (ch.20)
4. The new creation (ch. 21)

Almost all orthodox scholars accept 1, 3 and 4 events as belonging to the end of history and in that same order! But there is a widespread reluctance to include 2 in the sequence, though it clearly belongs there. This is due in turn to a long-standing tradition in the church which has rejected so-called '*pre*-millennialism' (the belief that 1 precedes 2 in time, that Jesus returns *before* he and his saints reign). This has resulted in extraordinary attempts to prove that Revelation 19–21 really intends the reader to understand the order of events as 2, 1, 3, 4 – in spite of the pattern in which they are there presented!

This subtle juxtaposition is not based on any clear indication in the text itself. It results from bringing to the text a prior conviction (the exact meaning of 'prejudice'), in this case the assumption that nothing intervenes between the return of Christ and the day of judgement. This has been the majority opinion in the church for many centuries and has been implied in its creeds (both the Apostles' and the Nicene). Christ was thought of as coming again to judge rather than to reign.

There are some scriptures which seem to uphold this compression of events and we shall look at them later. It is often claimed that they are 'plain' statements, whereas Revelation 20 is said to be 'obscure'. Having made this judgement, it is then argued that the latter should be interpreted in the light of the former – which usually means forcing the one to fit the other.

Even if it were 'obscure', that is no reason to dismiss it. Some seem to think that to say it is 'highly symbolic' excuses them from taking it seriously or even explaining what are the realities behind the symbols. And they seem ready enough to take the first and last visions at face value!

But is it so obscure? There seems to this writer very limited use of symbolic language in these visions. Most of the events are stated as fact, actual occurrences. The figures of speech are hardly mysterious: 'four corners of the earth' is perfectly obvious and need not be taken to mean the writer believed the earth was square. Who doesn't understand what 'the great white throne' stands for? The only really puzzling reference is to 'Gog and Magog', but a glance at Ezekiel 39 suggests them to be labels for the last prince and people to attack God's people *after* David's dynasty has been restored.

The time has come to study the passage (20:1–10) in detail, allowing the text to speak for itself before comparing it with other relevant scriptures. We shall seek to study it with the reverence due to the inspired words of God and the integrity of an open mind concerned with objective exegesis.

The first thing to notice is the repeated use of the phrase 'thousand years' – six times in one short passage. In two of these the definite article makes it still more emphatic: '*the* thousand years'. It could hardly be more precise.

Some want to take it as a symbol, citing ten cubed as an indication of completeness. But even those who do so usually say it represents an extended period of *time*, as opposed to a brief interval. It is much more than an interlude. It is an epoch which has significance in its own right.

The case for taking the phrase literally rests on the fact that other spans of time are specifically denoted in this book. For example, the duration of the 'Great Tribulation', or 'Big Trouble', is said to last for 'a time, times and half a time' (12:14), or '1,260 days' (12:6) or 'forty-two months' (13:5).

The contrast between these three and a half years of intense suffering for the saints and the following thousand years of reigning with Christ is very much in line with the whole purpose of the book – to encourage faithfulness in the present by thought about the future. As Paul wrote: 'I consider that our present sufferings are not worth comparing with the glory that will be revealed in us' (Rom 8:18).

In further consideration of the ten 'verses' as a whole, we can ask the usual basic questions: when, where and who?

WHEN do 'the thousand years' occur? The twofold answer is clear from the 'sevenfold vision' of which they are a part: *after* the rider on the white horse (Jesus) has defeated the beast and the false prophet and *before* the great white throne. In other words, the millennium lies *between* the second advent and the day of judgement.

WHERE do Christ and his saints reign? In heaven or on earth? The book of Revelation keeps alternating between heaven and earth (4:1;7:1;8:1, etc.). But there is usually a very clear indication of location. So which is the setting for chapter 20?

We must begin with chapter 19. Heaven is 'open' for the rider (19:11), but it is then very obvious that he comes to earth for the battle with evil forces (19:19). The angel binding Satan comes 'down out of heaven' (20:1). His later release also takes place on 'earth' (20:8–9). The 'earth' later disappears before the final judgement (20:11).

The whole focus is on 'earth', throughout this passage. In the absence of any hint to the contrary, we may take the millennial reign of the saints to take place on this 'old' earth before it disappears. A sudden shift to heaven in verses 4–6 would have been clearly indicated. Furthermore, the saints reign 'with Christ' (20:4) and he has by now returned to earth (19:11–21).

The wider context of the whole book confirms this in three earlier announcements. Those who overcome will be given 'authority over the nations' (2:26). Those who are redeemed by the blood of the Lamb will 'reign on the earth' (5:10). The 'kingdom of the world' will become the kingdom of Christ (11:15). None of these promises is fulfilled until chapter 20.

WHO is the central figure in this passage? Surprisingly, it is not Christ! He is only mentioned incidentally. Most of the attention is on Satan, though his part in the millennium is limited to the very beginning and the very end. The saints are in the forefront during the centuries between. The structure of the passage is therefore a 'sandwich':

1–3   Satan removed (brief)
4–6   Saints reigning (lengthy)
7–10   Satan released (brief)

A reason must be found for this extraordinary disproportion of content. Meanwhile, we will consider each of the three 'paragraphs' in greater depth.

SATAN REMOVED (20:1–3)

To understand what is happening here, we need to look again at the wider context.

Four alien and hostile figures have already been introduced. Three are actual persons, two of them human: Satan (hurled to earth in ch. 12), the 'antichrist' and the false prophet (emerging in ch. 13). Together they form an 'unholy trinity', taking over world government at the climax of history, causing the greatest distress for the people of God. They are all male. The fourth is female, but is not a person. She, a prostitute, is a 'personification' – of a city, 'Babylon', the commercial hub of the world.

These four dominate the final but very brief period of this 'present evil age'. They are dealt with in reverse order to their appearance:

Babylon falls (ch. 18).
Antichrist and false prophet are thrown into hell, the first humans to go there (ch. 19).
Satan is removed, released, then thrown into hell himself (ch. 20).

It will be noted that Satan's doom is phased and includes an astonishing development (in 7–10).

Phase 1 is his removal from the earth. His two human puppets, the political dictator and his religious accomplice, have already been consigned to the 'fiery lake' (19:20). But that is not to be his fate – yet. He is to be confined rather than consigned, taken into custody to await final judgement (as some of his colleagues are already; 2 Pet 2:4; Jude 6).

Who will remove him? Not God, not Christ, not the church, but one unnamed angel. What an indignity for one who has had the whole world in his power (1 John 5:19)! This point is important, for this act has sometimes been confused with statements in the Gospels (e.g. Matt 12:29; 16:19).

How will he be removed? This has misleadingly been called 'the binding of Satan' by those who want to identify it with Jesus' victory over the devil when tempted in the wilderness (Luke 4:13–14; Matt 12:29). But it is far more than being bound. There are five verbs, not one. Satan is seized, chained, thrown, locked, sealed. He is thus rendered totally ineffective as well as removed altogether from his earthly sphere of influence. The incident should be labelled the *banishment* of Satan. The master of disguise and distortion is no longer around. He is unable to 'deceive the nations' any more (20:3).

To say that this has already happened is surely to be self-deceived. Yet this is frequently done in the interests of identifying the 'millennium' with the present church age. His 'binding' is then limited to failing to prevent the spread of the gospel, while unbelievers remain firmly under his control. The absurdity of this application is obvious. If the world is like it is after Satan has been seized, chained, thrown, locked and sealed, what will it be like when he is 'released' again?! Who would dare claim that he is not deceiving the nations right now?

Where will he be confined? Not on the earth, but 'under' it. The word used for his location (in Greek *abussos* = bottomless) refers to the immeasurable underworld, the lowest region of the abode of the dead, the home of demons (cf. Deut 30:13; Rom 10:7; Luke 8:31); it is used seven times in Revelation (9:1,2,11; 11:7; 17:8; 20:1, 3). Another name for this place of imprisonment is 'Tartarus' (this familiar term from the pagan world is used in 2 Pet 2:4). Wherever this is, it is certainly not on earth.

However, this incarceration is not permanent. God has one more purpose for Satan, which comes as a complete surprise later in this chapter. What happens in the meanwhile, between his restraint and subsequent release?

SAINTS REIGNING (20:4–6)

The removal of the beast, the false prophet (19:20) and the devil (20:3) will leave a political vacuum in the world. Who will take over its government? But a prior question needs to be faced: will there be a need for anyone to take it over? To put it another way: will there be anyone left to govern?

Will anyone survive the 'Armageddon' conflict described in chapter 19? First impressions might suggest that no one is left alive on earth. The vultures are invited to consume 'the flesh of all people' (19:18). After the two leaders are taken captive alive, the 'rest of them' are killed (19:21). This has been taken to refer to the entire population of the world, but a more careful reading shows that these inclusive terms are qualified by the term 'the kings of the earth and their armies', that is, the vast host that had 'gathered' for the battle (19:19).

That many people are not involved is clearly indicated in the sequel, where Satan has to be restrained from deceiving 'the nations' (20:3) and later is able to gather a huge following on his release (20:8).

So there will still be a need for world government. Who will constitute it? The answer is both individual and corporate: Christ and his faithful followers.

The word 'thrones' is plural (the only other such in the whole book is 4:4). Since the scene is on earth, they are not to be confused with either God's eternal throne in heaven (chs. 4–5) or with the 'great white throne' of final judgement after earth has 'fled' (20:11). The collective noun covers all 'seats of government', local, regional, national and international. Their purpose is the administration of justice; they will be used by those 'given authority to judge' (20:4). But who are they?

Here we face a rather difficult grammatical issue: does the text indicate one, two or three groups of 'rulers'? At first sight, it seems that only those who have been martyred for Christ reign with him. They have been 'beheaded because of their testimony for Jesus and because of the word of God' (20:4; this dual charge was the reason for John's imprisonment and the basis of his call for endurance, 1:9; 14:12). They have been 'faithful, even to the point of death' (2:10), which means to the extent of dying, not just until the moment of dying; it is widely misapplied at funerals after natural death.

Closer examination reveals that 'those given authority to judge' are not necessarily the same as those 'beheaded'. Note the extra phrase: '*and* I saw' inserted between the two groups. It sounds as if they are not entirely the same, yet not entirely different! The simplest explanation is that the latter is a section of the former. John sees the faithful followers of Jesus sharing his reign and particularly notices among them those who chose to die rather than deny their Lord. This would fit in with the promise that *all* who hold on until he comes and do his will 'to the end' will rule the nations (2:25–27), while for *some* this will mean martyrdom (2:10).

222 WHEN JESUS RETURNS

It is easy to see why the latter should be singled out for special mention. What an encouragement to those hearing the death sentence pronounced on them by earthly judges to know that one day they would be sitting on their 'thrones'. This would combine vindication with compensation. At a deeper level, their own experience of injustice in court would strengthen their ambition to be absolutely fair when they come to carry the responsibility. What an amazing reversal of roles!

Some have seen yet another subgroup in those who had 'not worshipped the beast or his image and had not received his mark on their foreheads or on their hands' (20:4). This could refer to those who refused to give in, but escaped with their lives. That there will be such is hinted at elsewhere in Revelation (12:6,17 and 18:4, for example). If there were no survivors, there would be no living saints to greet Christ on his return, to be 'changed in the twinkling of an eye' (1 Cor 15:51–52; 1 Thess 4:17). But whether Revelation 20 specifically refers to these or is further defining the 'beheaded' is an open question; this author inclines to the latter. The former would be included in the larger body first mentioned.

So one overall group is in view, with focus on one section in the fore-ground – saints in general and martyrs in particular.

How can martyrs be reigning on this earth? Put out of the world for their faith, they are now back in it. They must have been brought back to life, their disembodied spirits re-embodied for life here on earth. In other words they have experienced a 'resurrection' (20:15; this noun, *anastasis*, used 42 times in the New Testament, always refers to a physical miracle, the raising of a body; it is never used of regeneration, the new birth). The language implies that John actually saw this happening in his vision of the future, so the 'picture' was a movie! He had earlier seen the 'souls' of the martyrs crying for divine retribution on their murderers (6:9). Now he sees them in resurrected bodies reigning on the earth.

This is yet another clear indication that the millennial reign follows the second coming of Jesus, since it is at that moment that 'those who belong to him' receive their new bodies (1 Cor 15:23; 1 Thess 4:16).

The distinction between this 'first resurrection' of the 'blessed and holy' and 'the rest of the dead' could hardly be clearer. We know from other scriptures that the whole human race, the wicked as well as the righteous, will be raised from the dead before the day of judgement (Dan 12:2; John 5:29; Acts 24:15). However, to refer to this *fact* as 'the general resurrection', an unbiblical term, is misleading, since it implies a single *event*. In Revelation we learn that the two categories are raised on different dates, widely separated in time. There will be two resurrections, the 'first' and the 'rest', at the beginning and end of 'the thousand years'.

That the two happenings are identical in nature is confirmed by the use of exactly the same verb for both (the third person plural aorist tense indicative of *zao*, which means: to exercise the functions of life, here translated as 'come to life'). It is true that this word can very occasionally be used in a spiritual sense (e.g. John 5:25, where the context indicates this metaphorical use); but its normal meaning is physical (as in John 11:25; Rom 14:9), particularly in this book so far (Rev 1:18; 2:8; 13:14).

There is the further point that 'came to life' in verse 4 is in clear contrast to 'beheaded', both physical events. They must have been 'spiritually raised with Christ' long before their martyrdom; and after it they were fully conscious and able to communicate with him (6:9). Like him, they experienced physical death and resurrection – but neither interrupted their 'spiritual' or even 'mental' life, which was continuous from their conversion. It was their bodies that 'came to life', enabling them again to function in this physical world.

Without labouring the point, it is important to emphasise it, since both a-millennial and post-millennial viewpoints give the verb two entirely different meanings – spiritual regeneration in verse 4 and physical resurrection of the body in verse 5, though there is not a hint of this switch in the text itself. This violates an elementary rule of exegesis: the same word in the same context has the same meaning unless *clearly* indicated otherwise. Let an older scholar, Dean Alford, summarise this inconsistency:

> ... if in such a passage the first resurrection may be understood to mean *spiritual* rising with Christ, while the second means *literal* rising from the grave; then there is an end to all significance in language, and Scripture is wiped out as a testimony to anything. If the first resurrection is spiritual, then so is the second, which I suppose none will be hardy enough to maintain; but if the second is literal, then so is the first, which in common with the whole primitive Church and many of the best modern expositors, I do maintain and receive as an article of faith and hope. (Quoted in William E. Biederwolf, *The Prophecy Handbook*, World Bible Publishers, 1991 reprint of 1924 original, p. 697)

This concept of two resurrections, of the righteous and the wicked, widely separated in time, was not original to this book. The idea was quite widespread among the Jews of Jesus' day. Many expected the 'righteous' dead to be raised before the Messianic reign on earth, while the wicked would only be raised for judgement at its end (some already said the interval between would be a thousand years). That is why Jesus could refer, without explanation, to 'the resurrection of the righteous', when talking to Pharisees (Luke 14:14). They already believed in two resurrections, while the Sadducees believed in none (Luke 20:27).

Three statements are made about those who 'have part' in the first resurrection. First, their *sanctity*. They are 'blessed and holy'. By implication those in the second are cursed and evil. Second, their *security*. At the second coming their salvation from sin will be complete (Phil 1:6; 1 John 3:2). They will be sure then that there will be no further risk of suffering 'the second death' which is 'the lake of fire' (20:6,14). Third, their *sovereignty*. Their 'kingship' will be combined with priesthood (compare 1:6

with 20:6). They will act as managers for Christ and mediators for the people. This dual function replaces the political role of the beast and the religious role of the false prophet.

This situation is not permanent. The 'reign' on this earth will end with the earth, though it will continue in the new earth (22:5). The 'thousand years' come to an end in the most surprising manner:

SATAN RELEASED (20:7-10)

The development revealed here is so totally unexpected that it could hardly have been invented by human imagination. Its very strangeness is a hallmark of divine inspiration.

We now see why Satan was not thrown into hell earlier, along with his two human agents (19:20). God is going to use him just once more. He is to be given a final fling! Released on parole, he is allowed to 'deceive the nations' one last time.

The nature of this deception has much in common with his very first trickery of the human race (Gen 3). Then it was two persons, now it is many ethnic groups. But the appeal is the same: moral autonomy, freedom from God's government (which now includes Christ and his saints). Since this 'kingdom' is now on earth, a literal 'body', it can be attacked with military might. A huge force is gathered from 'the four corners of the earth' to march on the seat of government, 'the city he [God] loves', clearly Jerusalem, the millennial headquarters of the 'United Nations' (20:9; cf. Isa 2:1-5; Mic 4:1-5; Matt 5:35).

This last 'battle' of all must not be confused with 'Armageddon', which was only the sixth bowl (16:16) and took place before the thousand years (19:19-21). It is identified by a different title, 'Gog and Magog', the names used by Ezekiel for the 'prince' and his followers who attack the land of Israel *after* God's people are re-established there and the Davidic dynasty restored to the throne (see Ezek 37-39). It seems that 'Gog' in Revelation is the last of a number of names given to Satan (like 'Apollyon' in

9:11 and 'Beelzebub' in Matt 10:25) and 'Magog' refers to the international army he persuades to fight for him.

The attempt to besiege and attack the world capital fails completely. The battle is never joined. Neither Christians nor Christ himself need to engage the enemy. God himself sends 'fire from heaven' (Gen 15:17; Lev 9:24; Judg 13:20; 1 Kgs 18:38; 2 Chr 7:1; Luke 9:54; Rev 9:18). Though the devil could tap such destructive power (13:13), it is now used to destroy his entire militia. He himself is thrown into the lake of fire, where his two human agents have already been for the thousand years.

Verse 10 is very important. It is the clearest statement of the nature of hell in the New Testament. The language is plain and simple; it cannot be dismissed as 'highly symbolic'. It is a place of 'torment', which can mean nothing other than conscious pain, whether physical or emotional, or both. This understanding goes back to Jesus himself (Matt 25:30; Luke 16:23–25). The suffering is continuous ('day and night') and never-ending ('for ever and ever' is an English equivalent of the Greek phrase *eis tous aionas ton aionon*, literally 'into the ages of the ages', the very strongest phrase in that language for everlasting time, cf. 4:9–10; 5:13–14; 7:12; 10:6; 11:15; 14:11; 15:7; 19:3; 22:5).

Since 'they', the subject of this statement, includes two human beings, the modern notion of 'annihilationism' (the belief that the 'wicked' are consigned to oblivion by extinction, either at death or after the day of judgement) is quite ruled out. Jesus taught the same punishment for all he would reject in judgement (Matt 25:41, 46). For a fuller treatment of this vital issue, see my book: *The Road to Hell* (Hodder and Stoughton 1992).

So ends Satan's reign in this world. Having been the prince, ruler and even 'god' of this world (John 12:31; 2 Cor 4:4), he now meets his doom and shares the common destiny of all who rebel against the kingly rule of God, whether human or angelic (Matt 25:41; Rev 12:4).

Did he not expect this to happen? Did he expect his last bid for earthly sovereignty to succeed? Was he self-deluded as well as the deceiver of nations? Did he really think he was stronger than God's people and therefore than God himself? Or did he, knowing his fate was sealed and his end near, seek to take as many as he could to share his ruin, in a last fit of frustrated rage? Perhaps we shall never know. Perhaps we don't need to.

In fact, this whole passage raises many tantalising questions, to which no answers are given. Hardly anything is said about the 'millennium' itself and how it will be worked out in practice. We can only conclude that such information was not relevant to the purpose of Revelation. It is enough to know that the forces of good will be publicly vindicated and the forces of evil finally removed.

So we have the basic facts. We are told *what* will happen at the end, but not *why* events will take this course. Of course, God is not obliged to give us his reasons for anything he does, as Job found out the hard way many centuries ago (Job 40:1–5; 42:1–6). There is a place for reverent agnosticism (Rom 9:20).

Yet the conundrum persists. Why 'on earth' is the devil given a final chance to do such damage at the very end of a thousand years of good government? And why 'on earth' is there such a thousand years anyway? While avoiding sheer speculation, we may feel our way towards an understanding by considering the spiritual effects of these two developments.

To take the positive one first, the millennial rule of Christ and his saints on this earth will be a visible vindication of him and them in the eyes of the world. It will demonstrate just what this world can be like when Satan is out of it and Jesus is back in it, indeed, what it could have been all along, had it not been polluted by sin.

At a deeper level, the millennium will affirm that this is God's world, that he made it for his Son and that it will all be in his hands again. The creation is basically good and the earth must not be written off as 'beyond redemption'. History must end with a consummation rather than a catastrophe, with redemption rather than ruin.

If it is asked why this climax should occur on the 'old' earth before the 'new' earth appears it can be pointed out that the 'world' (i.e. the unbelieving people on the earth) would otherwise never see the victory of good over evil.

And there is a remarkable parallel between our own redemption and that of our planet. In both cases the spiritual regeneration precedes the physical. We have to work out our salvation while still in the 'old' material body until it is 'transformed' into the 'new' one (Phil 3:21). This will mark the completion of the restoration to our original state. In much the same way, the new earth will mark the conclusion of the process begun during the millennium.

The negative aspect is a little more puzzling. Why is Satan released again at the end of this 'ideal' regime? One can only conclude that it is a convincing demonstration that conditions do not change the human heart. The big lie that sin is environmentally caused is finally exposed. After a thousand years of peace and prosperity, there are still ungrateful and discontented people around.

Of course it needs to be remembered that the millennial rule will not be democratic, but a 'benevolent dictatorship', not chosen by popular vote but imposed by divine choice. It is in this sense that both Christ and Christians will rule with a 'rod [or sceptre] of iron' (2:27; 12:5; 19:15). This is not a symbol of cruel tyranny, as might be supposed, but of strong rule that cannot be broken. It will include strict censorship, for example, which is always resented by the unrighteous.

In spite of the many benefits of this 'good' government, its impartial administration of perfect justice and its generous welfare of all, there will still be many subjects who would rather forfeit these to regain their moral, or rather immoral, autonomy. Their resentful, rebellious hearts will want to be free from the restraints imposed by the Lord and his people. This is why Satan can gather a worldwide force. He can only deceive those who desire what he offers.

It becomes apparent that the millennium is a fitting prelude to the day of judgement. The issue is made crystal clear – to accept or reject the divine rule, the kingdom of heaven on earth. This has been the issue all through history, but in the millennium it comes to a head. This provides the double proof of the need for an eternal separation within the human race. The new universe God intends to create can only be inhabited by those who have voluntarily and eagerly 'entered the kingdom', embracing the will of God for his creatures with glad and thankful hearts.

It is therefore entirely appropriate that the millennial passage (20:1–10) is immediately followed by that separation on the great day of judgement, for which 'the rest of the dead', even those lost at sea, 'come to life' again. For them the 'books' which contain the record of their godless lives on earth are sufficient evidence for their sentence. The 'book of life' contains the names of all who remained faithful to Jesus (3:5), who had part in the first resurrection and reigned with him for the thousand years.

CHAPTER SIXTEEN

The Broader Context

Our study so far has led to the 'pre-millennial' understanding of Revelation 20. That is, the second coming of Christ *pre*-cedes his thousand-year reign on earth, which in turn comes before the final judgement.

But this interpretation is far from universally held in the Christian church. It has been frequently attacked on 'biblical' and 'philosophical' grounds. We shall begin with the former, since divine revelation is more weighty than human speculation.

It is frequently pointed out that this chapter is the *only* passage in the whole Bible that speaks clearly about a 'millennium'. Some go further and would not admit that it is clear even here, since Revelation is 'highly symbolic' and therefore obscure throughout! For either reason or both, it is considered unreasonable to build a major doctrine on these verses.

Hopefully, the preceding exegesis shows that the passage is far from enigmatic when allowed to speak for itself without prior imposed conclusions. And even if it were the only reference, it is still part of the word of God. Once should be enough for God to say what he wants us to hear (and we need to remember the emphatic sixfold repetition of the 'thousand years').

Furthermore, the church has not shown any reluctance to build other teaching on one passage, even one verse! One thinks of the insistence on a trinitarian formula for baptism (based on Matt 28:19; all other references are in the name of Jesus Christ only). Then there is the application of the name 'Israel' to the church (based on one ambiguous phrase in Gal 6:16; over seventy other references in the New Testament all refer to the Jewish people).

It would seem that prejudice may be operating when it comes to the millennium!

But there can be genuine 'biblical' objections to building beliefs on one passage, two in particular:

i. Negatively, the absence of confirmation
ii. Positively, the presence of contradiction

Quite simply, if no other scriptures point in the same direction or if many other scriptures point in a different direction, a passage must be re-examined in this light. The latter is the more serious difficulty.

ABSENCE OF CONFIRMATION

Certainly, there is no other unequivocal statement about the millennium elsewhere in the New Testament. But there are a number of indirect references, perhaps all the more impressive because they are incidental.

There are, of course, some clear promises in the rest of the book of Revelation. 'Overcomers' will 'rule the nations' (2:26–27). The redeemed will 'reign on the earth' (5:10). The 'kingdom of the world' will become the 'kingdom of Christ' (11:15). Chapter 20 is clearly the fulfilment of these predictions.

When we turn to Paul's letters we find a number of hints. Perhaps the clearest is in his first letter to Corinth. Upbraiding the Corinthian believers for suing each other in pagan courts, he says: 'Do you not know that the saints will judge the world? And if you are to judge the world, are you not competent to judge trivial cases?' (1 Cor 6:3). This cannot refer to the final judgement, which is in the hands of the Lord alone. It points to a day when Christians will be responsible for the administration of justice. Note that Paul assumes they have already been told about this.

Later, in the same letter, dealing with the subject of resurrection, he describes the order in which people will be raised, apparently in three phases:

i. 'Christ, the *first* fruits;
ii. *then*, when he comes, those who belong to him.
iii. *Then* the end will come' (1 Cor 15:23–24).

Admittedly, the third phrase does not mention resurrection specifically. Nevertheless, he does not state that there will be a 'general' resurrection of the whole human race at the time of Christ's return. But the two Greek words translated 'then' (*epeita* and *eita*) both mean 'subsequent'; if the third event was 'concurrent' with the second, another word would have been used (*tote*). He immediately proceeds to talk about a 'reign' of Christ *preceding* 'the end' which culminates in the final vanquishing of death itself (1 Cor 15:25–26; cf. Rev 20:14).

That Paul believed in a resurrection of faithful Christians *before* the rest of mankind is confirmed by his use of a most unusual phrase (in Phil 3:11). Normally translated: 'resurrection from the dead', the Greek phrase actually includes a double preposition, *ek*, literally: 'the *out*-resurrection *out* from the dead', which may be paraphrased: 'out from among the dead'. In other words, this is not a general resurrection of all, but of a limited event predating that. Not surprisingly, it is used of Jesus himself (e.g. 1 Pet 1:3). Here, Paul is using it of Christians who 'press on' to '*attain*' it. Nothing needs to be done to attain the general resurrection (except to die!). Clearly, Paul is referring to the 'first resurrection' of the 'blessed and holy' (Rev 20:6).

In the same letter Paul looks forward to the day when 'at the name of Jesus every knee will bow ... and every tongue confess that Jesus Christ is Lord' (Phil 2:10–11; cf. Isa 45:23 and Rev 5:13). When did he expect this universal recognition to take place?

Writing to Timothy, and perhaps quoting an early hymn, Paul promises: 'If we endure, we will also reign with him' (2 Tim 2:12;

cf. Rev 3:21). This saying is a perfect summary of the whole message of Revelation. Note that almost all the New Testament references to Christians reigning are in the *future* tense (Rom 5:17 is one of the few exceptions; the primary reference here is reigning over sin rather than over others). Followers of Jesus must walk in his footsteps – suffering leads to glory, the cross comes before the crown.

These Pauline references may be few, but that is no excuse for dismissing them. He only mentions the Lord's Supper in one letter, and only then because of its abuse – yet his teaching on that is taken seriously. And his asides are significant precisely because they indicate what he takes for granted.

Working back through the New Testament we come to the Book of Acts. We note the same phrase: 'out from among the dead' in the apostolic preaching of Jesus' resurrection (Acts 4:2).

But the crucial reference is right at the beginning, the very last question asked by the disciples before Jesus returned to heaven: 'Lord, are you at this time going to restore the kingdom to Israel?' (Acts 1:6). All scholars agree that by 'kingdom' they meant political autonomy under a monarch of the Davidic dynasty. The question contains four 'premises' (prior assumptions):

i.   Israel once had this 'kingdom'.
ii. Israel has lost this 'kingdom'.
iii. Israel will recover this 'kingdom'.
iv. Jesus is the one to achieve this.

The only uncertainty they have is about the timing: now or later?

It is vital to notice that Jesus does not question the question as he often did when they were based on wrong assumptions (a modern example is the trick question: 'Have you stopped beating your wife?'). He accepts all four basic premises and deals only with the query about timing: 'It is not for you to know the times or dates the Father has set by his own authority' (Acts

1:7). In other words, this event will happen. It is already on God's calendar. But the dating is not their concern. There is other immediate business to attend to: to be his witnesses to the ends of the earth by the power of the Holy Spirit (Acts 1:8). That this is the thrust of Jesus' reply will become obvious by imagining another question: 'Lord, are you at this time going to assassinate Pilate and Herod?' Consider the implications if the reply is still: 'It is not for you to know the times or dates the Father has set'. What would the disciples have understood this to mean?

And there is a later indication that this was the conviction the apostles themselves came to in answer to their own question. In his second public sermon, Peter says that Jesus 'must remain in heaven until the *time* comes for God to *restore* everything' (Acts 3:21); the italicised words are exactly the same unusual Greek words as in Acts 1:6. It is hard to resist the conclusion that the apostles had put two and two together after the ascension and realised that the kingdom would be restored to Israel at his return, even though they still did not 'know the time or dates the Father has set' (Acts 1:7).

So Jesus is accepting their belief that one day the monarchy would be restored to Israel. But when can a descendant of David again sit on a throne in Jerusalem? And who will it be? If the answer is not Christ's millennial rule on earth, the New Testament gives no other possibility.

Turning to the Gospels, especially Matthew and Luke, we find the same sort of clues scattered throughout their pages. At the beginning of the story, an angel promises Mary that the Lord God will give her son 'the throne of his father David' (Luke 1:32). This was an earthly throne, not one in heaven, as Mary would have understood.

Jesus was born 'king of the Jews' (Matt 2:2) and he died as 'king of the Jews' (Luke 23:38). The placard of his crime, pinned to the cross on which he was executed, elicited the plea of a dying criminal: 'Jesus, remember me when you come into your kingdom' (Luke 23:42). In spite of all appearances and circumstances, he believed Jesus was the Messiah and would return one day to claim the throne of Israel. Jesus told him that long before then, even that very day, they would be together 'in paradise' (Luke 23:43; note that Jesus avoided the word 'kingdom' and used instead the Persian word for a palace garden, that is, to be in a privileged place with a royal personage).

Others had anticipated this coming monarchy. The ambitious mother of James and John requested that 'one of these two sons of mine may sit at your right hand and the other at your left in your kingdom' (Matt 20:21). Undoubtedly, she saw this 'kingdom' in earthly terms, a restored monarchy in Israel requiring prime and deputy ministers. Jesus accepts these assumptions but points out that he will not be responsible for the appointments. Again, the Father decides these things (Matt 20:23, note that the places are prepared for the people, not vice-versa).

Jesus did promise the disciples that 'when the Son of Man sits on his glorious throne, you who have followed me will also sit on twelve thrones, judging the twelve tribes of Israel' (Matt 19:28). Some place must be found in our thinking for the fulfilment of this, as well as for more general predictions like 'the meek will inherit the earth' (Matt 5:5). When will this happen?

On a number of occasions, Jesus offered earthly rewards for faithful service. He offered 'riches' and 'property of your own' to those who handled money and other people's possessions with integrity (Luke 16:11–12). In the parables about his return, reliable servants are awarded greater responsibility: to be put in charge of many things (Matt 24:21,23) or of five and ten cities (Luke 19:17). The councils, as well as the courts (1 Cor 6:2), will be in Christian hands.

That Jesus himself believed in two resurrections, separated in time, is indicated by his use of the common term: 'the resurrection of the righteous' (Luke 14:14) and his endorsement of moral qualifications for the first: 'those who are considered worthy of taking part in that age and in the resurrection from [literally, 'out from'] the dead' (Luke 20:35).

So far we have only been skipping through the pages of the

New Testament. But the apostles' expectations of the future have their roots in the prophecies of the Old Testament, to which we now turn.

There are, of course, many promises of an earth transformed under the rule of God himself, a time of unparalleled peace and prosperity in which nations can safely engage in multilateral disarmament. Harmony will be matched by longevity in human life. This vision of an earth restored to its original condition pervades the prophets, but is particularly clear in Isaiah.

There are, however, two ambiguities in this Hebrew hope. First, would it be brought about by a divine agent (God himself) or a human one (the Messiah)? Second, could it be done on this old earth or would it require the creation of a new one? This double tension is not resolved within the canon of Jewish scriptures, but by the time of Jesus a programme may be found in other writings (intertestamental literature known today as the 'apocrypha' and 'pseudepigrapha'). An emerging expectation anticipates a Messianic age on the old earth (estimates of its duration vary from forty to one thousand years) *before* God creates a new earth (Isa 65:17). This pattern is remarkably parallel to that outlined in Revelation 20.

There is one scripture which emphatically predicts a time when God's people will rule this world. Significantly, it belongs to the same 'apocalyptic' genre of literature as Revelation, namely, the second half of the book of Daniel. The two writings have a great deal in common and illuminate each other.

In particular, the seventh chapter is quite specific about a future reign of God's people on this earth, especially in verses 13–22. This section begins with 'one like a son of man, coming with the clouds' (verse 13), quoted by Jesus of himself (Mark 14:62) and clearly a reference to his second advent. This is followed by: 'he was given authority, glory and sovereign power; all peoples, nations and men of every language worshipped him' (verse 14). There follow three affirmations that he will share his authority with his people: 'the saints of the Most High will receive the kingdom' (verse 18); 'the Ancient of Days came and pronounced judgement in favour of the saints of the Most High, and the time came when they possessed the kingdom' (verse 22); 'then the sovereignty, power and greatness of the kingdoms *under the whole heaven* will be handed over to the saints, the people of the Most High' (verse 27). The kingdoms thus transferred are specifically defined as 'rising from the *earth*' (verse 17).

It is almost impossible to avoid linking Daniel with Revelation. The parallels are too many to be coincidental and extend even to such details as hair colour (Dan 7:9 and Rev 1:14). The overall picture of the Ancient of Days, Son of Man and the saints taking over the kingdoms on earth in Daniel surely corresponds to the millennium in Revelation.

In summarising this part of our study, it seems right to say that there is considerable evidence, both direct and indirect, that other scriptures confirm the concept of a millennial reign on earth. But what about those that seem to contradict such a notion?

PRESENCE OF CONTRADICTION

It is claimed that some texts actually preclude the possibility that Jesus will ever reign over an earthly kingdom.

There is his much-quoted statement at his trial before Pontius Pilate: 'My kingdom is not of this world' (John 18:36). The little word 'of' has been given many different meanings – not in this world, not like this world, not for this world, etc. However, the statement is more likely to concern the origin and source of his kingdom than its nature and location. Indeed, he went on to say: 'my kingdom is *from* another place'. But there is a practical aspect, namely the power with which it is established and protected, which will not be by military might. Significantly, in Revelation 19 and 20, when armies gather in the Middle East to attack and destroy God's people, the latter are not armed to defend themselves; Christ's word and God's fire achieve the victory on both occasions.

But the main claim for contradiction of the millennium rests on those texts which speak of events as *simultaneous* which would be widely separated in time by a millennial interlude.

For example, there are verses that appear to speak of a 'general' resurrection of all humankind, righteous and wicked, at the same time. The words of Jesus spring to mind: 'A time is coming when *all* who are in their graves will hear his voice and come out, those who have done good will rise to live, and those who have done evil will rise to be condemned' (John 5:29; but note that in verse 25 there is an earlier selective raising that anticipates this).

There are also verses which imply that the second advent and the final judgement occur together. '*When* the Son of Man comes in his glory, and all the angels with him . . . he will separate the people' (Matt 25:31–32). 'This [God's vengeance against persecutors] will happen *when* the Lord Jesus is revealed from heaven in blazing fire with his powerful angels' (1 Thess 1:7).

And there are passages which imply that the dissolution of the old heaven and earth and the creation of the new heaven and earth follow straight on from his coming (2 Pet 3:3–10). Actually, second century expositors widely used verse 8 as a proof-text for the millennium, since its mention of 'a thousand years' came *between* the discussion of his coming and the announcement of the new creation (see page 260)! Such exegesis sounds somewhat bizarre today, since that verse is a general statement that could be applied to any period in history, but its widespread use in this way bears testimony to the early belief in a millennial rule of Christ after his return.

In all these cases we may have an example of a common feature of prophecy – the foreshortening of separate future events into one prediction. The phenomenon is often illustrated by viewing distant mountains through a telescope, so that separate peaks are apparently linked. The outstanding example in the Old Testament is that only one coming of the Christ is seen, whereas later revelation shows that there will be two advents, widely separated in time. There is a specific case in Isaiah (65:17–25), which blends in one vision the millennium on the old earth and eternity in the new; people will die at a much greater age in the former, but not at all in the latter.

There are examples in Jesus' predictions as well. A simple one is his compression of the intermediate state of Hades with the ultimate state of hell in the parable of the rich man and Lazarus (Luke 16:19-26). A more complex case is his condensing of the fall of Jerusalem in AD 70 and the disasters preceding his return into one discourse, so that it becomes quite difficult to know to which he is referring (Matt 24; Mark 13; Luke 21).

Jesus did not need to give full details whenever he mentioned the future. That would have involved needless repetition and could have caused distraction. On each occasion he selected those aspects relevant to the point he was making, if necessary compacting separate items into one statement.

The same may be said of the phrase: 'day of the Lord'. This is used of both the second advent and the last judgement, but to insist that the two events must therefore take place within the same twenty-four hours is to miss the varied meanings of the word 'day', which can equally well refer to an epoch (as in 'the day of the horse and cart is over'). In the Bible 'the day of the Lord' is in contrast to the era when sin and Satan have been allowed to govern the world. It is the 'day' when the Lord directly intervenes in world affairs, to bring his purposes to completion. The 'length' of that 'day' is immaterial.

CHAPTER SEVENTEEN

The Philosophic Problem

Intellectual difficulties prevent some from embracing the idea of a future, earthly millennium. They simply cannot comprehend how such a state of affairs could be brought into being or maintained. The problem may simply be a lack of imagination, unable to envisage such a radical change in our social and natural environment.

Others find it hard to fit it all together. The most common riddle is how resurrected saints with new bodies can live alongside mortals still in their 'first' mode of existence – overlooking the fact that this precise situation has already occurred between Jesus' resurrection and ascension. He sat and talked with his disciples, ate with them, even cooked breakfast for them.

But mortals will still have sexual appetites and activity, while the risen saints 'neither marry nor are given in marriage' (Luke 20:35). How will they feel about this? Will they be above temptation?

Then there are questions about location and communication. If Jesus is reigning bodily he can only be in one place at a time. Will he stay in Jerusalem or travel? And how can his scattered deputies governing different regions be said to be 'with the Lord for ever' after his second coming (1 Thess 4:17)?

It is quite easy to compile a huge list of such perplexing questions. But it would be highly improbable if we get any answers beforehand. The fact is that the Bible does not deal with such matters. One of the most striking features of Revelation 20 is its total silence about conditions during the 'thousand years'. Clearly, it would not help us to know any more than we do.

Indeed, such speculative meditation could prove a dangerous distraction from the vital task of living this present decisive phase of our existence.

We also need to remember that it is just as hard, if not harder, to imagine what endless life on the new earth will be like. We would have had real problems picturing life in this world if we could have been told about it before we were born. Even our forefathers would have found it well-nigh impossible to picture men driving a car and playing golf on the moon, using televisions and computers, engineering genes. The important point is that our comprehension is limited by our present knowledge and experience and it is very foolish to say a thing is impossible simply because we don't understand how it could work.

However, we need to identify the reasons why we find it difficult to believe some things. Behind many of the practical questions already mentioned there lurks a major mental blockage due to the Greek influence on Western philosophy.

The millennium is essentially a Hebrew concept and therefore alien to Greek thought. Linked as it is to the hope of *bodily* resurrection, itself an object of ridicule to those who believed in the immortal soul needing to be set free from its physical prison (cf. Acts 17:32), the whole idea of a future period of existence in this material world is offensive.

For the Greeks never managed to get the spiritual and physical realities properly related. Unlike the Hebrews, whose doctrine of creation prevented them from segregating the two spheres, the Greek thinkers sharply distinguished between eternal and temporal, sacred and secular, heaven and earth, soul and body. Plato concentrated on the former and Aristotle on the latter; neither 'got it together'.

This led to an ambiguous attitude to the 'flesh', leading to extremes of indulgence or repression. Inevitably 'evil' came to be associated and even identified with the physical aspect of existence. Consequently 'salvation' was the liberation of the 'soul' from the body and its environment, either through discipline or death.

Nothing could be further from biblical truth, which affirms that the physical universe is basically 'good' (Gen 1), spoiled only by moral pollution. Physical appetites, including sex, were intended by God to be enjoyed. The body can be a holy temple, a dwelling-place for God's Spirit. His eternal purpose includes immortal bodies in a renewed universe.

Even in the days of the New Testament, the battle was 'joined' between these utterly different philosophies (see 1 Tim 4:1-5 for just one example). The insidious influence of such 'Gnosticism' (the claim to superior knowledge of reality, the opposite of 'agnosticism') became a major threat to the Judeo-Christian faith in the second century. Believers were in danger of becoming 'super-spiritual'.

The sad fact is that Greek philosophy took over the major part of the Christian church and has coloured, or rather discoloured, theology to this very day. Scripture is read through Greek spectacles by most Westerners (it is vital to realise that though the New Testament is written in the common, *koine*, Greek of its day, all but one of its writers and all of its thought were Hebrew).

This disaster happened in North Africa. Alexandria, on the Egyptian coast, boasted the most prestigious university in the ancient world after Athens. Being outside Greece, its unique contribution was to apply Greek philosophy to other cultures. It was here that the Old Testament was translated into the Greek language by seventy scholars, it is said (hence its name, the 'Septuagint' or 'LXX' for short). But with language can come thought and Jewish scholars began to 'think Greek', the most notable being Philo.

Much later, the same subtle process affected Christian theologians in this university, notably Clement and Origen. The latter developed a radically new method of handling scripture: the *allegorical*. He taught his students to look behind the literal statements in the Bible and find the 'spiritual' meaning and message. This was a major step away from the 'plain sense' and has persisted to the present ('You don't still take the Bible literally, do you?'). Its modern form treats scripture as a source of 'values' rather than facts.

This 'spiritualising' method was taken much further by a bishop in Hippo (now in Tunisia), called Augustine. His promiscuous youth left him with a strong association of 'physical' and 'evil'; for ever after he regarded all sexual activity as morally compromised, even within marriage. It is perhaps understandable that he wholeheartedly embraced Plato's detachment of the 'spiritual' from the material which he had thoroughly studied in his 'classical' education. But it was a disaster for the church when he recast Christian doctrine within this framework. More than any other, he has influenced subsequent thinking, both Catholic and Protestant. It is no exaggeration to say that he succeeded in changing the church's mind-set from Hebrew to Greek.

While this has affected many major doctrines, we are concerned with its influence on millennialism. As we shall see, the only view of which we have any record in the 'church fathers' (as the scholars of the first few centuries are called) is the 'pre-millennial' interpretation of Revelation 20 already expounded – that is, the bodily return of Jesus will lead to his reigning on earth, for a thousand years before the day of judgement. There is no trace of any discussion or difference up to the time of Augustine.

But he changed all that. There is evidence that in his earlier ministry he believed and taught what had up till then been the 'orthodox' pre-millennial position, apparently universally held without question. But this understanding is incompatible with Platonic philosophy. It is far too physical to be spiritual, far too earthy for the 'kingdom of heaven'. Radical adjustments would have to be made, two in particular.

The first was to break the sequence in Revelation, separating chapter 20 from chapter 19 so that the order could be reversed and the 'millennium' passage then claimed to be a 'recapitulation' of events preceding the second advent, rather than following it. It is said to be a description of the 'church age' (which by then had only been five hundred years; now, fifteen centuries later, the figure of 'a thousand' must be regarded as a 'symbol' of at least two thousand!).

This change planted the seeds of the *post*-millennial view – the belief that Jesus will return *after* (i.e. 'post') the millennium. But that raised another question: after what kind of a 'millennium'? Even in Augustine's day, after the Emperor Constantine's conversion and the establishment of Christianity as the only recognised state religion, it was still somewhat difficult to see the world as totally under the control of Christ. More especially, the evidence hardly showed that Satan was no longer at work in it. So another major shift in interpretation was made.

This second move made the millennium a 'spiritual' reign. Christ rules in heaven rather than on earth, though this rule is manifested on earth wherever the gospel is preached and the church established. It is only within this sphere (the 'City of God', as Augustine called it) that Satan can be bound and banished.

This change planted the seeds of the '*a*-millennial' view – that Christ will never rule on earth in the 'earthly' sense (as in the 'throne of David'). The pre-fix 'a-' really means 'non-' (as in 'a-theist') but there is widespread reluctance to use the term 'non-millennial' to describe this position, since that would seem to imply a rejection of Revelation 20. The careful reader may have already realised that most 'a-millennialism' is really a 'spiritual' form of 'post-millennialism', and we shall be treating it as such.

Augustine carried so much weight that the pre-millennialism of the first few centuries was actually condemned as heresy by the Council of Ephesus in AD 431! It has been widely suspected ever since, by Catholic and Protestant alike, though the last two centuries have seen a rekindled interest, not least because of a renewed longing for the return of the Lord, stimulated by the deteriorating state of the world, which few would now deny.

This historical/philosophical background is a necessary preliminary to looking at the range of attitudes today. The three main positions were all in place by the sixth century. The 'pre-millennial' early church had become the 'post-millennial' or 'a-millennial' later church, through the Augustinian influx of Platonic philosophy.

But time has not stood still. Nor has thought. There have been developments in all three positions:

Some post-millennialists have returned to the concept of an earthly, political reign of Christ, through a church which will take over world government for an extended period *before* he returns. We must therefore distinguish between 'spiritual' and 'political' post-millennialism.

Pre-millennialism reappeared early in the nineteenth century, but in a new guise. It was part of a novel theological framework which divided the history of the world into seven distinct epochs, called 'dispensations', in each of which God dealt with mankind on a very different basis, or 'covenant'. The final 'dispensation' will be the restored 'kingdom' of Israel ruled over by Christ in Jerusalem, while Christians remain in heaven. So we must now distinguish between 'dispensational' pre-millennialism of modern times and its 'classical' form in the early church.

True 'a-millennialism', in its proper sense of 'non-millennialism', is really the product of the widespread 'liberalism' in the twentieth century. This either rejects the whole idea of a Christian 'millennium' as absurd, dismissing Revelation 20 altogether; or it regards the chapter as a 'myth'; a non-historic fable containing insights but not foresight (the 'thousand years' is simply part of the 'poetic' framework, like the 'six days' in the creation 'myth' and does not refer to any particular period of time). We will refer to these as 'sceptical' and 'mythical' forms of 'a-millennialism'.

Though there are some minor variations within them, this sixfold classification is the best we can come up with for contemporary discernment and discussion. The reader who has already given the matter some thought may identify his or her position by working through the eliminating questionnaire below.

1. Do you believe that the phrase 'a thousand years'

in Revelation 20 refers to a particular period of earthly history?

NO:　　　　　you are an A-MILLENNIALIST; proceed to 2.

YES:　　　　　proceed to 3.

2. Does the passage have any meaning for us today?

NO:　　　　　you are a SCEPTICAL A-MILLENNIALIST.

YES:　　　　　you are a MYTHICAL A-MILLENNIALIST.

3. Will Christ return after or before the thousand-year period?

AFTER:　　　you are a POST-MILLENNIALIST; proceed to 4.

BEFORE:　　you are a PRE-MILLENNIALIST; proceed to 5.

4. Does the 'thousand years' symbolically cover the whole of church history from first to second advent or literally the final part?

WHOLE:　　you are a SPIRITUAL POST-MILLEN-NIALIST.

PART:　　　you are a POLITICAL POST-MILLEN-NIALIST.

5. Will the 'thousand year' period be essentially Christian or Jewish in character?

CHRISTIAN: you are a CLASSICAL PRE-MILLEN-NIALIST.

JEWISH:　　you are a DISPENSATIONAL PRE-MIL-LENNIALIST.

So now you know! Or do you? If you are still in doubt, read on. Hopefully all will become clear as we examine each of these six positions in detail. We shall look at each from three perspectives: historical (how, when and why it developed), exegetical (how Revelation 20 is handled) and practical (its implications for evangelism and social action).

Of course, it is virtually impossible to be totally objective, especially in the last area, which is based on observation rather than statistics. And the discerning reader will have already guessed this writer's position ('classic pre-millennialism', in case you hadn't!). This study will conclude with a personal statement of the reasons for this conviction.

Nevertheless, a sincere attempt will be made to make a fair presentation of the various views. None is without difficulties, but some have rather more than others! Nor is the matter settled by majority vote, which has varied greatly in time and place.

For 'evangelical' readers, one question ought to be uppermost: which 'correctly handles the word of truth' (2 Tim 2:15)?

CHAPTER EIGHTEEN

The Different Views

1. 'SCEPTICAL' A-MILLENNIALISM

This view can only arise in the mind of someone who no longer believes in the inspiration and authority of scripture; who says the Bible may 'contain' the Word of God, but does not constitute it. It is a mixture of divine inspiration and human imagination. Discernment is needed to distinguish the wheat from the chaff. What the criteria are for this exercise varies from person to person and is therefore highly subjective. It has been called: 'reading the Bible with a pair of scissors'!

Revelation 20 is usually dismissed, along with most of the book and other 'apocalyptic' portions of scripture, frequently with a certain amount of contempt.

Underlying these sweeping rejections is a rationalistic scepticism born of the Enlightenment, which contaminated theological and biblical studies in Germany towards the end of the nineteenth century. The movement was labelled, 'Higher Criticism' of the Bible (as opposed to 'Lower Criticism' which simply sought to reconstruct the most accurate text). The basic assumption was that the supernatural realm (if it even exists) cannot affect the natural (Platonic dualism again!). Thus, miracles are excluded, unless a 'naturalistic' explanation can be found for them; as is prophecy, when predicting the future. Since Revelation is largely the latter, it is highly suspect and virtually expunged from the Bible. So we are not able to critique the exegesis of this view!

However, it has to be admitted that some evangelicals, while disagreeing violently in principle with this approach, agree with it in practice! Whether consciously or unconsciously, they neglect the 'apocalyptic' scriptures in general and ignore the millennial issue in particular. They do not feel it important to wrestle with the meaning of Revelation 20, regarding the debate over it as an academic distraction of no practical or spiritual value.

This, of course, is to accuse the early church of error when Revelation was included in the 'canon' (= rule of measurement) of scripture. Incredibly, all the major Protestant Reformers (Luther, Calvin and Zwingli) were of this opinion!

The effects of this neglect vary according to how seriously other scriptures are taken. Heirs of the Reformation still hold firmly to the other major features of the end-time: the return of Christ, the day of judgement, hell and heaven. But there is less interest in the earth, both old and 'new'.

In the absence of a real meeting between the kingdom of heaven and the kingdoms of earth in the millennium, evangelicals concentrated on the former and the next world, while liberals concentrated on the latter and this world. Thus was born the 'social gospel', which interpreted 'kingdom' in terms of improved political and cultural conditions here and now; it would be established by human revolution rather than by divine intervention. This concept carries quite a high degree of motivation to be involved in society.

But the result is that there is very little difference between Christian and humanist hopes for the future. The second coming of Christ tends to slide from the centre to the periphery of expectation. It may still be a credal item, but has ceased to be the 'blessed hope' (Tit 2:13), the return of the only person with the ability to put this world to rights.

So there is great emphasis on love, some on faith, but little on hope. Readers should readily recognise this in preaching and practice.

2. 'MYTHICAL' A-MILLENNIALISM

This takes Revelation 20 more seriously, treating it as scripture
with a message. Yet at the same time its plain, simple sense as
a prediction of future events is rejected, by treating it as fiction
rather than fact.

It is important to understand the meaning of the word 'myth'
when applied to scripture. It does not mean 'untrue', though its
frequent association with 'legend' can give that impression. The
word defines the *kind* of truth to be found in it. The 'story' may
not report literal events that have happened or will happen but
may still contain moral or spiritual 'truths' which correspond to
reality. They range from Aesop's fables to Jesus' parables.

One characteristic of such myths is that not all their features
are significant for the truth. Some may simply be part of the
literary framework, the 'poetic licence' of the writer, to capture
and sustain interest. It is the 'essence' of the myth that contains
its message. The details must not be pressed too far. They are
not total allegories in which everything stands for something.

The first scriptures to be treated as 'myth' were the early
chapters of Genesis. This was partly because 'Higher Criticism'
could not accept the possibility of 'backwards' prophecy (the
divine revelation of the unknown past) any more than 'forwards'
(the unknown future); but it was primarily due to the scientific
discoveries that contradicted the biblical account. The earth took
four and a quarter billion years to reach its present state, rather
than six days (a slight discrepancy!). Missing ribs, magic trees
and talking serpents were seen as the stuff of fable. Yet the 'myths'
contained vital 'truths'. The difficult details were merely literary
decoration.

Once started, this resolution of the conflict between science
and scripture proved to be a slippery slope. The problem was:
where does myth end and history (that is, factual event)
begin? Soon the patriarchs Abraham, Isaac and Jacob were
suspect; then Moses and the exodus. But the 'stories' were still

valued – for 'values', those ideals and standards which govern our lives.

Inevitably, the New Testament came under the same scrutiny. All along, the parables had been understood this way as stories with a message in them. But now events presented as historical and formerly accepted as such came into question. The miracles of Jesus became 'acted parables' and then just parables. The virgin birth 'story' was simply a way of introducing Jesus' unique relationship with his heavenly 'Father' (who then was his earthly father and was he the result of fornication?). The German scholar Rudolf Bultmann took this to the extreme by applying it to the very heart of Christian belief – the bodily resurrection of Jesus – now considered an apostolic fable enshrining the truth that the influence of Jesus survived his passing.

Of course, the book of Revelation seemed ready-made for this 'demythologising' approach. Highly symbolic and full of picture-language, it was an easy target for the myth-makers. It contains insight into the present rather than foresight into the future, existential rather than historical truth. This became known as the 'Idealist' school of interpretation (see pages 101–106).

Mythical truth is timeless and timely; it is applicable anywhere and anytime. So it is unrelated to the passage of time, the flow of history, the order of events. This virtual removal of time reference from Revelation has serious consequences for the interpretation and application of its message, not least for chapter 20.

The 'millennium' is not a particular period of time; the 'thousand years' stands for any or all time. The truth it contains is that Christ and Christians together are able to take over the territory of Satan (assuming that the devil himself is not a myth, a mere personification of evil!).

Undoubtedly this is true and this truth is a great encouragement to believers under pressure, fitting in with the purpose of Revelation. But is it the whole truth contained in this passage? To limit its message to this single theme is to ignore many of the specific details – for example, the 'first' and 'the rest' resurrections and the release of Satan. Above all, it ignores the sequence of events in the series of visions of which this one is only a part.

So, while this interpretation is in one sense 'true', it is far from an adequate explanation. It rules out any real ground for believing that Christ will one day rule this world after Satan is banished from it. In theological terms, the 'eschatological' dimension of the gospel (what will *certainly* happen in the end) is changed into an 'existential' mode (what can *possibly* happen in the present).

'Mythical' is preferable to 'sceptical' a-millennialism, in that it does make something of Revelation, though not much. 'Spiritual' post-millennialism, to which we now turn, makes rather more. The two are not always easy to distinguish, since the difference seems to be one of degree rather than kind. Hence the common confusion around the term 'a-millennial'. This term should be limited to the view that 'the thousand years' has no reference to any particular period of time, whereas 'post-millennial' applies this term to the church age between the first and second advents of Christ, either in whole ('spiritual') or in part ('political').

3. 'SPIRITUAL' POST-MILLENNIALISM

As we have already seen, this is the second oldest viewpoint, appearing in the fourth and fifth centuries, primarily through the teaching of Augustine.

It was partly a reaction against somewhat unwise earlier preaching about the physical features of the millennial kingdom, which went beyond the scriptural and bordered on the sensual. Augustine said he was induced to forsake the pre-millennial view of the early 'fathers', because some had perverted the doctrine with 'carnal' notions.

However, it was primarily due to his embracing Platonic 'dualism', which distinguished between spiritual and physical, but not clearly between physical and evil ('carnal' covered both). To this thinking, the traditional concept of the millennium seemed far too 'earthy' (later Christians would use the word 'worldly').

So the millennium was transferred from the future to the present (the second advent being 'post' = 'after' rather than 'pre' = 'before' this) and shorn of its physical and political context. It was 'spiritualised', with Christ ruling in heaven and only on earth through his body, the church.

Revelation 20 is taken much more seriously than by true 'a-millennial' interpretation. An explanation is offered for every element. But the major innovation is to treat this chapter as a recapitulation of events leading up to 19, thus breaking the sequence of visions. This radical step involves quite different interpretations.

The 'thousand years' were taken quite literally at first as the length of the church age, but now, after two thousand years, it must be seen as a 'symbolic' pointer to an extended period, since the 'millennium' is considered to cover the whole age between the two advents.

Since it is obvious that Satan still has considerable influence in the world, his banishment is reduced to his 'binding', which only limits his 'imprisonment' to preventing the spread of the gospel. The 'angel' who bound him was Christ (Matt 12:29).

The martyrs are reigning with Christ in heaven; this began at the moment of death when they went to be with the Lord. The first resurrection cannot now be understood as a bodily event; it must refer to regeneration, that conversion experience in which we are 'raised' with Christ (Eph 2:6). It is not, therefore, corporate but a separate event for each individual.

The 'coming to life' for 'the rest' is a corporate and physical event, the 'general' resurrection of righteous and wicked at the second advent for the day of judgement. This means, of course, that all those who experience the 'first' resurrection (i.e. conversion) will also be included in the second. They will 'come to life' twice. This makes nonsense of 'the rest', since it now includes everybody!

The 'release of Satan' for the final fling will take place just before the second advent and refers to the battle of Armageddon. Thus Revelation 19:19–21 and 20:7–10 are parallel accounts of the same conflict, the destructive force being both the word of Christ (19:15) and the fire from heaven (20:9).

The reader must judge whether this is genuine *ex*egesis (bringing out of the text what is already there) or manipulated *eise*gesis (putting into it what is not already there). To put it simply, is the text being interpreted in line with a preconceived scheme? Is it being 'forced to fit' a predetermined pattern?

What is clear is that a number of the statements (e.g. 'the first resurrection') are taken metaphorically rather than literally, hence the superficial similarity with 'mythical' a-millennialism. Even more striking is the arbitrary switching from metaphorical to literal with the same phrase in the same context ('come to life').

Nevertheless, this line of interpretation has been the most widely accepted in the church through the ages. What has been the effect on Christian hope?

The answer is: pessimism about this world and optimism about the next. The world is expected to remain much the same. As the population increases, both the kingdom of God and the kingdom of Satan will expand. The wheat and tares will 'both grow together' until the time of the harvest (Matt 13:30). Indeed, just before the end, the situation will get worse, with the 'release' of the sower of tares.

The hopes of a whole world brought back under the rule of God are postponed until the 'new earth' appears, ushered in immediately after the second advent, when the judgement takes place. Then, and only then, will the kingdom have truly and fully come 'on earth as it is in heaven' (though there is a noticeable lack of emphasis on the 'new *earth*' among advocates of this position).

This whole scheme appears to offer a satisfying explanation of the present state of the world, combined with a stimulating expectation for the future. The latter provides quite a strong motive for evangelism but the belief that this world is unlikely to get much better tends to inhibit social action. The underlying Platonic dualism tends to emphasise 'saving souls' rather than bodies at the individual level (consistently, Augustine taught the cessation of healing miracles after the 'apostolic' age; he was forced to revise his opinion towards the end of his ministry when such things began to happen in his own church!).

Ironically, a much more optimistic version of post-millennialism also claims Augustine as its father. There was an ambiguity in his thinking about this world, wavering between pessimism and optimism about the church's influence upon it. We shall now look at the more hopeful version.

4. 'POLITICAL' POST-MILLENNIALISM

At the time of Augustine, two political developments had taken place which radically affected Christian thinking about the future. On the one hand, the Roman Empire had become 'Christian'. The 'conversion' of Constantine (at the battle of the Milvian bridge north of Rome, when he had seen the logo of Christ in the sky and heard a voice saying: 'In this sign, conquer') had led to the 'establishment' of Christianity as the imperial religion and later to the suppression of other religions (including Judaism). The church had conquered the world, though the discerning wondered if it wasn't the other way round as they saw the world come into the church in more ways than one! It was the birth of 'Christendom', as it was later to be known, an earthly 'kingdom of Christ' – ruling through his vicarious (= delegated) people and subsequently his 'vicar', the papa (= father) or pope of his people. Conquering Rome in the name of Christ seemed a harbinger for the 'conversion' of the whole world.

On the other hand, the empire itself was under attack on its borders, notably by 'barbarians' from the north. Rome would be sacked and the Emperor would move east to the new capital of Constantinople. All this did nothing to discourage Augustine's belief that the church would survive such political disasters, that fallen empires would be replaced by 'the City of God'. Rome might disappear, but the church of Rome would take its place (it is interesting to note that to this day the popes have used the imperial title 'pontifex maximus', insignia of office and even vestments of the former Emperors).

So the church, or kingdom of Christ, would rise like a phoenix from the flames of war threatening all political states. It would survive and grow, despite all apparent setbacks, for God was with it.

This more confident strand in Augustine's thought inevitably raised the question: will the church, then, reach the point where Christians will be able to take over the government of the whole world? Over the centuries this hope has kept coming – and going.

During the great age of exploration, when new continents were being discovered, Catholic priests, motivated by this ecclesiastical imperialism, sailed with the explorers. Many Protestant mission-ary hymns of the nineteenth century ('Jesus shall reign where'er the sun') reveal the same global ambition. This view has always been popular when the church is enjoying a wave of advance.

This outlook has had its setbacks in the twentieth century (not least two 'world wars' centred in 'Christian' Europe, which were a contributory factor to the spreading secularism that has followed). Yet, surprisingly, there has been a recent revival of post-millennial optimism.

This has centred in the Western world with 'Restoration' move-ments in Britain and 'Reconstruction' movements in America. A 'Dominion' theology teaches that the redeemed are called to rule the earth (Gen 1:28 is by implication extended to include humans as well as animals) by 'discipling the nations' (Matt 28:19 is taken to refer to political states rather than various ethnic groups). In a word, the church is called, even commanded, to 'take over' the world and establish a 'political' kingdom of heaven on earth, thus bringing the 'millennium' into being. Note that this is without Jesus needing to return and therefore before he returns – to find his kingdom all ready for him!

This latest form of post-millennial thinking obviously carries an extremely strong motivation for social action and not much less for evangelism (since the 'take-over' depends to some degree on the proportion of Christians in the population). The world can be 'Christianised' without everyone in it becoming a Christian. The important thing is that the power and authority will need to be in Christian hands. The church 'militant' will become the church 'triumphant', not just in heaven, but here on earth.

How does this outlook handle Revelation 20 (though this is not a primary basis for their case)? Most of it is taken in exactly the same way as the 'spiritual' post-millennialists (see the previous section) with two significant exceptions.

First, the 'thousand years' is taken quite literally as the final millennium of the church age, ten centuries of peace and prosperity under Christian government. It is important to notice that this era has not yet begun.

Second, the millennial rule is wholly on earth and of an earthly kind. It is political. It will be recognised by the whole population, believer and unbeliever alike.

In both these aspects, this form of post-millennialism is much nearer the pre-millennialism of the early church. But the biggest difference remains – it is achieved without the return of Christ and his bodily presence.

And there are some major theological objections to this scenario. For one thing, it tends to confuse 'church' and 'kingdom', which are not identified in the New Testament. The church may be a community, a 'colony', of the kingdom, but it is not the kingdom itself, which extends far beyond the church. When the church thinks of itself as a 'kingdom', its leaders start behaving like kings and build their own little kingdoms. Imperialism replaces evangelism.

More serious, there is a failure to recognise the tension between the 'now' and the 'not yet' of the 'kingdom' in the New Testament. It has come and it has not come. It has been inaugurated but not consummated. Half of Jesus' parables envisage its coming as a gradual process of human infiltration and half as a sudden crisis of divine intervention (the parable of the wheat and tares combines both concepts; Matt 13:24–30, 36–43). The kingdom may be 'entered' now, but it will not be universally 'established' until the king returns.

This failure leads to a comparative neglect of the second coming, which was so central to the apostolic preaching. This event is mentioned over three hundred times in the New Testament and the expectation figures largely in its practical application of belief to behaviour. But in the viewpoint we are considering, this advent fades almost into insignificance. Obviously, if the millennium has to precede the return and has not even started yet, the 'hope of his coming' is too far away to affect us deeply. It belongs to the dim and distant future – whereas previous generations expected him 'soon', hopefully within their lifetime, which profoundly affected their way of living.

Finally, there is one major difficulty – does it look as if the church will soon be governing the world? After two thousand years, is the church any nearer this goal? Some cynics might observe that the church seems incapable of running its own affairs, never mind everyone else's!

Whatever else it is, political post-millennialism is a 'triumph of hope over experience'. Can such high expectations be sustained? The Bible recognises that 'hope deferred makes the heart sick' (Prov 13:12), but we are asking whether the hope is true or false, not just whether it will be soon or late. Has God promised it or not?

Will Revelation 20 be fulfilled before Jesus returns? If so, then most believers may hear of it in heaven or even see it from there (Heb 12:1?), but they will not be part of it. They will never experience it for themselves. It will have come too late.

If it is fulfilled after Jesus returns and the 'first resurrection', all believers will have the joy of living in a world under Christian control. We will now turn our attention to this 'pre-millennial' view.

5. 'CLASSICAL' PRE-MILLENNIALISM

This view takes a middle course between the *pessimism* of 'spiritual' post-millennialism, which believes this world is not likely to get much better, and the *optimism* of 'political' post-millennialism, which believes this world will be 'Christianised' by the church. It can make a fair claim to *realism*, by believing that this world will only recover its original state when Christ is back in it, and Satan is cast out of it.

It takes Revelation 20 in its plain, simple sense (if that is taken to be its 'literal' sense, its exponents plead guilty). The sequence of visions is accepted, placing Christ's millennial rule on earth with his saints, particularly the martyrs, after the second advent and before the day of judgement. The righteous will be raised first at the beginning of the thousand years and the rest at the end. Satan will be totally restricted for the greater part but released for the final denouement. In fact, ask a pre-millennialist what he believes and he might well say: 'Read Revelation 19–20 without listening to anyone else'!

This is probably why this seems to have been the unanimous position of the church for the first few centuries. They simply had the scripture and were not faced with the bewildering variety of interpretations we have to choose from today.

'Classic' means that this was the earliest belief – and the only one for a considerable time. The early fathers believed in 'the corporeal reign of Christ on this very earth' (to quote Papias, bishop of Hierapolis in Asia). Some (for example, Justin Martyr) associated this with the restoration of the kingdom to Israel, though not all were agreed on this. Many other names are cited as holding this 'pre-millennial' position – among them Barnabas, Hermas, Ignatius, Polycarp, Irenaeus, Justin Martyr, Tertullian, Hippolytus, Methodius, Commodian and Lactantius.

There is negative as well as positive evidence from these early centuries. Not a single trace has been found of any alternative view in the many documents that have survived. Michael Green,

commenting on the quotation of Psalm 90:4 ('With the Lord a day
is like a thousand years, and a thousand years are like a day') in 2
Peter 3:8, says: 'This verse, Ps.xc.4, became, in the second century,
the main proof-text of chiliasm, the doctrine that Christ would
reign for a thousand years at the parousia. This belief became
almost an article of Christian orthodoxy from the time of the
writing of Revelation to Irenaeus' (in the Tyndale Commentary
2 *Peter and Jude*, Inter-Varsity press, 1968 p.34).

Criticism of the prevailing view only surfaced with Clement and
Origen (significantly, in the 'Greek' culture of Alexandria). The
first direct challenges are associated with Eusebius, Tyconius and
Constantine in the fourth century and Augustine in the fifth. The
latter's post-millennialism was to become the orthodoxy of the
'Catholic' church, which later condemned the earlier 'chiliasm'
as 'heresy'.

However, it never died out. In small groups that studied
the Bible for themselves, during the centuries when most
simply accepted the traditions of the church, pre-millennialism
reappeared – for example, among the Paulicians, Waldenses,
Lollards and Wycliffites.

Even when the 'magisterial' Reformers (so-called because
they relied on the Constantinian church-state alliance to bring
about change) hung on to the Augustinian post-millennialism,
pre-millennialism was rediscovered by the radical left wing of
the 'Anabaptists'. Alas, a few of these became extremist and
gathered in Munster, Germany, to set up the millennial kingdom.
Though this fiasco is often cited to discredit chiliasm, it needs
to be pointed out that, in practice, this was a fanatical form of
political post-millennialism!

Among pre-millennialists of a later age is the eminent scientist,
Sir Isaac Newton. In the nineteenth century a surprising number
of Anglican bishops held this view (Ryle, Westcott and Lightfoot,
for example), though few, if any, would today.

So there has been a continuous witness through the ages,
though after Augustine it often dwindled to a small minority.
It is currently attracting renewed interest as an alternative to

'dispensationalism' (see below), which is losing credibility. The writings of George Eldon Ladd and Merrill C. Tenney have done much to encourage this. Leading pre-millennialists of our day have included Dr Francis Schaeffer and Dr Carl Henry.

However, it is not yet widely held again, so it is difficult to assess the practical effect on evangelism and social action. In theory this should be beneficial because it offers hope for both this world and the next, avoiding both extremes of pessimism and optimism.

Evangelism becomes worthwhile because of the glorious future envisaged. The faithful followers of Jesus will share his 'reign' in both the old and the new earth (Rev 20:6 and 22:5). This destiny is available to all who will repent of their sin and believe in the Saviour. The alternative is unspeakably horrible (Rev 20:10, 15; 21:8).

Social action becomes worthwhile precisely because it will ultimately be successful. There will come a day when good will overcome evil, justice will replace injustice, peace replace war, plenty replace poverty, and health replace sickness. If a Communist is prepared to sacrifice all for a classless, crimeless society which he may never live to see (and which we now know no Communist will ever live to see!), how much more will a Christian live and work for a 'millennium' which he is certain to see and in which he will play a part?

There is a further personal incentive. If the responsible positions then will be delegated according to integrity and faithfulness now (as Jesus clearly taught; Matt 25:21-23), what a stimulus to be such right now. If the courts are to be in the hands of Christians who can administer justice fairly (1 Cor 6:2), lawyers and judges can be qualifying now. The millennium will need honest bankers, caring councillors and a host of loving men and women to provide truly 'civil' service. In this perspective a whole host of 'secular' jobs become 'sacred' vocations. Taxi-driving and washing-up are as important to God as saving souls. Worship and work come together again.

Of course, some will argue that if it's all going to come right at the second coming, why bother to try to improve the world now, against such heavy odds? Apart from overlooking the fact that sloth can forfeit the future altogether (Matt 25:26–30), such thinking has missed the very essence of Christian motivation. Those who really do believe in what the second coming will bring will seek to have as much of that as they can beforehand. To take a parallel case, those who 'know that when he appears, we shall be like him, for we shall see him as he is' will seek to purify themselves now, 'just as he is pure' (1 John 3:2–3). Those who expect to inherit a fortune are not content to wait if they know they can have a good part of it immediately!

This world is not written off. Jesus is coming back to reclaim it. The more we can reclaim now in his name, the better that will be for his glory, the good of others and even our own future. We can give ourselves 'fully to the work of the Lord' (which for the believer means daily work just as much as 'church' work) because we know that our 'labour in the Lord is not in vain' (1 Cor 15:58).

But there is another version of pre-millennialism which has exactly the opposite effect. Unfortunately, it is the one with which most today are familiar.

6. 'DISPENSATIONAL' PRE-MILLENNIALISM

This is a relative newcomer, of which there is no trace before 1830. This raises the question as to why, if it is the correct interpretation, no one had seen it in scripture before then.

Revelation 20 is taken in much the same way as the 'classical', but the whole thing is then put into a novel framework, the singular features being:

First, the division of world history into seven 'dispensations', eras in each of which God relates to humans on a different basis. The last of these is the millennium, the only one truly deserving the title 'kingdom', since only then is the earth directly ruled by the Lord.

Second, it is this 'kingdom' which Jesus offered to the Jews at his first advent. On their rejection, it was withdrawn and postponed until the second advent. The church age is therefore a 'parenthesis' in God's purpose, which centres on Israel. Jesus' teachings on the kingdom, including the Sermon on the Mount, are primarily applicable to the millennium rather than the church.

Third, the future destiny of Christians is in heaven (they are God's 'heavenly people'), while the Jews will remain on earth (they are his 'earthly people'). For all eternity, 'never the twain will meet'!

Fourth, the church will be 'snatched away' from the earth before the 'Big Trouble' preceding the second advent. This event is called 'the secret rapture', or simply 'the Rapture' (see the section on this on pages 175–182). It is the next event on God's calendar and could happen at 'any moment', without warning. Christians will therefore be absent during the catastrophic events described in Revelation 4–18, but will return to earth with Christ in chapter 19. Whether they stay around with him after that is somewhat vague. What is clear is that:

Fifth, during the millennium the Old Testament kingdom of Israel will be fully restored. A rebuilt temple will see the revival of the sacrificial system (though it is usually qualified to be a 'memorial' to Christ's sacrifice on the cross, a kind of Jewish 'Eucharist', rather than an atoning ritual).

This whole 'dispensational' scheme significantly altered previous pre-millennial thinking. In particular, the millennium became more Jewish than Christian. In spite of its novelty, it took rapid hold, first in Britain and then in America, where it is probably now the majority view among evangelicals.

It originated with a man called John Nelson Darby, an Anglican curate in Dublin who became the founder of the 'Brethren', sometimes known as 'Plymouth' Brethren after one of the strongest early centres of the movement. Originally aimed at uniting Christians from all denominations in spontaneous worship around the 'breaking of bread' and in serious study of scripture, it soon became a denomination of its own, eventually splitting into many separate groups, some very 'open' to other believers and some very 'exclusive'.

From the first there was a deep interest in biblical prophecy to see what would become of the church in its 'ruined' state, as Darby described it. It was he who embraced and taught the 'dispensational' focus on Israel rather than the church and the 'secret rapture' of believers before the 'Great Tribulation'. His views did not go unchallenged; men like Benjamin Newton, S.P. Tregelles, and George Müller (of Bristol orphanage fame) never accepted them. But his dominant personality prevailed and his method of interpreting scripture became Brethren orthodoxy from which few dared to dissent.

Crossing the Atlantic, he convinced a lawyer, Dr C.I. Scofield, of its rightness. He in his turn produced a Bible with notes, in which he incorporated 'dispensational' comments. This 'Schofield' Bible sold exceptionally well among evangelicals in the United States. The danger was that readers found it difficult to remind themselves of the difference between the inspired word of God and the human commentary, accepting the latter as 'in the Bible'.

Today there are seminaries which teach nothing else (Dallas is the best known; the books of one of its students, Hal Lindsay, are known the world over and have sold by the million). Some missionary organisations will only consider candidates with dispensational convictions.

There is no questioning the enormous influence of this teaching.

On the positive side, it has to be said that it has done more than anything else to restore pre-millennialism to the church. Millions again believe that Christ is coming back to earth to reign over this earth for a thousand years.

But the negative results outweigh the positive. The packaging has polluted the contents. The theological framework in which the millennium is enmeshed is fatally flawed.

The most serious error concerns the 'kingdom'. If political post-millennialists have overemphasised the 'now' dimension and seen it largely in its present manifestation, dispensational pre-millennialists have overemphasised the 'not yet' dimension and seen it as exclusively future. This fails to do justice to the now/not yet dialectic of the New Testament.

This inevitably leads to the sharp separation of Jewish and Christian destinies and an unbalanced emphasis on the Jewishness of the millennium. This is contrary to Jesus' prediction of 'one flock and one shepherd' (John 10:16), Paul's concept of one olive tree into which shall be grafted 'the full number of the Gentiles' and 'Israel as a whole' (Rom 11:17–26) and John's vision of a new Jerusalem descending from heaven to earth and bearing the names of the twelve tribes of Israel and the twelve apostles of Christ (Rev 21:12–14).

The division of history into seven dispensations is highly suspect. At the opposite end of the theological spectrum, 'Reformed Calvanists' lump them all together in 'the covenant of grace' (a phrase not found in scripture). The biblical position seems to deal with two covenants, old and new, law and grace, Moses and Christ; though the 'new' incorporates the covenants with Abraham and David, while all mankind benefits from the covenant with Noah.

This leads on to another problem. The letter to the Hebrews is at pains to show that the 'old' covenant is 'obsolete and ageing' and 'will soon disappear' (Heb 8:13). This includes the whole sacrificial system in Leviticus, which has been 'done away' by Christ's supreme sacrifice on the cross. Its reappearance during the millennium would be an anachronistic anomaly!

The tragedy of all this is that pre-millennialism has become inextricably bound up with dispensational thinking in so many minds that it is assumed they belong together and that it is impossible to have one without the other. When the faults of dispensationalism are discovered, especially by those brought up under it, the tendency is to discard the whole teaching rather than sort out what is true from what is false. The millennium is rejected as one of the dispensations. The baby is thrown out with the bathwater!

Many who do this don't know what to put in its place and vaguely regard themselves as 'a-millennial' – in the true sense of non-millennial. It is not that they are rejecting Revelation 20 in principle, but in practice it is no longer part of their thinking or preaching. Mostly, they are quite unaware of 'classical' pre-millennialism, the view of the early church (one Bible college principal told this author he'd never heard of it!). When they do hear about it, the reaction is usually one of real relief – that it is possible to be pre-millennial without being dispensational.

There is one more aspect to be considered: the practical effect of dispensational pre-millennialism. Of all the views, this probably produces the highest motivation for evangelism. The imminence of Christ's return ('he could come tonight') prompts an urgency in the saved to save others and in the unsaved to be saved. Perhaps the majority of evangelical missionaries sent out from the United States are impelled by this kind of thinking.

However, zeal does not justify motive. Cults produce enthusiastic missionaries (Mormons and Jehovah's Witnesses are good examples), as did the Pharisees in Jesus' day (Matt 23:15). All motives must be tested by scripture.

But if dispensationalism produces the highest motivation for evangelism, it probably has the lowest for social action. The combined beliefs of an any-moment 'rapture' and a 'Jewish' millennium sap the desire to try and make this world a better place. The attention is focused on heaven rather than earth. What is the point of getting involved in long-term social betterment when Jesus and a saved Israel will be putting it right? For a fascinating study of the effect of this teaching on political endeavour, see: *Living in the Shadow of the Second Coming: American Premillennialism 1875–1982* by Timothy P. Weber, (Zondervan 'Academie', 1983).

While both forms of pre-millennialism stimulate evangelism, there is a sharp contrast between them when it comes to social action. Now that more evangelicals are recovering a balance between the two aspects of 'mission', it is very important to draw attention to this marked difference.

CHAPTER NINETEEN

The Personal Conclusion

Our study of the millennial views is over. Hopefully the reader's thinking has been clarified rather than confused! At least by now it will be realised that the debate has a very practical purpose and is not just an academic exercise. Our real convictions on the subject have a quite profound effect on our attitude to life.

I have not hidden my own conclusions, which I arrived at quite independently of others. Brought up in the Methodist Church, I never heard the millennium mentioned, much less discussed, though they did sometimes sing about it, perhaps without realising it; one of my favourite hymns as a boy was: 'Sing we the king who is coming to reign . . .'. It was when I began to teach the Bible systematically, as a Royal Air Force chaplain, that I began to consider and then study this question. After reading as much as I could of the very different opinions and checking these against scripture, I became convinced that the early church had been right after all and indicated this in my first book (*Truth to Tell*, Hodder and Stoughton, 1977).

Let me summarise my pilgrimage by listing the reasons for my position as a 'classical' pre-millennialist:

1. It is the most 'natural' interpretation of Revelation 20. I felt that others were forcing this scripture into their own mould, giving artificial, even arbitrary, meanings to some of its features. It is a fundamental principle in my Bible study to let the passage speak for itself, taking it in its plainest, simplest sense unless there is a clear indication to the contrary.

2. It gives the most logical explanation for the second advent. What can he only do by coming back here? Why should Jesus return to planet earth at all? Certainly not for the final judgement, which takes place after earth has 'fled' (Rev 20:11). So for what? And why do we have to come back here with him (1 Thess 4:14)? If he and we are not going to 'reign' on earth for a considerable time, it is difficult to find another adequate reason for his return, or ours.

3. It puts the most emphasis on the second coming. This is related to the point above. Both a-millennialists and post-millennialists tend to play down the second advent, which does not then have the central place it occupies in the New Testament. The reason is simple. If the only, or even the main, desire for his return is to be with him, this will have already happened for the believer at the moment of death (Phil 1:21).

4. It made sense in itself. I could understand why God would want to vindicate his Son in the eyes of the world and stage a final demonstration of what this world was meant to be like and could be like in the right hands. I could even see why he would add a final revelation of the rebelliousness of sin, even in an ideal environment, before the day of judgement. The phased transition from the old earth to the new matched my own redemption, first in my old body, only much later in the new.

5. It 'earths' our future destiny. Those who deny a future millennium rarely talk or even think about the new earth. Everything in the future centres in heaven. But heaven is only a waiting-room for believers, until they come back to this earth and later on to the new earth, where Father and Son will dwell with us. Instead of going to heaven to live with them for ever, they come to earth to live with us for ever (Rev 21:2–3), as at the beginning (Gen 3:8). All this gives our planet an eternal significance.

6. It strikes a note of realism. It avoids both the gloomy pessimism of those who think this world will never be

much better than it is and the naive optimism, even triumphalism, of those who think the church can dethrone Satan and enthrone Christ by taking over the nations herself. Pre-millennialism avoids both extremes, accepting that the world will get worse before it gets better, but certain that it will get better after it gets worse.

7. It has fewer problems than others! It has been frankly admitted that *all* the views have some difficulties. But classic pre-millennialism has far less than the alternatives, especially when it comes to interpreting Revelation 20. There are still many unanswered questions, but I can live with these. It is the easiest to preach with confidence, because it is the one which the common reader is most likely to find in the appropriate passage.

8. It is what the early church believed. The unanimity of the first few centuries is very impressive. They were not infallible, but they were the nearest generations to the apostles. The absence of any debate is striking, as is the fact that differences only appeared when Christian doctrine was polluted by Greek philosophy.

For these reasons, I am able to pray the daily prayer Jesus gave to his disciples with real meaning and desire – 'your kingdom come . . . on earth as it is in heaven' (Matt 6:10) – as much as it can before the coming of Christ and the rest of it after.